Historical Problems
Studies and Documents

Edited by
PROFESSOR G. R. ELTON
University of Cambridge

14

THE DISSOLUTION OF THE MONASTERIES

THE DISSOLUTION OF THE MONASTERIES

Joyce Youings
University of Exeter

LONDON: GEORGE ALLEN AND UNWIN LTD
NEW YORK: BARNES AND NOBLE INC

FIRST PUBLISHED IN 1971

BRITISH ISBN 0 04 942089 5 *cased*
         ISBN 0 04 942090 9 *paper*
USA   ISBN 389-04454-7

Printed in Great Britain
in 10 point Plantin type
by Cox and Wyman
Fakenham

TO B.S

AUTHOR'S NOTE

A fraction only of all the available material relating to the Dissolution of the Monasteries is available in print. Where suitable this has been used, although in some cases the author has introduced minor corrections where reference to the originals indicated that these were necessary. A good many of the documents printed here *in extenso* are already well-known from their being calendared in the *Letters and Papers of Henry VIII*. By and large the more formal documents, including the enrolled accounts, are in Latin, and these have been translated. In all cases spelling, punctuation, and the use of capital letters have been modernized. Place and personal names, as far as possible, have been given in their modern form. Explanations of archaic or technical words and phrases have been added in italic type, and, where necessary, sufficient words have been supplied to make the sense clear, all such editorial insertions being placed within square brackets. The notes preceding each document are largely factual and are intended to assist the reader to understand the text by placing it in its historical context. For a bibliography the reader is referred to the end of Dom David Knowles's great classic, *The Religious Orders in England* III, but an appendix is included here of work on the Dissolution and allied topics published since 1959.

The author wishes to thank the following for permission to print documents: the Trustees of the British Museum; the Controller of Her Majesty's Stationery Office, for Crown copyright material in the Public Record Office and for the map on p. 247; Professor V. H. Galbraith for Doc. 1; the Town Clerk of Exeter for Doc. 12; Professor the Rev. M. D. Knowles and the editor of the *English Historical Review* for Doc. 24; and the editor of the Dugdale Society for Doc. 26b. Her debt to the many scholars who have worked in this field, especially in recent years, is, she hopes, sufficiently acknowledged in the appropriate places. For assistance with the final stages of the book's preparation she is particularly grateful to Professor G. R. Elton, the editor of the series, who read and commented on an early draft, to Monica Channer who typed the manuscript so patiently and efficiently and to Peter Lock who helped substantially with the preparation of the index.

CONTENTS

CONTENTS

ABBREVIATIONS

Ag. Hist. IV	*The Agrarian History of England and Wales*, vol. IV, 1500–1640, edited by Joan Thirsk, Cambridge, 1967
BIHR	*Bulletin of the Institute of Historical Research*
BM	British Museum
EcHR	*Economic History Review*
EHR	*English Historical Review*
Knowles, *RO* II & III	M. D. Knowles, *The Religious Orders in England*, vols. II & III, Cambridge, 1955, 1959
LP	*Letters and Papers, Foreign and Domestic, of the reign of Henry VIII*, edited by J. S. Brewer, J. Gairdner, and R. H. Brodie, 1862–1910 (References relate to documents, not pages)
PRO	Public Record Office
Statutes	*Statutes of the Realm*, edited by A. Luders *et al.* 1810–28
TRHS	*Transactions of the Royal Historical Society*
VE	*The Valor Ecclesiasticus*, edited by J. Caley and J. Hunter, 1810–34
Wright, *Letters*	*Three Chapters of Letters relating to the Suppression of the Monasteries*, edited by T. Wright, Camden Society, 1843

INTRODUCTION

Problems and Documents

THE Dissolution of the Monasteries in England and Wales in the reign of Henry VIII was an act of resumption, a restoration to secular uses of land and other endowments provided over many centuries, very largely by laymen, for the support of houses of regular clergy and nuns. What was achieved in the 1530s was the reversal of a series of acts of donation, but with the important proviso that all the property passed in the first instance not to the original donors or their heirs and assigns but to the Crown. By various means, by statute, by legal process, and by simple deed of gift, the monastic lands became vested in the king, to be at his absolute disposal. The communities of men and women religious were never, in so many words, actually dissolved. Nowhere in the formal instruments were they forbidden to pursue their corporate existence, to follow their liturgical routine, or indeed to adhere to their Rule. Much, of course, was implied in the statutory forfeiture of all their ornaments and church furnishings, and in the provisions made not only for the maintenance but also for the legal status of the dispossessed who were regarded as having returned to the secular world. Some of the monks and nuns, though in no case as far as we know whole communities, did actually stay together. But the general assumption of all concerned was that shorn of their lands the religious communities would disappear. And this is what in fact happened. Institutions which for the most part traced their foundation to gifts of landed property came to an end with the surrender of that property.

To approach the Dissolution thus may be thought to be to take too legal and materialistic a view of an event, or series of events, which was a landmark in the ecclesiastical history of England and Wales. It is true that the Dissolution had very substantial religious, as well as social and economic, consequences, but its inspiration and execution owed little to religious considerations. There was not even any sustained effort to convict the religious of harbouring Roman loyalties, which indeed very few of them did. It is arguable that the Dissolution formed neither an integral nor an essential part of the Reformation in England and Wales. Might not some quite considerable diversion of monastic resources have taken place even if there had been no breach with Rome? Or, once accomplished, might not the Dissolution have remained final even if there had been a healing of that breach in his later years by Henry VIII? It is even conceivable that had they not been great landed proprietors all but a few of the English and Welsh monasteries might have remained, slightly changed though not necessarily reformed, within the Anglican system. It can hardly be argued that they formed, or were seriously thought by Henry VIII and his ministers to form, a challenge to the royal supremacy. It is indeed difficult to claim of any single religious house in the middle and late 1530s that its members stood united against any encroachment on its affairs by the secular world.

Historians of widely different religious persuasions are today in remarkable agreement that the monasteries of early Tudor England and Wales were no longer playing an indispensable role in the spiritual life of the country, certainly not one to justify their continued enjoyment of so large a part of the landed wealth of the kingdom. Those who are most critical of Henry VIII condemn him not so much for dissolving the monasteries as for failing to apply the proceeds of the Dissolution towards the educational, social, and religious betterment of his subjects.[1] Both sides, in fact, find considerable common ground in the writings of Thomas Starkey (Doc. 14). Even those who seek to defend the continuance of monasticism succeed only in demonstrating the extent to which the religious were involved in the more mundane aspects of contemporary life, playing a part in the public life of town and countryside more or less commensurate with their status as local landed proprietors. Of very few communities is it now seriously argued that they either shunned the world and its temptations, or, in their contacts with it, set an example to laymen or to their secular clerical brethren. On the other hand we now discount official pronouncements about the moral shortcomings of the monks and nuns, and have learned to view the evidence placed on record by bishops and other 'visitors' in its true perspective.[2]

But the attitude of ordinary early Tudor laymen, and the extent to which they regarded the monasteries as a necessary part of their present and future life, still very largely eludes the historian. Perhaps it is as well to remember that in general people gossip when it suits them. The scurrilous stories in circulation about monastic morality were only what contemporaries chose to believe: they were not derived, like so much present-day historical data, from the highly confidential records of episcopal visitations. May it not be the case that the concern of most

[1] J. J. Scarisbrick, *Henry VIII*, 1968, p. 511.
[2] For a realistic assessment based on a wide range of evidence see A. G. Dickens, *The English Reformation*, 1964, pp. 52–4.

laymen, when it came to the point, was less with the more venial sins which were the business of bishops, and more with the degree of devotion shown by the religious in the discharge of pastoral responsibilities, particularly when such responsibilities seemed to be of the monks' own seeking? Partisan statements are not the best kind of historical evidence, but the submissions of the parishioners of Wembury in Devon (Doc. 3) have about them the ring of authenticity, and may well reflect a state of affairs not uncommon up and down the country. The neglect of which they complained arose on account of the widespread late-medieval practice, which had gained both episcopal and royal sanction, of monastic appropriation of parish churches, with all the revenue appertaining thereto, saving only the obligation to provide a parish priest. The object, of course, was not to provide pastoral experience for members of the community concerned but rather to augment its regular income, and it was on such grounds that it had been sanctioned. The ultimate effect of the Dissolution was to place such resources and responsibilities in the hands of laymen, or, in the particular case of Wembury, of a corporation of secular clergy. This may or may not have been a change for the better, but clearly any change stood a good chance of winning the parishioners of Wembury to the king's side. Such relief as came their way, however, came not as part of a movement for religious reform, but simply as the result of a great redistribution of rights of property.

The Dissolution of the Monasteries has taken its place in historical studies primarily as a revolution in landownership, second only to that which followed the Norman Conquest. In making the first attempt to analyse the Dissolution on a national scale the Russian scholar, Alexander Savine, seized upon the *Valor Ecclesiasticus*, the survey of the income of the church in England and Wales carried out in 1535.[3] His findings have stood the test of time. Work on narrower fronts, especially at county level, has very largely confirmed his confidence in the *Valor* as a remarkably reliable, if conservative, survey of monastic resources. The *Valor* has indeed become, for historians of the monastic estates, and especially of their disposal by the Crown, almost as indispensable a work of reference as it rapidly became for contemporaries. What Savine was unable adequately to do, and what few historians since his time have even attempted, is to use such late monastic records as are available, together with the great mass of post-Dissolution material relating to the years immediately preceding, to add momentum to the somewhat static picture of the monastic economy afforded by the *Valor*. There is still a great deal we do not understand about what was happening in those vital years from 1535 to 1539, and a good deal may yet be

[3] A. Savine, *English Monasteries on the Eve of the Dissolution*, Oxford Studies in Social and Legal History I, 1909.

revealed from a thorough study of the use made of conventual seals during those years.

The next major aspect of the Dissolution to be tackled by twentieth-century scholars was, appropriately enough, the provision made for the dispossessed religious. Most of the essential material relating to the initial awarding of pensions had long been available in print, and this, together with the still largely unpublished records of later Government inquiries, enabled Mr Baskerville to upset the older impression that the religious were left to the mercy of their friends and relations.[4] In his pursuit of the subsequent careers of the religious Mr Baskerville is now thought by many historians to have painted rather too rosy a picture. It is generally acknowledged that in terms of the current value of money the pensions awarded were reasonable, and in the case of the governors even generous, and that such obligations towards the religious as it accepted the government to a large degree honoured.[5] But there is still considerable doubt whether the names which appear on the pension lists provide anything approaching an adequate estimate of the total number of professed monks and nuns who left the cloister at, or not long before, the Dissolution. One recent estimate has put the total number of unpensioned religious as high as 10 per cent.[6] As for the later careers, about which we seem to know so much, those who figure in the written records are only too likely to be those, possibly no more than a minority, who were either more fortunate, or better fitted to cope with life in the secular world. There is even less certainty about what happened to the very considerable number of monastic servants, both indoor and outdoor, to say nothing of the elderly and infirm lay persons who depended on monastic charity. It is arguable, but far from easy to demonstrate, that the outdoor servants were re-employed by the monks' successors. What assistance, if any, was provided by the government no one seems to know for certain. Moreover, apart from the treatment meted out to the relatively destitute, there still needs to be calculated the total liability assumed by the early Tudor Government

---

[4] G. Baskerville, *The English Monks and the Suppression of the Monasteries*, 1937, is a general and somewhat popularized summing up of the author's more scholarly work in the counties of Gloucester, Surrey, and Norfolk, publication of which marked the first substantial corrective to the work of Gasquet. For a recent addition to the source material available concerning the later history of the religious see G. A. J. Hodgett, *The State of the ex-Religious in the Diocese of Lincoln*, Lincoln Record Society LII (1959).

[5] A. G. Dickens, 'The Edwardian Arrears in Augmentations Payments', *EHR* LV (1940).

[6] G. A. J. Hodgett, 'The unpensioned religious in Tudor England', *Journal of Ecclesiastical History* XIII, ii (1962), but cf. the cautionary note struck in D. S. Chambers, *Faculty Office Registers, 1534–49*, 1966, pp. xlii–xlix. The most up-to-date survey is in G. W. O. Woodward, *The Dissolution of the Monasteries*, 1966, pp. 139–57.

in fees and other annual payments to laymen, to those, in fact, to whom the monks bequeathed to their successors a legal rather than a moral obligation, and for how long all such burdens formed a substantial drain on the new royal resources.

It has long been recognized that the Dissolution did not lead to the permanent augmentation of the annual income of the Crown, and indeed that the former monastic lands were 'dissipated' to a very great extent by Henry VIII during the later years of his reign. This failure to achieve what most historians see as the main object of the exercise is usually ascribed to the disappearance from the scene, in 1540, of Thomas Cromwell. But this is to ignore the fact that by the time of Cromwell's fall four years had passed since the first assault in 1536, years during which not only very substantial but very many grants had been made, and that in December 1539 Cromwell himself was named as one of the first commissioners to sell monastic and other Crown lands. We are indeed still very far from knowing just how great an immediate increase in annual spending power the Dissolution afforded to the government. The treatment given to the subject in the only general work on early Tudor government finance is, by present-day standards, quite inadequate.[7] Enrolled accounts, very few of them available in print, exist in abundance, though it must be admitted that it was never the intention of their compilers that they should illuminate the financial position of the Crown. However, it should be possible, now that the principles underlying the new-style government accountancy are fairly well understood, to draw up an overall balance sheet. It will not be enough to discover in any given year how much cash reached Westminster. The new resources could be tapped not only at times convenient to government needs but could also be made available for use on the Crown's behalf very much nearer the source of supply. Only after all the accounts, spreading over more than a decade, have been analysed, right down to the level of local bailiffs, will it be possible to compile a really satisfactory balance sheet of the whole operation. Meanwhile, however, such evidence as is available about the administration of the new Crown lands suggests that, quite apart from the disposal of its capital assets, the Crown extracted nothing like the maximum possible return from its new resources. Whether this was through design or administrative inertia still remains to be determined.

There are two, closely-related, fields in which considerable progress has been made in recent years. From the work of Professor G. R. Elton and Professor W. C. Richardson we now know a great deal about the administrative machinery established to deal with the former monastic lands, how it worked and how it fitted into contemporary administrative

[7] F. C. Dietz, *English Government Finance, 1485–1558*, Illinois, 1920, reprinted 1964, pp. 139–40.

B

developments.[8] On the work of the central office and of the central officers of the court of Augmentations there is probably very little which remains to be said, but there is still no general study of the court's operations in the field. It is, however, clear that a great deal depended on the personal attitudes and capabilities of the regional officers, and also that certain broad principles of policy emanated from the central office. The notoriety which the court enjoyed among would-be grantees of the former monastic lands took little account of the magnitude of its task. Its slow-moving efficiency may well turn out to have been its chief contribution to the successful carrying out of the whole operation.

The printed calendars of patent rolls have long served as the chief, and indeed only, source of information about the alienation or disposal of monastic estates by the Crown. But by supplementing these with evidence from the Augmentations records, including the Treasurers' Accounts, and especially the Particulars for Grants, a good deal has been learned about the terms on which the former monastic property was sold or otherwise disposed of.[9] It is becoming clear that absolutely free gifts were few and that such generosity as the Crown evinced was carefully controlled. Certainly from 1539 until the end of Henry VIII's reign the matter was largely one of business not politics, and least of all one of religion. Few of the king's subjects had conscientious reservations about buying monastic property, whatever the shade of their religious views. But further analysis of the grants made between 1536 and 1539, when there were not only rather more gifts but also a number of exchanges of property with the Crown, may serve to complicate the picture. Moreover, careful comparison of the dates and contents of these early grants with the actual dates of dissolution may well lead to a greater appreciation of the part played by laymen, both within and outside government circles, in determining the course of events.

The challenge presented by Professor R. H. Tawney in 1941 in the paper which sparked off the controversy over the relative progress as landowners of the gentry and the aristocracy has still not been adequately met by those especially concerned with the disposal of monastic lands.[10] Tawney taught us to pursue them beyond the initial Crown grants but for very few counties do we yet know into whose possession they had fallen by 1547, let alone 1558. Work so far achieved has on the whole confirmed Tawney's impression that with the passage of the years

[8] G. R. Elton, *The Tudor Revolution in Government*, Cambridge, 1953, especially pp. 203–19, and W. C. Richardson, *History of the Court of Augmentations*, Baton Rouge, 1961.

[9] For an analysis based on a single county see J. A. Youings, 'The terms of disposal of the Devon Monastic Lands, 1536–58', *EHR* LXIX (1954) and for the only attempt to deal with the problem in general terms, H. J. Habakkuk, 'The Market for Monastic Property', *EcHR* Ser. 2, X (1958).

[10] R. H. Tawney, 'The Rise of the Gentry', *EcHR* XI (1941).

more and more went to make up smaller or medium-sized estates. It is now clear that there was less purely speculative buying than Tawney believed, but as yet there is little known about how the purchase money was raised.[11] Are we even sure that it was all paid? It may well be that the time has already passed for a reply to Tawney's challenge in the terms he suggested. For one thing it is possible to take too long a view. The fact that a piece of former monastic property changed hands for the third time, say in the early 1560s, may be regarded as of far less significance than its immediate re-sale, even at a modest profit, in the early 1540s. More important, once a piece of former monastic property had left Crown ownership are we to regard its re-sale as of any special significance compared with the sale of any other property? Should we not be concerned with the land market as a whole, and not only with the purchases being made but also with private sales of property, especially when these latter were associated, chronologically, with the purchase of monastic lands? By such means the real significance of the availability of monastic lands in the quickening of the early Tudor land market may eventually be determined.[12]

Most of the problems so far considered lend themselves to a quantitative approach, and, faced with the amount of material available, most historians have tackled them on a local, usually for convenience a county, basis. The work of assimilating the results and building up a national picture has not yet proceeded very far.[13] There is even a danger in a local approach for monastic estates were not contained within county or even regional boundaries, and not until its last stages did the Dissolution itself proceed on any kind of territorial pattern. It was an operation carried out on a country-wide basis and communications were not so bad in Tudor England that men did not know what was happening several counties away. How in fact was the Dissolution carried through with so little opposition, lay or clerical? Certainly it was not with the use of armed force. There is little or no evidence of any of the religious or their friends being man-handled, and indeed very little sign of any attempts to use force to hinder the Dissolution. Some will argue that success was assured in advance by the installing of well-chosen governors, abbots and prioresses who could be relied upon to surrender without protest when called upon to do so. But this is to

[11] Habakkuk, *op. cit.*, pp. 377–80, but see also G. W. O. Woodward, 'A speculation in monastic lands', *EHR* LXXIX (1964).

[12] For a short but pioneering study of this kind see J. E. Kew, 'The Disposal of Crown Lands and the Devon land market, 1536–58', *Agricultural History Review*, XVIII, ii (1970).

[13] Recent published work is listed on p. 254. Some attempt to reach general conclusions in the field of agrarian history will be found in *The Agrarian History of England and Wales* IV, 1500–1640, ed. J. Thirsk, Cambridge, 1967, pp. 306–55 (England) and 383–7 (Wales).

assume a working together of court, aristocracy, gentry, bishops, and all who took a hand in monastic elections, in a way which was inconceivable even if there had been time in which to plan and carry out such a policy. Others will suggest that the religious were won over by the promise of pensions, and laymen persuaded to co-operate by the promise of grants. This explanation is probably nearer the truth but it is an oversimplification. Both explanations rest on the assumption that there was a sharp and persistent division of interest between the Crown and secular society on the one hand and the religious communities on the other. But many laymen at all levels of society had a very considerable vested interest in the continuance of monasteries of which they were 'founders', or from which they derived regular income as lay officials, as employees, and as tradesmen. Above all they were tenants of monastic lands (Doc. 2). The point has recently been made yet again, in connection with the Lincolnshire rising, that lessees of monastic lands would naturally fear a change of landlord.[14] But the monastic tenant existed in his thousands in all counties and it needs to be explained why men should, on this account, oppose dissolution in Lincolnshire more than in, say, Devonshire. Their attitude to possible dissolution was bound to be moulded by their expectations of the way it would affect them. A great deal must surely have depended on the information generally available about the Crown's intentions as successor to the monks, both as landlord and as paymaster. It may well be that the greatest single factor ensuring the success of the Dissolution was that it proceeded slowly enough for almost all concerned to know exactly where they stood.

It is, then, vitally important that the chronology of the Dissolution should be accurately established. This has been achieved, at least in essentials, by Professor David Knowles in the final volume of his great history of the religious orders in England.[15] Here we have, for the first time, everything in proper sequence, from the pre-Reformation suppressions, including those of Wolsey, through Cromwell's successive and hitherto very confused visitations and commissions, to the statutes, the forfeitures, and the surrenders. Against this chronological sequence one is able, with the help of the voluminous state papers of the period, to watch how government policy and action developed and proceeded, not smoothly or swiftly but slowly and often very unpredictably, moulded always by circumstances, public reactions, even by pressures from individuals, both at court and in the counties. But many questions still call for an answer. How far did the government fear opposition and what steps were taken to avoid trouble? A study of the dates of

---

[14] M. E. James, 'Obedience and Dissent in Henrician England: The Lincolnshire Rebellion, 1536', *Past and Present* 48 (1970), p. 36.
[15] D. Knowles, *The Religious Orders in England* III, 1959.

dissolution indicates that up to a point it was a piecemeal business but
that particularly in 1536, and again in 1539, the Dissolution took the
form of territorial sweeps.[16] Was the pattern accidental or did it follow
administrative convenience? What trouble, in fact, did the government's
agents encounter? With how much publicity was the operation effected?
Why was it found necessary to proceed by so many different methods of
effecting the legal transfer of monastic resources to the Crown? How
important were the parliamentary statutes in this respect, and what
exactly was the role of Thomas Cromwell?

It has perhaps been inevitable that those who have deprecated the
dispersal of the religious communities, both contemporaries and
historians, should have placed responsibility not on the king but on his
chief minister, Thomas Cromwell, and also that those who have recognized Cromwell's energy and efficiency as an administrator should
instinctively regard the Dissolution as his personal achievement. Such
an assumption is reinforced by the survival of so many letters, some of
them couched in the most obsequious terms (Doc. 17c), from governors
of religious houses, anxious above all else to obtain his support. It
must be remembered, however, that the instinctive reaction of the
head of any religious community in time of crisis was to seek help from
the Crown. All that was new was the recognition that in Cromwell's
interest lay the best hope of royal favour. Such people were by no
means ill-informed and a careful analysis of the gifts and fees showered
on Cromwell throughout the 1530s, but with varying intensity, might
cast an interesting light on his political credibility at various times.
Many of his correspondents quite clearly believed that, once informed
of their anxieties, he would serve their best interests. Are we not too
ready to assume that Cromwell intended the ultimate ruin of his clients
from the beginning of his political career? The question still remains
as to his personal responsibility for the devising, timing, and organizing
of the Dissolution. But again it must be remembered that Cromwell
was nothing if not the servant of the Crown and that, particularly after
his appointment as the king's Secretary in April 1534, what are so
often referred to as his papers were those of the king's. There were at
least two other ministers whose part in the planning and carrying out
of the Dissolution should not be ignored, namely Thomas Howard,
third duke of Norfolk, and Sir Thomas, later Lord, Audley. But even
if one still believes, and most historians will continue to do so, that
Cromwell was the key figure, one does not have to assume that he was
able to plan the whole operation to serve only the interests of the Crown,
nor that he, or for that matter anyone else in government circles, knew

[16] For the calendar years of dissolution see D. Knowles and R. N. Hadcock,
Medieval Religious Houses, England and Wales, 1953, with additions in *EHR*
LXXII (1957). Some further revision of dates is necessary.

very long in advance how far it would be safe to go. It is also possible that there were times when the ease with which the Dissolution was achieved took even Cromwell by surprise.

One of the most valuable contributions of Professor Knowles's great book to the background of the Dissolution is the insight it provides into the internal administration and economy of the early Tudor monasteries. At the more superficial level, that at which reform was always possible, there was in a large number of religious houses chronic bad management, lack of discipline, and a high degree of petty squabbling. There was also a good deal of debt, though Professor Knowles thinks that this, and also the ratio of domestic servants, has been exaggerated. But he also finds something deeper and far less capable of being reformed, an almost universal concern for material comfort, an assumption that the monastic life need not deprive a man or woman of the standard of living or of the pursuits and pleasures, most of them harmless enough in themselves, enjoyed by laymen. There had been a great deal of mitigation of monastic Rules, both official and unofficial, in the later middle ages but particularly in the half century preceding the Reformation so that,[17]

'With the exception of the Carthusians, the Bridgettines and the Observant Franciscans, the religious life in England was humanly speaking less spiritually stimulating in 1530 than it had been a century earlier.'

To the word 'spiritually', and with the same important exceptions, Professor Knowles might also have added the word 'intellectually'. There were indeed notable exceptions and some communities were still fulfilling their obligation to send their potential scholars to the universities. But historians seem to be agreed that education and the pursuit of learning in early Tudor England did not depend upon the continuance of life within the cloister.[18] Was it not perhaps the growing awareness of this fact during the 1530s which, in the eyes of Cromwell and his particular associates, tipped the balance against the monasteries, as well as the more obvious objective of effecting a really substantial augmentation of royal resources?

Such conclusions about the quality of early Tudor monastic life are of vital importance to anyone seeking to take a long view of the Dissolution, but they do not necessarily contribute to our understanding of the Dissolution as it actually happened. Do they explain why, with few exceptions, the religious put up so little resistance? If they were so comfortable how were they apparently so easily dispersed? If there was so little internal unity, so little respect for their superiors, how

[17] Knowles, *RO* III, p. 460.
[18] J. Simon, *Education and Society in Tudor England*, 1967.

were those same governors able to obtain, apparently so readily, the consent of their entire convents to an act of surrender? Would the monasteries have enlisted more lay support if they had still been centres of education and scholarship? Would laymen have shown greater respect for asceticism, had it been more widespread? None of these questions admits of an answer in general terms. Indeed Professor Knowles's candid admissions may well deceive the unperceptive reader. The internal condition of the religious houses of England and Wales, even on the eve of the Dissolution, varied to such an extent, both as to material comfort and disciplinary standards, that neither an excess of the one or a lack of the other can really have determined events. Moreover any attempt to gauge lay attitudes must always take into account the passage of time. In normal times, that is before there was serious talk of widespread disendowment, few influential laymen nourished strong feelings about the future of the religious houses.[19] They were longstanding neighbours, with all that that implied in terms of personal friendship, hospitality and not infrequent litigation. Although the monastic life commanded little real lay respect, by and large there was no widespread popular hostility, except that reserved for landlords in general, and no great desire to see the monasteries completely closed down. Many thought they were too well endowed, and some degree of disendowment had been canvassed for a long time (Doc. 1), but not even the formidable combination of Henry VIII and Simon Fish could have roused laymen against the monks in a hurry. Indeed in 1529 it might have seemed a much easier task to play upon and enlist the far more deepset and persistent rivalry felt by the secular clergy for their regular brethren. What we have to do is to chart the course whereby, in the decade which followed, the natural cupidities of most influential laymen were aroused and harnessed to those of the Crown, to the ultimate destruction of the monastic life throughout England and Wales.

Monasticism itself was, indeed, virtually extinguished by 1540. The monastic lands became, for the most part, reabsorbed into the secular landed wealth of the country. But the monastic buildings lasted very much longer, and still remain in a very large number of cases today, in various stages of survival. They too serve as source material for the historian. The recovery of bare monastic site plans has long been a favourite pursuit of archaeologists, but in recent years the possibilities of more extensive topographical studies – always understood, if not fully pursued by the masters such as Sir William St John Hope – have been increasingly exploited. What is called for now is a wider exploration

[19] The point is made most succinctly by Professor A. G. Dickens in his Introduction to *Clifford Letters of the Sixteenth Century*, Surtees Society Clxxii (1962), p. 32.

of all the relevant sources.[20] Not only in the Dissolution surveys, with their lists of lead roofs (Doc. 22) and interior furnishings, but in many other classes of post-Dissolution records lie rich stores of information, not only concerning the monastic churches and conventual buildings, but also the extensive monastic precincts and their relation to their topographical environment, both urban and rural (Docs. 19, 34, 37). To what extent, we must ask, both in the physical and the human sense, was the monastic gatehouse and the precinct wall a barrier between the secular and the regular world? And what were the possibilities presented to laymen of converting monastic fabric to secular use?

The Dissolution is indeed one of the best documented episodes in Tudor history, especially as regards the taking over and disposal by the Crown of monastic resources. The variety of material accumulated and produced by the court of Augmentations alone is formidable, and to this may be added the voluminous state papers of Henry VIII's reign, as well as relevant material in other sections of the public records, including the records of parliament. Local records, especially those of towns and cities, and private archives, contribute a certain amount, mostly to the later history of the monastic property. There are, of course, gaps which are most frustrating, especially to anyone pursuing the suppression of a particular religious house.[21] But in the selection of the documents which form the second half of this book the problem has been one of finding room for examples both of the more familiar types of document, those which on the whole have been most used by historians, and also of the rarer and less-used sources which illuminate a particular aspect of the subject and suggest lines of further inquiry. In spite of the limited space available an effort has been made to provide documents substantial enough in themselves to offer the reader the opportunity to judge whether he or she agrees with the interpretation put upon them in the introductory chapters.

[20] For some useful suggestions see J. C. Dickinson, 'The Buildings of the Austin Canons after the Dissolution of the Monasteries', *British Archaeological Journal* xxxi (1968).

[21] A good example of what can be achieved, even without a convenient *corpus* of source material, is S. F. Hockey, *Quarr Abbey and its Lands, 1132–1631*, Leicester, 1970.

2

The Crown and the Smaller Monasteries

'AS concerning . . . the extirpation of the state of monks and friars, the enterprise . . . requireth politic handling . . .'[1]

So wrote Henry VIII in 1543 for the edification of his cousin, James V of Scotland and although the advice he proceeded to offer implied that in England and Wales all had gone smoothly, in accordance with care-fully-laid plans, Henry can hardly have forgotten so soon what had been one of the most complicated and long-drawn-out operations of his reign.

The lands and other sources of income which English kings and their subjects had given to the Church over a period of more than eight hundred years had always been regarded as being, in a very special sense, sacrosanct. The anathemas of the earlier charters and, by im-plication, the solemn verbiage of countless later gifts, 'to the church of St . . . and the monks there, serving God', had consigned to eternal fire any who should violate such arrangements. It was, in fact, not an abbot but a bishop who, at a time when the 'voluntary' surrender of monasteries was proceeding apace, reminded the king of this. Stokesley of London, on being called upon in 1538 merely to effect an exchange of property, recalled that most of the endowments of his see had been given by St Ethelbert, its first founder, or by King Offa, 'and their gifts are written with terrible words and strange imprecations *contra alienatores*'.[2] Perhaps the bishop had a shrewd idea as to which of the parties to the exchange would come off best. Straight exchanges of land between laymen and clergy had, of course, quite often taken place, for their mutual convenience, ecclesiastical estates had been resumed by laymen and redistributed among other religious or quasi-religious institutions, and ecclesiastical corporations had both sold and bought land, but the general understanding had always been that the total re-sources of the Church were not thereby diminished. Indeed, in the eyes of the anti-clerical party the total landed wealth of the late medieval

[1] M. St Clare Burne, *The Letters of Henry VIII*, 1936, p. 315.
[2] *LP* XIII i, 1500.

Church in England and Wales was always increasing. Up to a point, and in its own interests, the English Crown had, by the Statute of Mortmain of 1279, placed a brake on the Church's acquisition of property. Moreover in the course of some of the more substantial late medieval redistributions of Church lands the Crown had not only been deeply involved but in the course of each operation had almost certainly added marginally, if only temporarily, to its own resources. The dissolution of the Knights Templar by Pope Clement V in 1312 had set free a large English estate which, as provided for by Rome, was ultimately transferred to the Knights of St John of Jerusalem, though not, it is thought, without some advantage accruing to Edward II and his associates. Even more important was the seizure by the Crown of the alien priories. Begun by Edward I and culminating in dissolution by act of parliament in 1414, this placed very considerable landed wealth virtually at the Crown's disposal. For the Crown to have retained substantial amounts of such property permanently in its possession would have been too much of an offence against the public conscience of the time and in fact most of the confiscated alien priory property was eventually applied by the Crown to the endowment of various schools, colleges, royal chapels and Henry V's new Carthusian monastery at Sheen.[3] In the long run the Church had nothing to fear from late medieval English kings and indeed by the Lancastrians in particular its interests were consistently protected. This was in spite of considerable parliamentary pressure to effect, with the help of the estates of the Church, and of the monasteries in particular (Doc. 1), some more permanent augmentation of royal resources. Even during the Yorkist period and the reign of Henry VII, when royal policy was directed towards the more permanent acquisition of Crown lands, the Church was never seriously threatened.[4] Temporary, and often quite prolonged, enjoyment by the Crown of ecclesiastical temporal revenues during vacancies was, of course, an accepted and regular perquisite of all medieval kings, including Henry VII and his son, but the pre-Reformation English Church on balance suffered little if any permanent loss of resources. Nor were the rights and privileges of its army of lay patrons seriously invaded, except as the result of attainder and forfeiture and other hazards affecting the landed subjects of the Crown. In this respect the laymen's losses were the Crown's gain, but as yet no religious house had anything to lose by exchanging an aristocratic for a royal patron or 'founder'.[5]

[3] M. McKisack, *The Fourteenth Century*, 1959, 291–5 and E. F. Jacob, *The Fifteenth Century*, 1961, 300–1. See also Knowles, *RO* II, 163–5 and B. P. Wolffe, *The Crown Lands, 1461–1536*, 1970, pp. 32–3.

[4] For the further re-disposition of church property in the later fifteenth century see Knowles, *RO* III, 157–8.

[5] 'Founders' were the lineal descendants, or legal assigns by gift, purchase, marriage, etc., of the original donors of monastic estates. A proprietory interest

Up to a point the suppression of religious houses by Thomas Wolsey was very like the earlier redispositions of ecclesiastical resources of which mention has already been made, including the passage of the property through the hands of the Crown. Between 1524 and 1529 by the authority, real or assumed, of a series of papal bulls, the Cardinal achieved the closure of some twenty-nine monastic communities. The net income from their property was about £1,800, that of one fairly wealthy house.[6] It is worth noting that the papal bulls of 1528–9 authorized the closure of an unspecified number of small houses, each however having less than six religious persons, up to a carefully specified total annual revenue, implying an understanding in Rome that diversion of resources rather than reform for its own sake was the primary intention. Wolsey was also authorized to unite houses with less than twelve religious to other houses of the same order, but if this was ever part of his plans he had no time in which to put it into effect. Clement V also gave his approval to a scheme for converting certain of the larger abbeys into seats for new bishoprics, with the turning of some of the monks into secular canons, but this too was one of those ideas which Wolsey's fall consigned to a temporary limbo in the minds of many laymen, including no doubt Wolsey's right-hand man, Thomas Cromwell.[7] Wolsey's main, and probably for the time being his sole, objective was to release revenue which could be applied to the endowment of his new Oxford college and his new school at Ipswich. There was no reason why his scheme should not be carried to a successful conclusion. In 1524 Bishop Fisher of Rochester had diverted the resources of two, admittedly decayed, nunneries to St John's College, Cambridge. Wolsey's choice of victims was indeed, on grounds of their condition, open to question but a careful study of the location of the individual properties would probably reveal some well thought out plan. The total suppression, even by a papal legate, of an entire English religious community, no matter how impoverished, required, however, more than a papal bull. Indeed the latter invariably laid down that before proceeding Wolsey must obtain the consent, in each case, of the patron or 'founder'. The king's approval was also, of course, essential, and there had to be in each case a legal instrument, however formal and essentially meaningless, whereby the voluntary surrender of the property by the convent to the Crown was affected. No one was necessarily deceived thereby, and any misgivings about the ability of the religious

---

of this kind in a religious house was a form of real property. It carried with it a certain amount of influence in the choice of new governors, i.e. abbots, priors, etc., rights to nominate to corrodies and to receive hospitality, and, of course, to benefit from the prayers of the community: Knowles, *RO* II, 283–7.

[6] Knowles, *RO* III, 161–2, 470.

[7] *ibid.*, 164, and *LP* IV iii, 5607–8. See *infra*, pp. 84–6.

to surrender the corporate endowments of their communities was no doubt overcome on these, as on earlier, occasions by the knowledge that the operation had both papal and royal sanction.[8]

Conveyance of the property to the Crown, if it was to be at the latter's free disposal, involved certain other technicalities besides the mere conveyance. In accordance with statutory requirements (8 Henry VI, c. 16 and 18 Henry VI, c. 8) in each county in which parts of the property lay there had to be juries empanelled, to declare, before the king's Escheator, the nature and annual value of each property coming to the Crown.[9] Moreover it was also necessary that in the case of each of the monasteries concerned the king should be declared, or 'found', by the local juries to be the undoubted 'founder', that is the representative of the original patron, and thereby entitled to property deemed to have escheated to the Crown following the renunciation of their rights by the religious. It should not have been difficult for Wolsey to have confined his choice to houses which really were of royal foundation or whose patronage had by some means come into Crown hands, but it was later held against Wolsey that he had overstepped the mark and 'found the king founder where other men were founders',[10] an invasion of rights of property which English landowners did not readily forgive. When the property was securely in Crown hands most, but not quite all, of it was conveyed to the Cardinal by letters patent under the Great Seal, with licence to proceed with the establishment of his new foundations. At his fall in 1529 Wolsey's interest reverted to the Crown: the school at Ipswich ended its brief existence and Cardinal College at Oxford was re-endowed with some of the property by Henry VIII in 1532. Some at least of the residue was later disposed of by the king to other laymen, including the Duke of Norfolk, and as late as 1536 the site of Stansgate Priory in Essex was granted by Henry VIII to the knights of St John of Jerusalem in exchange for property which included the manor of Hamton Court.[11]

The most valuable residual profit accruing to the Crown from Wolsey's suppression of monasteries was without any doubt the experience gained

---

[8] For the text of Wolsey's bulls see T. Rymer, *Foedera* (1704–35) XIV, 23. The heads of some of the houses dissolved by Wolsey went through a form of legal surrender. The relevant original documents (calendared in *LP* IV i, 1137) would probably repay inspection.

[9] *Statutes* II, 252, 306. The actual terms of the statutes were that the king was prohibited from disposing of the property unless inquisitions had been held and returns made establishing his legal ownership.

[10] Knowles, *RO* III, 163.

[11] Most of the property was in Essex. For the mechanics of the provision of the landed endowments of both Cardinal College and the Ipswich Grammar School see J. Oxley, *The Reformation in Essex*, Manchester, 1965, pp. 70–81, especially pp. 74–5.

in the course of the operation by Thomas Cromwell. As one of the Cardinal's men he was deeply involved in the surveying and subsequent administration of the property before Wolsey's fall. His first-hand knowledge of the problems involved in the confiscation of monastic lands, as well no doubt as a shrewd idea of the possibilities of further depredations, he carried with him into the royal service. That Wolsey's ill-fated scheme, conceived entirely in the interests of his own personal prestige, should, even to this extent, have shown the way towards the augmentation of the resources of the Crown is ironical. The Cardinal would never have robbed the Church in the interests of the State: his way of financing government was by way of forced loans from laymen and by direct taxation.[12] In so far as Wolsey took Church lands he did so only by robbing Peter to pay Paul, merely a stage in the centuries-old conflict between the secular and regular clergy. The real seculari-zation of Church property had not yet begun.

While it is impossible to defend Wolsey's suppressions simply on the grounds that they concerned only small or decayed religious houses, there can no longer be the slightest possible doubt that in the early 1530s a considerable number of houses, and not only the smaller com-munities, were in very poor shape and had been so for quite a long time. Dwindling numbers of recruits and lack of discipline, as well as and probably more than moral and spiritual weaknesses of a more venial nature, had brought many houses to the point where only inertia on the part of all concerned kept the community in being. The trouble which most often came to light was debt, but this will rarely have been unaccompanied by other weaknesses, and for some communities the very impossibility of extricating themselves from this economic quag-mire was almost a blessing in necessitating some drastic action. It was surely such a situation which led the prior and canons of Christchurch, Aldgate, to surrender their entire estate to the king in February 1532. This surrender has been interpreted by some historians as a trial run by the Crown, a testing of popular reactions, without any reference to the Pope and at a time when Henry VIII had not yet slipped the bonds with Rome. But there is in fact no evidence of the exercise of Crown pressure in the matter, except that the canons later alleged that they had been jockeyed into complete and irrevocable surrender when all they had intended was some temporary succour. There seems no sound reason for doubting the statement in their deed of surrender that of their own free will they handed over all they possessed, including their liabilities, to the king, their undoubted founder. This is not to suggest that their action came as a complete surprise to the king and there is evidence that he had plans for devoting the surrendered property to another foun-dation. In fact about two years later most of it was granted to Sir Thomas

[12] On this point see Wolffe, *op. cit.*, pp. 87-8.

Audley, More's successor as Lord Chancellor.[13] It was indeed Audley who, in the course of making arrangements for the necessary local inquests concerning the property, put forward the opinion that the deed of surrender did not give the king an adequate title. He advised a special act of parliament. This he no doubt calculated would not only place the king's title – and hence ultimately his own – above all possible doubt, but would be a neat way of avoiding the necessity of empanelling a jury of Londoners to declare the king's title. Far in fact from testing public opinion the facts suggest that the government was anxious to avoid inviting competing claims from citizens as co-founders with the king. The statute (25 Henry VIII, c. 33), after citing the surrender document and declaring the site, precincts, and the entire priory estate to belong to the king 'as true and just founder', proceeded to declare,

'that our said sovereign lord shall have the actual and real possession of and in the premises and every part thereof in as large and ample manner as though office and offices [inquests] had been duly found thereof according to the laws of this realm, and that all letters patent made and to be made by his highness to any person or persons of or in the premises or any part thereof shall be good and effectual in the law to all intents and purposes according to the tenures, forms, and effects of the same letters patent, albeit none office or offices be or shall be found of the manors, lands, tenements, or hereditaments to be contained and expressed in any such letters patent.'[14]

Here then, in the very first surrender of monastic lands to the king without any pretence of papal authorization, and probably because no less a person than the Lord Chancellor himself already had expectations of a share of the proceeds, every possible care was taken to make the transfer legally unassailable. It was a story that was to echo and re-echo during the decade which followed.

The surprising thing is that so few other communities followed the Christchurch example. There were plenty whose situation was far worse and who were even less capable of setting their affairs in order. It would have required very little persuasion, only the appearance of someone authorized to put them out of their misery. In fact the visits of royal agents in 1534 and 1535 led to the immediate surrender of some half-dozen houses.[15] Had there not followed some more positive action

[13] *LP* VII, 419, g. 28 and 587, g. 10.

[14] *Statutes* III, pp. 489–90. For a detailed account of this episode see E. Jeffries Davis, 'The beginning of the Dissolution: Christchurch Aldgate, 1532', *TRHS*, Ser. 4, VIII (1925), pp. 127–50. While the facts are not in dispute some of the author's conclusions are open to doubt: see Knowles, *RO* III, 200–1.

[15] For a list of the houses, four in Kent, two in Yorkshire, and one in Essex, with the dates of their surrender (taken from the Chancery enrolments of the

by the government there might well have been, in the later 1530s, a trickle of genuinely voluntary surrenders, perhaps increasing to a point which would have satisfied those whose only concern was reform. Indeed, in July 1536 it was reported to Cromwell that many houses in the north were ready to surrender by documents under their convent seals.[16] Be that as it may, in pursuing the development and maturity of government policy regarding the dissolution of religious houses allowance must always be made, right up to the time when, sometime late in 1539, only a hard core of stubborn resistance remained, for a high degree of willingness on the part of whole communities to surrender their corporate possessions and, by implication, the life that went with them. The case of Christchurch is, above all, a reminder that in times of financial and other crises the religious communities sought help, not from other houses of their order, least of all from their secular brethren the bishops, whose attentions they never encouraged, but from influential laymen, including, *par excellence*, the king. In so doing they were instinctively following historical precedent, and for practical purposes the breach with Rome was irrelevant.

Thomas Cromwell played no very obvious part in the dissolution of Christchurch, Aldgate, and not until December–January 1534–5 did he figure officially on the monastic scene with authority to carry out a general visitation. But he had never ceased to meddle with monasteries since his period of service with the Cardinal, and many abbots and other governors of religious houses were among the first of the king's subjects to recognize his escalating power and influence at Westminster. One of the earliest in the field was the abbot of Pipewell in Northamptonshire who in June 1531 granted to the king's new councillor an annual fee of 26s 8d (Doc. 4b). Cromwell's experience, his first-hand knowledge of the monasteries as institutions, his familiarity and sympathy with the parliament men, among whom it is said there was talk of dissolving monasteries during the parliamentary session of 1529,[17] and above all his interest in government finance, combined to make him particularly well equipped to advise the king as to the possibilities of expropriation and indeed to devise government policy towards the monasteries. In fact, however, the first positive evidence of official intentions to confiscate the property of the Church at large comes indirectly from the king himself. On 15 March 1533 the imperial ambassador, Eustace Chapuys, reported to the Emperor Charles V a conversation he had recently had with Henry. The latter had been full of 'imperial' ideas, of his intention of reversing the submission to Rome of

---

deeds) see Rymer, *Foedera* XIV, 557–8. See also Knowles, *RO* III, 289–90. In each case the king was said to be 'founder'.

[16] *LP* XI, 75.
[17] Scarisbrick, *op. cit.*, p. 250, n. 4.

his predecessors, Henry II and King John. Henry had told Chapuys that he also intended 'to reunite to the Crown the goods which church-men held of it, which his predecessors could not alienate to his prejudice'. This, he said, he was bound to do by virtue of his coronation oath, per-haps a typically-Henrician rationalization but it was in effect almost exactly the line of talk by their Commons in parliament which had met with such stubborn resistance from the Lancastrian kings (Doc. 1). Henry VIII was in fact thinking of a 'resumption' of one-time Crown lands which his predecessors had granted to the Church.[18] As an idea it was much more sophisticated and legalistic than the crude and general approach of someone like Simon Fish who simply wanted the Church at large disinherited.[19] Under canon law not only a founder but also his descendants could require a religious foundation to provide succour in time of need, an idea no more far fetched in the early sixteenth century than that which lay behind the fiscal feudalism which both Henry and his father had been adopting with marked success in respect of their lay landowning subjects.[20]

The months which followed Henry's revelations to the ambassador were taken up with the crucial legislation putting into legal effect the breach with Rome, and the importance of the clergy to Henry and Cromwell was measured not so much by their possessions as by their collaboration in carrying through the legislative programme. In the Lords and in Convocation the heads of virtually all the religious houses for men were involved, and by implication had involved their communi-ties, in each stage of the breakaway from Roman jurisdiction.[21] Their agreement, in the Act of Dispensations (25 Henry VIII, c. 21), passed early in 1534, to the section prohibiting English monks from going abroad in an official capacity, cut the last link of the English men and women religious with Rome and, in the opinion of a recent writer, affected the virtual nationalization of English monasticism at one blow.[22] Of more immediate practical consequence the act provided that in future all dis-pensations and other ecclesiastical licences were to be supplied in England and not at Rome, including licences to members of the regular religious

[18] *LP* VII, 235, p. 109. For the arguments underlying Crown resumption see B. P. Wolffe, 'Acts of Resumption in the Lancastrian Parliaments', *EHR* LXXIII (1958), pp. 583–613.

[19] The relevant part of Simon Fish's *Supplication of the Beggars* will be found in G. R. Elton (ed.), *The Tudor Constitution*, 1960, pp. 322–4. See also Dickens, *English Reformation*, pp. 99–101. Fish's statement that the clergy, secular and regular, between them possessed more than a third of the landed wealth of the kingdom was, in fact, no exaggeration.

[20] Knowles, *RO* II, 286, and J. Hurstfield, 'The revival of Feudalism in early Tudor England', *History* XXXVII (1952), pp. 131–45.

[21] Knowles, *RO* III, 175–7.

[22] *Statutes* III. 464–71 and Scarisbrick, *op. cit.*, p. 324, fn. 2.

orders to become secular priests. The oath required of all the king's subjects early in 1534 by the Act of Succession brought not only the governors but each member of each religious community to the point of accepting or rejecting the new regime, and at this stage even the Carthusians submitted. The real climax came, however, with the Act of Supremacy (26 Henry VIII, c. 1) late in 1534. With the notable exception of the Observant Friars, the Bridgettines at Syon (but only temporarily) and the London Carthusians, all the religious who were called upon to do so subscribed. The clergy at large had indeed proved to be no obstacle to the Henrician Reformation and any scheme of dis-endowment on the grounds that the regular orders were potential enemies of the king could not possibly form an essential part of royal policy. Lay opinion still had to be tested, and in fact at this stage it suited Henry and Cromwell very much better to obtain the consent of the religious to the breach with Rome rather than to be left with no alter-native but to destroy them. The long-drawn-out pressurizing of the Lon-don Carthusians was a measure of the government's desire at this stage for a moral, not a material, victory. The Observant Friary at Greenwich was actually refounded, the London Charterhouse was not finally sup-pressed until November 1538, and the community at Syon was not dispersed until yet another twelve months had passed.[23]

There was, however, at least as early as 1534, some thought being given by one or more persons within or on the fringes of the Court to the augmentation of royal revenue. There was never really enough money but it seems likely that the rebellion of certain Irishmen in the summer of 1534 made the problem more urgent. There survives among the papers of Thomas Cromwell, now the king's Principal Secretary as well as his most influential servant, a series of draft proposals which may even represent his own thinking in the early autumn of 1534 if not before. The suggestions (Doc. 5) are nothing if not radical and comprehend all the clergy, both secular and regular, above parish level. All endowments were to be forfeited to form a central fund out of which the higher secular clergy and the religious communities would be provided with fixed allowances. The residue would be at the king's disposal 'for the defence of his realm and maintenance of his royal estate'. In a typically Tudor effort to have it both ways the author envisaged not only a salaried clergy but also the payment to the Crown of first-fruits (the first year's income). In addition the cathedral clergy and archdeacons were to contribute a substantial regular proportion of their annual income. Finally all clergy, with laymen, were to pay a special, *ad hoc*, tax on their income or mov-able wealth. For present purposes the most interesting proposal con-tained in the document is the provision (clause 5) that the endowments of all religious houses where the number of religious persons was, or

[23] Knowles, *RO* III, 211, 237, 221.

a

lately had been, under thirteen should be surrendered *in toto* and, the
implication is obvious though it is nowhere expressly stated, there being
no provision for maintenance, such communities would cease to exist.
Whoever drafted this clause, whether consciously or not, showed a way
whereby a considerable number of religious houses might be dissolved:
without endowments, it could safely be assumed, a religious community
must vanish. This was resumption carried to its logical conclusion, the
process of foundation in reverse but without the inconvenient necessity
of discovering whether or not each of several hundred small communities
were of royal foundation. Had the scheme as it stood been put into effect
the Crown would not have actually taken possession of the endowments
but would have had the use of a considerable part of the income arising
therefrom. The plan also provided (clause 10) for the gradual phasing out
of the order of St John of Jerusalem, so that its resources in England
might be diverted towards the reduction of the Turks, or of those
enemies nearer at home, the Irish.

In the event the scheme was never implemented. The parliament
which met on 3 November 1534 passed, as well as the Act of Supremacy,
a subsidy act and also a simple measure whereby the king was to enjoy
not only the first-fruits of each clerical benefice but also one-tenth of its
annual income (26 Henry VIII, c. 3).[24] For the time being the clergy's
endowments were left in their own hands. As Chapuys described the
situation on 28 November,

'The king, who, as head of the Church in his kingdom, was intending
to take back into his hands all church property and distribute only a
frugal sustenance to ministers of the Church, is for the present satisfied
to leave the churchmen in possession of their property, provided they
will contribute. . . . Since the king was determined to bleed the church-
men he has done much better to do it thus than to take all their goods,
to avoid the murmur and hatred, not only of the clergy but of the people,
especially of those who have endowed churches or their successors.'

This last phrase, together with his oftquoted comment which followed
that had wholesale confiscation taken place it would have been necessary
to give most of the proceeds to 'gentlemen' to keep them quiet, shows
Chapuys at his best as an acute observer of the English scene.[25]

What the imperial ambassador can hardly have anticipated was the
vital part to be played by the Act of First Fruits and Tenths in the future
dealings of the Crown with the monasteries, and more particularly with
their landed revenues. It would be a safe assumption that at this time
no one in England knew how many monasteries there were in existence,
their geographical location, how many were autonomous houses and

[24] *Statutes* III, 493–9.
[25] *LP* VII, 1482.

how many were cells only, and least of all the identity and value of their lands and spiritual revenues. To have embarked, in 1534 or later, on any scheme of confiscation without such information would have been foolhardy; to have launched a survey with confiscation in view even more so. As it was, the task was completed at a time when any suspicions people may have entertained were certainly groundless and even the suspicions can easily be exaggerated. Contemporaries always assumed that government inquiries inevitably meant taxation. Not for at least another three years did Cromwell find it necessary to make public declaration that the government had no plans for wholesale suppression.[26]

The Act of First Fruits and Tenths provided for the appointment of local commissions under the Great Seal, the commissioners to consist in each case of the bishop and others to be named by the king, to inquire into the true annual value of each ecclesiastical benefice. Detailed instructions were prepared, those relating to the monasteries being as follows:

'Item, to search and know the number and names of every abbey, monastery, priory, and house religious and conventual, as well charter-houses [Carthusian] as other, founded and edified within every deanery or elsewhere within the limits of their commission as well in places exempt as not exempt and in whose dioceses and jurisdictions they be and the number, names and certainty of all the manors, lands, tenements, rents, farms, possessions, parsonages, portions, pensions, tithes, oblations and all other profits as well spiritual as temporal appertaining or belonging to every such abbey . . . [etc.] and in what shires, towns, hamlets and places the said manors . . . [etc.] lie and be. And their whole and entire, distinct and several yearly values. And the true certainty of such annual or perpetual rents, pensions, alms, and fees for receivers, bailiffs, auditors and stewards only, and none other officers, yearly given and paid out of the same. And the several names of the said officers to whom such fees be limited. And the names of the persons for whose souls such alms is distributed and given and the names of the persons and places whereunto and to whom such annual and perpetual rents and pensions be yearly paid . . . '

On completion of their inquiries the commissioners were instructed to have prepared 'a fair book after the auditors' fashion', that is a valuation showing the extent and source of gross income, less allowable deductions. Religious houses and parochial benefices were to be arranged according to the deaneries in which they were situated, the entry for each benefice being complete in itself, 'and nothing to be allowed or deducted thereof for reparations, fees, surveying of cures or any other causes or things whatsoever they be except only such annual and perpetual rents . . .

[26] See *infra*, pp. 68–9.

[etc.] as before specially is mentioned'. Finally the returns were to be certified by the commissioners and sent under their seals to the king's Exchequer, 'as they will answer unto the king's highness at their uttermost peril, to the intent that the tenth of the premises may be taxed'.[27]

The letters patent appointing the commissions were dated 30 January, 1535, one for each county. Apart from the bishop the persons appointed in each case were local gentlemen, for the most part men not otherwise heavily committed in the king's service. Indeed they were asked to complete their task by 30 May but although continually harried by Cromwell it was well into the autumn before the returns were anything like complete and after the New Year before the last arrived. Even at county level the compilation of what became known as the *Valor Ecclesiasticus* was an enormous undertaking and this, rather than idleness or reluctance on the part of the commissioners, most of whom were at pains to proclaim their zeal, accounted for the delay. The *rentier* nature of most of the estate assisted the commissioners, provided the necessary rentals were available and forthcoming. The most difficult part of the survey must have been the evaluation of land still in the monks' or nuns' occupation or of tenements the income from which came partly in kind. Both were required to be expressed in cash terms. It is in the valuation of demesne in hand that the *Valor* has been found by modern scholars to be fairly consistently unreliable. But when the *Valor* figures are compared with other, mostly post-Dissolution, evidence the discrepancies are only glaring when seen against the quite remarkable reliability of the returns as a whole. The survey of the revenues of Walsingham Priory in Norfolk (Doc. 4a) is typical of its kind except for the fact that, as the commissioners make very clear, the monks enjoyed a relatively large income from offerings at the shrine of Our Lady. As far as the gross income from land and the 'spiritual' revenues were concerned the valuation was as accurate as anyone could have wished and in fact more accurate than some would have thought possible, given on the one hand the anti-clerical temper of the times and on the other the disposition of some laymen to do their best for their clerical friends. The notorious undervaluation of some of the Lancashire monastic lands – the facts of which are not in dispute – has recently been convincingly explained as being due to there being three houses in the north of the county which were surveyed by commissioners appointed for the diocese of York who had a very large territory to cover.[28] It is true, of course, that for the most part the *Valor* figures can only be checked by compari-

---

[27] *VE* I. vii-x, and also in *English Historical Documents* v (1485–1558), ed. C. H. Williams, 1967, pp. 751–2.

[28] C. Haigh, *The Last Days of the Lancashire Monasteries and the Pilgrimage of Grace*, Chetham Society, Manchester, 1969, pp. 37–8.

son with post-Dissolution accounts which, thanks to administrative inertia, were to a large extent themselves prepared by reference to the *Valor*. However, a large number of entirely new surveys, especially of demesne, were made after the Dissolution, and it is upon comparison with these that confidence in the *Valor* has been built up.[29] In the case of five of the smaller Sussex houses newly surveyed in 1536-7 (Doc. 13) the later commissioners could add only £16 odd, or barely 3 per cent, to the earlier, i.e. *Valor*, gross valuation of £552 odd. One-third of this could be accounted for by a more realistic valuation of demesne. In the case of the sixth house, Hastings, the value of its property had 'decayed for certain lands in Peasmarsh now surrounded by sea'.

It has been suggested, though without any very substantial evidence, that Cromwell was in favour of concentrating any Crown attack on the property of the bishops but that the king preferred to deal first with the regular clergy as being less indispensable.[30] The *Valor Ecclesiasticus* points neither way and in any case whatever its future utility may have been there is no justification whatsoever for regarding it as anything more than a taxation assessment. However, almost simultaneously Cromwell was making use of the powers conferred upon him in January 1535 when he became the king's vicegerent in matters spiritual, and in-directly of the duty placed upon the king by the Act of Supremacy of 1534 (26 Henry VIII, c. 1) 'to visit, repress, redress, reform . . . [etc.]', to appoint his own deputies to visit monastic houses up and down the country. The way was now clear for him to step into the shoes of the diocesan bishops and indeed, with the right to visit the former exempt houses as well as the rest, he possessed powers considerably greater than had been enjoyed by the secular hierarchy and the opportunity, if he cared to use it, of reforming the English Church root and branch.[31] His 'Visitors', especially Richard Layton and Thomas Legh, have received more than their fair share of attention from historians and others concerned with the Dissolution, at least as far as their peregrin-ations in 1535-6 are concerned. Their methods were not by any means as indefensible as has often been claimed, and even if the conventional view be accepted that their mission was to gather sufficient evidence to condemn the religious in the eyes of parliament, careful reading of their letters to Cromwell – their so-called '*comperta*' are very terse and by no means all have survived – does not reveal a story of unrelieved villainy. They not infrequently commended whole communities to the Vicar-

[29] See especially Savine, *English Monasteries*, pp. 42-75.

[30] L. Stone, 'The political programme of Thomas Cromwell', *BIHR* XXIV (1951-2), p. 8. The only evidence actually cited by Professor Stone comes from April 1536 and calls for a very different interpretation: see *infra*, p. 41, n. 38.

[31] S. E. Lehmberg, 'Supremacy and Vicegerency: a re-examination', *EHR* LXXXI (1966), p. 226.

General and the worst of their gossip was only what circulated in every market place in England, and probably in Wales too. Incidentally the speed with which the Visitors moved does not need to be explained in terms of the urgent need to gather evidence but, as the Visitors themselves were well aware, it was important that Cromwell should be seen to be exercising his new powers by as many people as possible without delay.[32]

Besides their letters to Thomas Cromwell, we have the text both of the *questionnaire*, or Articles of Inquiry, provided for the visitors to put to the monks and nuns, and also of the Injunctions which they were ordered to administer, not, be it noted, in the light of the answers to the questions but prepared in advance for universal application. The questions, apparently drafted in the previous year by Dr Richard Layton, were on the whole reasonable and not unduly inquisitorial.[33] If plied with patience they could have provided much useful information and a basis upon which to plan a programme of necessary reform. Among the useful information sought was the names of the first and subsequent founders of each house, on the face of it an innocuous question the answer to which, in the light of the part played by founders or patrons in the choice of new governors, the Vicar-General had every right to know. The Injunctions, however, (Doc. 7) were anything but conventional, being shot through with current politics, no opportunity being lost of reminding the religious of their obligations to the new regime (nos. 1–3, 25). The items relating to the domestic routine of the monasteries, although largely along the familiar episcopal lines, were reasonable and sensible. But it is a reflection, not so much on the slackness of recent episcopal visitation as upon the general air of uncertainty and upon currently accepted standards that the inclusion of the by no means unprecedented order 'that no monk or brother . . . go forth of the precincts' aroused among the religious dismay and consternation. What exactly did the Vicar-General mean by this injunction? Did the prohibition include the abbot or the monastic officials concerned with the administration of abbey property? Worse still, did an abbot really have to obtain permission (no. 5) to employ women domestic servants, or to entertain distinguished lady guests? If intended to be interpreted literally such injunctions were, of course, unreasonable and virtually impracticable. The storm of protest which they evoked suggests that the Visitors did little to allay the worst fears of the monks. Whatever Cromwell's real intentions, there is no reason to think that, in the few years left, the Injunctions were strictly observed or that individual monks and nuns suffered any penalty for breaking them. Was it indeed a deep-laid plot

---

[32] *LP* IX, 424.

[33] T. Wilkins, *Concilia*, etc. 1737, III, 786–91. For Layton's part in their compilation see Wright, *Letters*, p. 157 (wrongly dated) and Knowles, *RO* III, 275–8.

to make monastic life so intolerable that the religious would welcome the opportunity, when offered to them, of changing their habits? Obvious as such a conclusion may appear it is on the other hand not unreasonable, in the light of all we know of the mental make-up of that remarkable man, to credit him with an officious but nevertheless sincere desire to use his new authority to restore order and discipline to those monasteries which were still capable of salvation. When, in July 1538, the abbey of Glastonbury received an episcopal visitation, many, particularly of the younger, monks, whose knowledge of the 'King's Injunctions' was admittedly a little hazy, actually invoked them in their representations against their superiors. May we not interpret as sincere, rather than as grimly ironic, Cromwell's reminder to himself sometime in February 1536 of 'the abomination of religious persons throughout this realm and a reformation to be devised therein'?[34] The worst motive that can in all fairness be imputed to him at this stage is a desire to have the governors of the religious houses dependent on him for any degree of relaxation. The result, if such was his objective, must have been most gratifying. The most revealing aspect of the shower of letters which reached Cromwell from distracted abbots, especially regarding their confinement to the precincts, was its indication of the degree of anxiety which the abbot of a great monastery such as St Augustine's, Bristol sustained (Doc. 8) not only to minister to the weaknesses of his fellow monks but to avoid upsetting the Vicar-General. There exists a letter to Cromwell dated 6 October 1535 from no less a person than the prior of Christchurch, Canterbury, indicating that the latter was willing not only to confine his community within the priory walls but also that Cromwell's own servant and emissary, one John Anthony, should take over the Wardenship of the priory's manors. Apparently quite resigned to the arrangement, including the payment of a fee, the prior stipulated only that the new Warden render his accounts promptly and, being a 'mortal man', provide surety for his efficient exercise of the office.[35] Evidence piles up from the latter months of 1535 of the impression which Cromwell had made on the regular clergy. The first thought of the bereaved monks of Osney (Oxon.) in November 1535 was to inform him of the death of their abbot.[35a] True, he was their chief steward, but it was to the Vicar-General that they appealed for help in procuring the election of a new

[34] Watkin, A. (ed.), *Somerset Record Society* LVI (1941), pp. 159–65, and *LP* X, 254.

[35] BM Harl. MS. 604, fo. 71, calendared in *LP* IX, 550. Although not as radical in its implications as the scheme of 1534 (Doc. 5), the idea that laymen should be appointed, presumably by the Crown, to administer the monastic estates, was widely current about this time. If pursued it would have been difficult for the monks to resist accepting a practice which they themselves had followed, at least in theory, in enrolling laymen as stewards, etc.: Savine, pp. 245–60.

[35a] *LP* XII, ii, 1120.

abbot of their own choice. His regular income by way of monastic fees rose quite sharply in the latter part of 1535.

What was almost certainly unknown, even to the Visitors, was the very real difference of opinion which existed during the winter of 1535–6 among the king's chief ministers and members of his Council as to what should be done about the monasteries, and Cromwell's own probably somewhat uncertain position as the power behind the throne. At some point very early in 1536, and possibly late in 1535, the decision was taken, probably on financial grounds, but also, by a process of rationalization, in the light of the reports of the Visitors, to proceed with the 'resumption', or confiscation, of the landed endowments of some of the houses of regular clergy. The problem was two-fold: which communities to single out and how legally to effect such a scheme. Any idea of a general attack on some proportion of the 'superfluous' income of all houses seems not to have been entertained. An attack on the smaller houses was obviously easier to justify and would arouse less opposition. On the second point it could probably have been argued that the Act of Supremacy empowered the king to dissolve unsatisfactory houses, but no doubt the lawyers would have felt uneasy about using that act as the king's authority for diverting the property of the Church to his own use.

Thomas Cromwell's predilection for parliamentary statute should not be taken for granted. It will be recalled that one of the questions addressed to the governors of religious houses by his Visitors concerned the identity of founders. In spite of the decision in the case of Christchurch, Aldgate, there was considerable precedent, both in Wolsey's time and since, for the escheat of monastic property to the king as founder. The use of the Visitors' reports for the selection of houses which could be shown either to have failed to maintain a minimum complement or in some respect to be disordered or decayed almost certainly had some attractions for Cromwell. He was indeed assured, probably early in 1536, that by such means there might accrue to the Crown landed property worth £40,000 a year.[36] The houses to be suppressed had, of course, to be of royal foundation. Failing the production by his Visitors of long lists of these it would perhaps have been sufficient to have revealed such uncertainty that the Crown could assert its own claims fairly widely. There is indeed evidence that in October 1535 Cromwell had himself written to the prior of Bridlington inviting the house to recognize the king as its founder. In rebutting the suggestion (Doc. 9) the prior was unable to name the present representatives of his house's founder, Sir Gilbert de Gaunt, but he did assert very firmly that the priory had hitherto been free from such 'interference' as Cromwell seemed to be threatening. A letter of 1 November from Dr Rowland Lee to Cromwell is even more explicit: he referred to a small house which

[36] *LP* x, 242, quoted in Knowles, *RO* III, 291.

was ripe for suppression and added that he supposed that the founder-ship could very easily be obtained from my lord of Northumberland.[37]

To have proceeded thus would have been a lengthy and tedious busi-ness and it may be doubted whether Cromwell was really serious. But there has recently come evidence from quite another source that he was loathe to resort to statute. This occurs in an anonymous and far from contemporary chronicle among the Wyatt papers recently edited by Dr Loades and takes the form of part only of a speech reported to have been made by Cromwell to the Council in the early months of 1536. He was apparently referring to the 'disquiet' aroused by Wolsey's suppressions in spite of his having procured papal licences and having proceeded gradually and circumspectly, 'Whereof,' Cromwell is reported to have continued, 'mine advice is that it should be done little by little and not suddenly by parliament.' Then, according to the chronicle, he proceeded to suggest that in view of the unpopularity of the monks' religion – by which he presumably meant their religious life – they should be per-suaded to 'change their coats', that is become secular clergy, and 'render their possessions to your majesty, by whose progenitors they were first created'. Whether this really represents Cromwell's views or not it is an interesting juxtaposition of ideas. The statement follows that the Council, confident of the king's power to deal with any trouble, decided to proceed by statute.[38]

There were other, and as they may have seemed to Cromwell, more compelling reasons why founders' rights could not be made to serve the king's interests. The early months of 1536 brought a stream of letters declaring the interests of numerous laymen up and down the country in the future disposition of the lands of monasteries rumoured to be scheduled for suppression. Sir Peter Edgcombe wrote from Cotehele about the Devonshire priories of Totnes and Cornworthy of which he was founder by virtue of a grant to his father by Henry VII of former Yorkist estates. He, and no doubt many other of the king's subjects, also had ideas of resuming some of their ancestors' ill-considered gifts to the Church, although Sir Peter did suggest that the worthy prior of Totnes might continue to enjoy his spiritual revenues.[39] It was, in effect, the situation relating to Christchurch, Aldgate, and the citizens of London in 1532–4 writ large, and only an act of parliament could

[37] Wright, *Letters*, p. 82.

[38] *The Papers of George Wyatt Esquire*, ed. D. M. Loades, Camden Society, Ser. 4, v. 1968, p. 159. Further evidence of Cromwell's last-minute caution comes in a report by Chapuys to Charles V on April 1, 1536 in which the am-bassador relates that the minister's change of mind had incurred the king's displeasure: *LP* x, 601, p. 244. In this context the new evidence turns out to be less 'completely unassessable' than was recently suggested: see G. R. Elton, *Political History*, 1970, p. 93.

[39] *LP* x, 551.

effectively bar such claims. In fact the very circulation of rumours to the effect that some monastic lands were to be confiscated, far from bringing laymen unreservedly to the side of the Crown as is so often assumed, served at once to place the Crown and large numbers of laymen in the position of competitors in what was to be the long-drawn-out business of permanently secularizing monastic resources. The extent to which laymen were already enjoying a substantial, albeit terminable share of monastic income by way of fees was by now, of course, laid bare in the *Valor*.

The first general act (Doc. 10) concerned with the dissolution of the monasteries was passed in mid-March 1536. As a piece of parliamentary legislation it was crudely drafted, being heavily overlaid with official propaganda and pious jargon. If it was Cromwell's handiwork it does him little credit. However it was apparently first introduced into the Lords chamber and the anonymous Elizabethan chronicler already referred to stated that it was the work of Audley, the Lord Chancellor and Sir Richard Rich, Solicitor-General, both able lawyers.[40] It contains one outstanding inconsistency which probably reflects as much as anything prolonged argument and indecision, both in Council and in parliament, about how to determine which monasteries to dissolve. The preamble to the act roundly condemned 'religious houses of monks, canons and nuns where the congregation of such religious persons is under the number of twelve persons', that is the conventional minimum number for a convent, other than the abbot, the line of demarcation suggested in the plan of 1534 (Doc.5). But the enacting clause (section II) clearly provided for the dissolution of 'religious houses . . . which have not in lands . . . [etc.] above the clear yearly value of two hundred pounds', a figure, be it noted, slightly above that laid down in the 1534 plan as providing adequately for a community of twelve priests and a governor. In fact when it came to the point it was the information contained in the *Valor Ecclesiasticus* and not the reports of the Visitors which determined the fate of each community. Useful as the latter no doubt were for propaganda purposes they were by no means as comprehensive in their coverage of the religious houses as the *Valor*, and provided inadequate information for drawing a line between the large and small communities. Once legislation had been decided upon not even Cromwell could have contemplated any sort of subjective judgement, deciding the future of each house on its merit, with all the argument and the lobbying which this would have led to. It could legitimately have been argued that a redistribution both of religious personnel and of property by closing the smaller houses and concentrating on the larger ones might result in overdue reforms, but there is no evidence that any redistribution of property

[40] S. E. Lehmberg, *The Reformation Parliament, 1529–36*, 1970, pp. 225–6 and *Papers of George Wyatt, op. cit.*

was ever contemplated by the government. Certainly none was affected. The idea of reform was now quite clearly a means, not an end, as far as the acquisitive government was concerned. Moreover the *Valor* had been compiled almost entirely by many hundreds of laymen up and down the country. To make use of their quite remarkable achievement would be, to them, gratifying to say the least and give them a sense of involvement. It was one of the ironies of the implementation of the act that in the case of those religious houses whose income was in the region of £200 a year those whose lay friends had returned minimal assessments had little cause to be grateful. At the risk of flogging a dead horse it must also be pointed out that the evidence of the Visitors, such as it was, did not bear out the creed which Henry and his advisers chose to adopt, namely that only the wealthier houses were worthy to continue.

The act did not in fact provide for dissolution in so many words but (section III) 'that his majesty [should] have and enjoy . . . such monasteries . . . which have not in lands . . . above the clear yearly value of two hundred pounds . . . and in like manner . . . all the sites . . . manors . . . appertaining or belonging to every such monastery . . . in as large and ample [a] manner as the abbots . . . [etc.].' Section VII assured to the king all the monastic movables of the houses concerned, including all ornaments and jewels and all money owing to them, as at March 1, 1536, and section IX made it unnecessary, in view of the late valuation, to hold any further inquisition or 'office'.

The government might have gone one stage further and obtained a statutory declaration that all contracts entered into by the monks, including leases, fees, corrodies, annuities, etc., were null and void. In fact the act included (section V) a general safeguarding of their interests in the property to all except the abbots themselves and 'such as pretend to be founders, patrons or donors' and declared invalid (section VI) only gifts, grants, leases, etc., made within one year before the passage of the act and then, where leases for lives or years were concerned, only those upon which the old and accustomed rent was not reserved,[41] or, in respect of grants of offices, etc., only those newly created. It would be an interesting exercise to discover, with the help of the *Valor Ecclesiasticus* of 1535, how many members of both houses of parliament in 1536 were in receipt of monastic fees as lay officers. It is hard to conceive of many of them having no such interest, and many will no doubt have felt, at least at the outset of the debate, that their interest might be better served by preserving the *status quo*. It may well be that some at least of the opposition which is said to have been voiced against the bill stemmed from more calculating considerations than the spiritual well-being of the country or its social needs. The effect of this very limited upsetting of

[41] The objection, from the Crown's point of view, was, of course, to leases upon which abnormally low rents had been reserved.

conventual grants was to give statutory protection to long leases for years which the common law courts frowned upon as probably fraudulent in intent.[42] Out of the many thousands of laymen who already enjoyed a share in the monastic resources, including Cromwell, only the founders were left out in the cold. To have devised any method of compensating them would have involved an altogether different formula, for theirs was a continuing interest while that of leaseholders, officers, annuitants, etc., was a terminable one. Section XVIII underlined the utter exclusion of founders from any rights they might claim to a resumption of the property.

Some provision had to be made for the 'governors' who, in spite of their 'detestable lives', could not be allowed to become martyrs but had to be encouraged to retire contentedly. They were to be provided (section X) with 'such yearly pensions and benefices as for their degrees and qualities shall be reasonable and convenient', with the promise of more generous provision for those who conserved their property pending the Crown's take-over. The rank and file of the religious were to be granted capacities, that is licences to become secular priests, with a gratuity, or to be accommodated in other houses of their order, this second alternative, incidentally, having been put forward in the act's preamble as the only hope of reforming their miserable lives and filling the 'great and honorable monasteries'. Section XI re-emphasized such hopes.

Section XIII reserved to the king the right at his discretion to exempt certain houses, by letters patent under the Great Seal, from the operation of the act. It has recently been convincingly demonstrated that in Yorkshire the exemption of an unusually large proportion of the smaller houses was necessary in order to provide accommodation for those religious, especially nuns, who decided to remain in the cloister.[43] But that is not quite the same thing as proving that when the act was being drafted and debated anyone foresaw the accommodation problem. The government's information on this score was by no means complete or up to date and the Visitors of 1535 had usually stressed the anxiety of the religious to be dismissed from their vows. There might even be some truth in Gasquet's contention that the government anticipated collecting large fines for exemption. It certainly did so (Doc. 28a) and although in each case it would have been more profitable to proceed with dissolution, Tudor governments had a propensity for imagining that they could both have their cake and eat it. The exemption clause, which may have been added at a late stage in the passage of the bill

[42] cf. E. Kerridge, *Agrarian Problems in the Sixteenth Century*, 1969, p. 85, where it is implied that this was the result only of the act of 1539.

[43] G. W. O. Woodward, 'The exemption from suppression of certain Yorkshire priories', *EHR* LXXVI (1961), pp. 385–401.

through parliament, is probably best explained as a way of retaining for the government some freedom of action, even a way of retreat should there be undue popular opposition.[44] For while we can safely impute both to the king and Cromwell considerable determination in 1536 to dissolve a substantial number of the smaller monasteries, we can also be sure that at this juncture neither of them had the slightest idea how far and how fast they would be able to go. Even discounting as propaganda the statements in the preamble about the excellence of the wealthier houses there are provisions in the enacting clauses – such as the option offered to the rank and file to go to other houses of their order – which are quite meaningless and irresponsible if in fact anything approaching wholesale suppression was at this stage seriously envisaged. It might be argued that the government was never, either at this juncture or later, prepared to show its hand, but it seems far more likely that like most governments it embarked only upon what seemed possible in current circumstances, with little or no idea what the future might bring within its grasp. Had real opposition shown itself Cromwell might well have left the more efficiently-administered even of the smaller houses alone, or only tapped their 'superfluous' income. It was presumably well known in England that wholesale state expropriation of monasteries had been well in train in Denmark and Sweden by 1527 and even earlier in Zürich, but the Henry VIII of the mid-1530s would have thought that no good reason for following suit.[45]

This seems to be the point at which to pose the question how far Henry VIII's government was influenced in the matter of the Dissolution by the ideas and practical suggestions of the so-called 'commonwealth' men, that group of humanist intellectuals whose existence was certainly not unknown to Thomas Cromwell. Such men, though highly critical of the Church, especially in the realm of education, relief of the poor, etc., were not fundamentally opposed to monasticism. Thomas Starkey, the friend of Reginald Pole, seems only to have accepted the idea of dissolution, rather than radical reform of the monasteries, under the pressure of events in England.[46] It was with all the enthusiasm of the convert that he applied himself, in the summer of 1536, to defending what had been done in the last session of the Reformation Parliament. He was, indeed, greatly concerned about the effect of the recent statute on the

[44] cf. the view of Professor Woodward, *ibid.*, p. 399, that 'the exemption clause was designed as an integral and necessary part of the statute of suppression, and not merely included as a money-raising afterthought'.

[45] Knowles, *RO* III, 165–71.

[46] G. R. Elton, 'Reform by Statute: Thomas Starkey's *Dialogue* and Thomas Cromwell's policy', *Proc. British Academy*, 1968, p. 170. See also Lehmberg, *Reformation Parliament*, p. 224, n. 1, where it is suggested that a draft bill providing for much less drastic treatment for the monasteries than was contained in the act of 1536 may have come from 'commonwealth' circles.

reputation of the English government, both at home and abroad.[47] In his letter, intended for, if not actually read by, the King (Doc. 14), he was at pains to defend the diversion of monastic endowments to uses other than those intended by founders, and he certainly assumed the existence of a regime which, in such matters of conscience, was prepared to be paternal, if not outright autocratic. He had obviously been won over to the idea of dissolution by the prospect of the benefits which might accrue to the king's subjects. This, from the government's point of view, was very useful propaganda. But he also argued passionately for the application of the proceeds of the Dissolution towards the immediate relief of poverty, and to the support of education, the profession of arms, and the economy generally. A conservative in matters of doctrine, Starkey still believed in the efficacy of prayers for the dead, but not to the exclusion of other deeds of charity. His unqualified approval of the act was clearly conditional on its limited application and it seems unlikely that, at this stage, he would have supported wholesale dissolution, even for 'commonwealth' ends.[48] If Cromwell had a sheet-anchor in 1536 may it not have been Thomas Starkey? The latter's insistence, in his letter to the King, on the need to maintain 'hospitality' on the sites of the dissolved monasteries does however strike one as a little odd in one who must have been familiar with the details of the act (Doc. 10), including sections XVII and XVIII. Is it too far-fetched to suggest that these, contained as they are on a separate sheet and headed by the king's sign manual, were added, not by the Commons but, prompted by Starkey, on the king's authority alone, after the Reformation Parliament had dispersed?

Be that as it may, had the government of Henry VIII rested content with what it was enabled to achieve as a result of the act of 1536 he at least, if not Cromwell, would no doubt have gone down in history as an astute and humane reformer. For nearly two centuries English monasteries had been lacking their full complement of religious, and some movement for consolidation from within had long been desirable. The houses which gained full exemption from the act of 1536 were technically, according to the terms of their patents, re-founded, and as late as 1537–8 the king was engaged in the re-founding of Chertsey, Stixwould, and Kirklees.[49] Even in 1539, as we shall see, many men believed that not all the monasteries were doomed.

The sixth session of the Reformation Parliament also passed an act

---

[47] *LP* XI, 73.

[48] Starkey's old friend, Reginald Pole, was shortly to be pressing in Rome itself for a pruning of decayed limbs of the regular orders: Knowles, *RO* III, 171–2.

[49] *ibid.*, 350.

establishing an altogether new and virtually self-contained government department, the court of Augmentations, for the purpose of administering the property which would shortly come into Crown hands. Its personnel and how the new department functioned will be dealt with in a separate chapter. The point will be made there that the establishment of this separate department is the strongest possible argument for the government's determination not only to augment its revenues but to retain its new resources permanently in its own hands. But in 1536 when the court of Augmentations was 'new begun', no one knew with any certainty how extensive its responsibilities would, sooner or later, become.

Parliament dispersed on April 14th and by the end of the month not only had the officers of the court of Augmentations been appointed but also bodies of commissioners had been appointed under the seal of the court to visit those monasteries which, in accordance with the recent act, were due to be dissolved, that is all those with net incomes of less than £200 a year. But speed was not everything and no community was to be dispersed, unless it was a question of voluntary surrender, until the property of the house had been newly surveyed and certain other information obtained. Commissions were appointed for each county, or, where appropriate, for groups of counties, or, in the case of Wales, for dioceses, consisting in each case of the two appropriate regional Augmentations officers,[50] one of the clerks employed in the compilation of the relevant part of the *Valor Ecclesiasticus*, and three local gentlemen. Instructions were issued (Doc. 11) indicating the procedure to be followed and the kind of additional information to be obtained. An advance on the visitations of 1535 was the instruction to the commissioners to make an inventory, to be agreed with the head or governor of each house, of movable goods, both plate and other valuables, and household stuff and farm stock. They were also to survey the demesne, especially that still in hand. Title deeds and other 'writings' concerning the property were to be taken care of, but no instructions were given to the commissioners, either now or on later occasions, about books and literary manuscripts. All the information was to be contained in a 'brief certificate' which was to be sent to the Chancellor, or chief officer, of the court of Augmentations. Before departing the commissioners were to enjoin each governor to commit no waste of his goods, to continue to till those fields still in the monastery's occupation, and to collect no rents except what were necessary for the maintenance of the covent, all this until such time as the king's further pleasure should be made known. The instructions to collect no rents suggests that it was intended that the operation should be complete if possible by midsummer or at the very latest by Michaelmas, the end of the financial year. The instructions also

[50] See *infra*, pp. 92–3.

included an appendix applicable to houses whose future had already been decided and whose goods and inmates were to be dispersed immediately. This followed exactly the relevant sections of the act of dissolution (Doc. 10) but also pointed forward to the procedure to be followed in all cases at such times as the fate of each house was finally decided.[51] That so few houses threw in their hand at the commissioners' first visit is probably to be explained by the lack of any financial provision for the rank and file and the uncertainty whether such would be made welcome in other houses of their order.

The commissioners, we may be sure, arrived at each of the monasteries within their purview in some style, though not necessarily with any considerable entourage. They expected, and for the most part received, the support of local officials. Many years later John Hooker, city chamberlain and chronicler, put on record his memories of the slight commotion which occurred in Exeter (Doc. 12). Not the least significant aspect of the episode is the very real suspicion in Westminster that such a disturbance of the peace could not have been caused by mere women. For the most part, as far as can be gathered from surviving records, the passage of the commissioners was uneventful. In the north of England, so soon to be much more troublesome to the king than was ever the case with the south-west, the dissolution of the smaller monasteries was later put forward as a grievance. But there was little attempt even there, by laymen or monks, to hinder the commissioners during the summer of 1536, and only at Hexham and to a lesser extent at Norton in Cheshire was there any show of resistance.[52]

The commissioners' task, even to the point of completing the 'brief certificates', was no light one. Progress inevitably varied from county to county, especially because of the necessity of having the Augmentations officers present, most of whom were responsible for more than one county. It was a lesson which Cromwell certainly learnt and, as we shall see, in 1537–8 he made different arrangements. At some date subsequent to the preliminary 'supervisions' the commissioners returned to those houses whose suppression had been finally decided upon to put it into practical effect. There being no question of any formal deeds of surrender it is not always easy to discover exactly when any particular house closed its doors for good and for the most part we have to rely on such information as may be gleaned from the accounts later prepared by the appropriate Augmentations Receivers, accounts in which they were careful to assume responsibility only for income arising since the statutory vesting day (Doc. 10, section v), namely March 1st, less the running expenses of each house up to the actual day of dispersal (Doc. 27a). By no means all the houses suppressed in accordance with the act

[51] Woodward, 'The exemption of Yorkshire priories', pp. 388–90.
[52] Knowles, RO III, 324–5.

of 1536 were in fact dispersed before the end of the year. By the autumn, when all further progress was halted by the outbreak of the Lincolnshire Rebellion and the Pilgrimage of Grace, some houses had received only their 'supervision', and some had not even received any attention at all from the commissioners.[53] For example, Hempton Priory in Norfolk was first visited early in August 1536 by Sir Roger Townshend, Sir William Paston (both local gentlemen), and the two Augmentations officers, Richard Southwell and Thomas Mildmay. Inventories were compiled and the house's movable goods formally placed in the custody of the prior, Henry Salter. Not until January 24, 1537 did they reappear and proceed to disperse the religious and arrange for the sale of movables. The Hertfordshire houses were not visited at all until March 1537. On the other hand some houses were dealt with very expeditiously. In Yorkshire, whose Augmentations officers had no overlapping responsibilities, all the smaller houses had been 'supervised' by the end of June 1536 and those whose suppression had been decided upon were dealt with by the beginning of August.[54]

The problem of accommodating those religious who expressed a wish to remain in the cloister was undoubtedly an important factor in deciding which houses were to be exempted from the implementation of the act. Not until the 'brief certificates' were to hand was it known at Westminster how many of these there were. An unknown number had already departed, many who had been professed when under age had been released by the visitors of 1535 on the authority of the Vicar General, and little or no official obstacle had been put in the way of others who sought capacities (licences) to go into the secular world before their communities were in imminent danger of suppression (Doc. 6). But, when it came to the point, a very large proportion of those who remained chose to stay (Doc. 13), especially the women, for whom there was little by way of alternative occupation in the outside world. For all of these accommodation had to be found by a government very much concerned, in spite of the widespread lay indifference to the value of the religious life, not to make martyrs. Indeed, such men and women were in many cases the friends and even the relations of influential laymen, even of the officers of the court of Augmentations. Be that as it may, in the opinion of Professor G. W. O. Woodward it was, in Yorkshire at any rate, the problem of accommodating those who in

[53] S. Jack, 'The last days of the smaller monasteries in England', *Journal of Ecclesiastical History*, XXI ii (1970), pp. 104–6, 117, 120–2. This paper and that of Professor Woodward already cited have been indispensable in the reconstruction of the procedure followed in 1536.

[54] *LP* XII i, 231, Jack, p. 122, and Woodward, p. 390. In some counties lay 'curators' were installed to supervise the monks' activities pending the commissioners' return: Jack, p. 115.

1536 wished to remain in religion which led to a considerable number of houses, especially those for women, being granted exemption.[55] As is clear from the commissioners' instructions (Doc. 11) the decision was reached as early as April 1536 to exempt the whole Gilbertine order. This may have been due to an anticipation of the problem of finding alternative accommodation for the seven smaller communities of this order which contained both men and women but is far more likely to have resulted from the influence of the Master of the Order of St Gilbert of Sempringham, Robert Holgate, president of the Council of the North.[56]

Lest there be a danger of imputing only the purest of motives to the Henrician government, it must not be forgotten that some very substantial fines were paid by about half of the houses selected for exemption, and that an even greater, but unknown, number at least undertook to find large amounts of cash. This is clear from the accounts of Thomas Pope, Treasurer of the court of Augmentations, for the period from April 24, 1536 to Michaelmas 1538 (Doc. 28a). Thirty-three houses paid a total sum in fines of nearly £6,000 and, without giving details, the accounts indicate that further sums were due from houses which, by Michaelmas 1538, had already surrendered as part of the 'voluntary' movement by then well under way. To these official fines must be added the payments made to Cromwell and other influential laymen, though not necessarily, as is so often assumed, in order to procure stay of execution. Possibly some decisions were influenced by timely gifts but more often than not there were other and more legitimate objectives. Decisions made had still to be implemented and formalities completed. Leonard Beckwith, Augmentations Receiver for Yorkshire, certainly accepted various fees and life pensions from houses which gained exemption but the services he rendered were in many cases to expedite the issue of letters patent rather than to procure the crucial verdict.[57] How the money for the fines was raised by the religious is rarely revealed. Some of it no doubt came from friends, or more particularly where the nuns were concerned, from relations, and a good deal was probably found by the religious themselves by dint of selling long or otherwise beneficial leases of their property. Rather more than three hundred separate houses were potential victims of the act and of those it appears that about eighty, or rather over one quarter, were exempted.[58] Not

[55] Woodward, pp. 398–9. See also Knowles, *RO* III, 316–17 where the exemptions are explained as arising, in the course of events, out of the accommodation problem.

[56] cf. Knowles, p. 317 where this evidence of an early decision is not mentioned, and also Woodward, pp. 386 and 389.

[57] Woodward, *op. cit.*, pp. 393–4.

[58] In a recent work (*Dissolution of the Monasteries*, 1966, p. 68) Professor Woodward puts the figure quite categorically at 67, but Professor Knowles, who

all received the statutory letters patent immediately and at least a dozen never in fact obtained even this degree of security. The last recorded patent was that issued as late as July 12, 1538, by which time 'voluntary' surrenders were well in train, to the Cistercian nunnery of Nunappleton, Yorkshire.[59] But while some patents were delayed at least until all or part of the agreed fines had been paid, many were formally exempted without fine at all. These latter are the ones most likely to have been reprieved in order to solve the problem of accommodation.

To return to the two hundred odd houses which were in fact suppressed in 1536–7, all were duly surveyed by the commissioners and as a result we know rather more about the physical state of the buildings, the amount of demesne in hand, the number of servants, etc., of these smaller houses than we do of the monasteries whose later dissolution was rather more summarily dealt with.[60] From their formal reports (Doc. 13) and more particularly from such of their letters as have survived it is clear that the commissioners did not go out of their way to uncover scandal; in fact where they did comment it was more often than not in order to commend, either as justification for treating the departing religious with humanity, or as a direct recommendation for exemption on grounds of local usefulness. George Gifford, Augmentations Receiver for Northamptonshire and his fellow commissioners wrote to the Chancellor of the Augmentations on May 12, 1536 commending the Cistercian nuns of Catesby, not only for the 'very perfect order' of the house but also on account of local reports about the amount of relief extended by the nuns to the poor. They also commented on the 'discreet entertainment' extended to them and their party, and it appears that the king, on being shown their letter, suspected that they had been bribed. However, they were unrepentant and did not hesitate, a month later, to put in a good word for Ulverscroft Priory in Leicestershire.[61]

The central officers of the newly-created court of Augmentations very quickly got to grips with some of the more detailed problems raised

---

seems to have made the most exhaustive count, sets it (*RO* III, pp. 315–16) at between 70 and 80 in England alone.

[59] *LP* XIII i, 1519, g. 44. This house finally surrendered on December 5, 1539: *LP* XIV ii, 636.

[60] Knowles, *RO* III, 306–15. A good deal of the detail, especially concerning the sale of movables, which most writers have culled from the limited number of so-called 'paper surveys' of 1536–7, can be obtained for practically every single house, including those dissolved in 1538–9, from the earliest Receivers' Accounts: see *infra*, pp. 106–7.

[61] Wright, *Letters*, pp. 129–30, 136–7. Ulverscroft survived temporarily but Catesby was dissolved in 1536. The 'brief certificates' for Leicestershire, Warwickshire, Rutland, Huntingdonshire and Lancashire are calendared in *LP* X, 1191.

by the transfer of monastic property. They were indeed quickly pressed for guidance by their more established, if in this respect not more experienced, colleagues of the duchy of Lancaster. The latter's statutory duties in regard to monastic lands, being so much the less, had enabled them to proceed with 'supervision' and so to dissolution (see p. 94) with greater speed than the Augmentations. To their question concerning the pensions to be assigned to the late governors the reply they received from John Onley, Attorney of the court of Augmentations, was that these should be 'the tenth part of the clear yearly value of the whole possessions of every such house as they be now valued at this second visitation', plus a further £2 to £3 at the Chancellor (of the duchy's) discretion, 'according to the degree and quality of the person,' this last phrase being a repetition of the words in the act (Doc. 10, section VIII). Thus was laid down, administratively, the principle that pensions were to be related basically to the value of the lands and other sources of income being forfeited, a useful rule of thumb for busy government officers which relieved them from too close an adherence to the more subjective principle embodied in the act. The commissioners probably adherred only when convenient to the threat implied in the statutory promise that the king would have 'most tender respect to such of the chief governors as well and truly conserve and keep the goods and ornaments of their houses to the use of his majesty'. John Onley also dealt with men and women in receipt of regular alms, who were to be provided for at discretion. He himself, he recalled, had assigned to some ten or twelve such persons at the Elsing Spital hospital in London about £10 a year, altogether, for their lives. With regard to disabled persons dependent on houses being dissolved, whether lay or religious, he had advised his commissioners 'to give unto such persons some honest reward in money and some small stuff of household' at their discretion and further, 'if they see any great or urgent cause of pity or charity in any such persons that in such cases they should deal with them more largely by their discretions, but no yearly living to be allowed . . .'. Here again was laid down another useful rule of thumb: the Crown was to incur no regular obligation beyond that assumed by the monasteries themselves but all payments which the latter had been required to meet, by the terms of the original donation, should be faithfully honoured. Servants, Onley continued, should have 'their full [i.e. outstanding] wages and some honest reward besides', and, after careful inquiry, all true debts owed by the religious should be paid, 'especially all such as be claimed for meat, drink and victuals and such other necessaries used and bestowed in the house'. In general, John Onley concluded, his office left it to the commissioners to act 'as to them upon the execution thereof shall seem most convenient for the avoiding of clamour of the people . . . and [he] thinketh that it will the easier be allowed when it is done than when it is put in question'.[62] In other words, in the opinion of this shrewd lawyer and intimate friend of Thomas Cromwell, people will accept their lot, however meagre, much more readily if, at the earliest possible moment, they know where they are. It was a policy which the court of Augmentations pursued, with marked success, not only in these early days but in the years which followed.

The dissolution of the majority of the smaller monasteries, it is now generally agreed, was only a minor cause of the rebellion of 1536,[63] and in any case although, as already indicated, it held up for a few weeks or months the completion of the current programme, it did not result in the postponement of any more ambitious plans simply because, as far as one can guage on present available evidence, no further advance beyond the statutory provision of 1536 was yet contemplated. However, the reckoning which followed close upon the defeat of the Northern Rebellion brought a further small but significant group of monasteries, with all their possessions, into the hands of the Crown. Henry himself gave the order that 'all the monks and canons that be in any wise faulty ... be tied up without further delay or ceremony, to the terrible example of others' and Abbot John Paslew of Whalley was executed at Lancaster on March 10, 1537. Within a matter of days the king wrote to his agents on the spot (Doc. 15), commending their action, not only in executing the abbot but in safeguarding the abbey buildings and lands. These were to be taken possession of in his name, 'as by our laws we be justly, by the attainder of the said abbot, entitled unto it'. His right to seize the entire estate of a religious house whose governor alone had been convicted of treason was not, as has sometimes been suggested, an *ad hoc* invention of the king but, as he himself claimed, was grounded in statute. Section IV of the Treason Act of 1534 (26 Henry VIII, c. 13) excluded from a general saving of interests in the property of convicted traitors, the traitors themselves, their heirs and successors.[64] The king's

---

[62] PRO, Duchy of Lancaster Records, Miscellanea (DL 41), 12/11–12. For the somewhat earlier dating of the exchange between the Duchy officers and John Onley see Haigh, *Lancashire Monasteries*, pp. 38–41 and cf. Elton, *Tudor Revolution*, pp. 209–10.

[63] A. G. Dickens, *The English Reformation*, pp. 124–8. An attempt by Dr C. S. L. Davies ('The Pilgrimage of Grace reconsidered', *Past and Present*, 41 (1968) to reinstate the Dissolution as a major cause of the risings offers little by way of evidence other than the fact that the smaller religious houses were thicker on the ground in the north than they were in the west of England, where there was no trouble in 1536. Even more recently, in his penetrating study of the Lincolnshire rising, Mr. M. E. James has found little direct connection between the early stages of the Dissolution and the revolt against the government: 'Obedience and Dissent', *Past and Present*, 1970.

[64] *Statutes* III, 509. It may be questioned whether the act itself really admits of the interpretation put upon it by the king and his lawyers (and by Miss I. D, Thornley in 'The Treason Legislation of Henry VIII', *TRHS* Ser 3, XI (1917),

intention regarding Whalley Abbey to 'devise for such a new establishment thereof as shall be thought meet ... [etc.]' may be taken as a
merely conventional and meaningless expression but it probably points
to a residuum of uncertainty in the king's mind. He certainly had no
intention of allowing the rest of the Whalley community to remain in
possession, although they were to be encouraged to remain in religion.
The heads of Hexham, Northumberland, and of Kirkstead and Barlings
in Lincolnshire were also attainted early in 1537 and all their estates
forfeit to the Crown. It is perhaps ironic that Mathew Mackerell, abbot
of Barlings, pleaded guilty to having sold plate and ornaments from his
house, his defence being that he was only anticipating the suppression
of the greater abbeys. Such anticipation was not to the Crown's liking,
and his action was more conveniently interpreted as an anticipation of
the rebellion.[65] Bridlington Priory and Jervaulx Abbey, both in Yorkshire,
completed the list of religious houses dissolved by the attainder of their
governors in 1537, but the same procedure was followed in 1538 in the
case of Lenton Abbey, Nottinghamshire and Woburn, Bedfordshire.
In similar manner towards the end of 1539 the Crown made an end of
the great Benedictine abbeys of Reading, Glastonbury and Colchester.
But it was never the Crown's intention to procure the wholesale suppression of monasteries by judicial process, nor indeed to make martyrs
and popular heroes. The king was very well aware of this latter danger
in March 1537 when (Doc. 15) he enjoined his agents to use their
'dexterity' so as to 'frame [the monks of Whalley] to that point that they
may enter into other [houses]'. Nor, among the rank and file of the
religious during the whole period from 1536 to 1540 did more than a
mere handful face trial and execution, and only the conviction of the
governor of a house had any implications at all for the rest of the community.

The takeover by the Crown's officers of the attainted monasteries in
1537 proceeded in a leisurely way. A great deal of the initial responsibility was undertaken by the duke of Norfolk as part of his duties as
the king's chief agent for the pacification of the north. He took possession
pending the arrival of Richard Pollard, one of the General Surveyors of
Crown lands, into whose charge, rather than that of the court of Augmentations, the lands of the attainted monasteries were placed. Pollard
was hard at work by June 1537 and seems to have worked amicably
enough with various local gentlemen who had assisted Norfolk at the
suppression of the various houses. He was obviously anxious to arrange

---

p. 118), but that such an interpretation was intended is clear from Cromwell's
note of 1533 about a bill 'whereby any bishop, dean, abbot, etc., convicted of
high treason [shall] forfeit the lands held in right of their corporations': *LP* VI,
1381 (3). On the attainted abbots see Knowles, *RO* III, 332.

[65] Knowles, *RO* III, 333.

everything to the king's utmost advantage and spoke scornfully of those who expected to obtain leases of the new Crown lands at the old rents. There is an interesting letter written by Norfolk on June 19th, to Cromwell asking, somewhat peremptorily, that James Rokeby and William Blithman (Augmentations Auditor and Receiver respectively for Durham county) should be sent up to join Pollard for the surveying of the property of the abbey of Jervaulx, 'to the intent they may instruct him in divers things touching the king's highness's profit in the same'. What Pollard thought of the suggestion we do not know, but Norfolk will almost certainly have known that the policy of the court of Augmentations was not to raise rents, to protect existing tenancies and to favour local men in letting the former monastic lands. We know from Norfolk's own letters that he himself was much in sympathy with such a policy, no doubt regarding it as offering the best hope of reconciling laymen to what had taken place. From Bridlington a week or so earlier he had written to Cromwell advising that local men be preferred in the letting of the priory's demesne, 'every man severally to him so that he shall not alien[ate] nor put away the same . . . whereby it shall not come to one man's hands and thereby many men shall be relieved'.[66]

[66] For the text of Norfolk's letters to Cromwell see J. W. Clay, *Yorkshire Monasteries, Suppression Papers*, Yorks. Arch. Soc., Record Ser., XLVIII (1912), pp. 44–55.

3

The Great and Solemn Monasteries

'. . . WHEREIN (thanks be to God) religion is right well kept and observed': from the Act of Suppression of 1536 (Doc. 10).

The political crisis of 1536–7 over, and the remaining smaller monasteries scheduled for suppression finally dealt with, the situation returned almost to normal. Bishops resumed once again their visitation of religious houses, showing no more than ordinary zeal in the discovery of either temporal or spiritual lapses. The so-called 'exempt' houses, those freed by papal decree from the attention of their diocesans, no doubt congratulated themselves on the fact that the Dispensations Act of 1534 (25 Henry VIII, c. 21, section XIV) had provided that despite the barrier now separating them from the Roman Curia they were not to be 'visited or vexed' by any bishops or even archbishops but only by commissioners appointed by the king under the Great Seal.[1] The surrender of the London Carthusians on June 10, 1537 brought to a conclusion the long campaign to remove the most formidable of the king's clerical opponents, and the birth of a male heir to the throne on October 12th no doubt led many to hope that a period of political calm and adjustment to the new order would now follow. Whatever private misgivings may have been nourished by the religious the great majority of them had not only subscribed to the oath of succession in 1534 but had been in no way involved in the late rebellion. To most people, including the religious themselves, there can have appeared no reason why the larger religious houses, and the remaining smaller ones, should not look forward to a new lease of life within a national, if not exactly nationalized, Church.

In fact the religious houses of England and Wales were now in their last years to be drawn into closer links with the secular world than ever before, so much so that seen purely in an economic and social context the eventual and actual dissolution of any particular community may appear as a relatively unimportant event. That the chronology of the Dissolution needs both to be established and properly understood goes without saying, but it still remains important to show how far lay

[1] *Statutes*, III, 469. Wolsey's authority, by Papal grant, to visit even the hitherto exempt houses had not endeared him to the regular clergy.

encroachment on monastic resources had gone before the final *coup de grâce* came. Easiest of all, perhaps, to explain is the plight of many of the smaller houses who were still endeavouring, in 1537 and even in 1538, to find large sums of money to pay for their licences of exemption from the act of 1536. Some were able to borrow from friends and relations but others, and it came to much the same thing, were driven to grant new or more advantageous leases of their property in return for substantial entry fines. But the need for the money to buy their licences, or indeed the need for money at all, does not explain the large number of grants of all kinds made to laymen under convent seal, grants of leases of property, of pensions or annuities, and of fee-carrying offices in the monastic temporal administration. Such grants were not, of course, novel in themselves but only in their multitude. A really comprehensive survey, with the help of post-Dissolution records, of all the grants made by monasteries to laymen in the 1530s would almost certainly point to the middle of 1537 as the real beginning of the great lay encroachment which preceded the actual Dissolution of 1538–9. It would also show how very inadequate is the *Valor Ecclesiasticus* of 1535 as a record of the charges or 'incumbrances' laid on their estates by the last generation of monks and nuns. It is from the accounts rendered by the Crown's officers immediately after the Dissolution that we learn (Doc. 26a) of what happened in the chapter house of Cockersand Abbey, Lancashire. In November 1537, for example, the abbey leased most of its estate at Hutton in Leylandshire, all in fact except the freeholdings and the turbary which was already let, for 99 years to one Henry Audley of St Albans. What fine or other consideration Audley paid is not recorded but the same source provides evidence that in the following year the abbey let its lands in Tarleton and Sullam to a local gentleman, Sir Robert Hesketh, for terms of 99 and 61 years respectively and that he paid fines of 20 marks and 'divers large sums of money . . . towards the repair of their monastery'. Leases for three and four score years were not unknown, even before 1535, as may be seen from references to some still running on the estates of Merevale Abbey, Warwickshire, in 1546–7 (Doc. 26c), but taking the evidence as a whole there is no mistaking the sharp upward trend in the length of terms of monastic leases in 1537–8. It is not always easy to be sure whether any particular piece of property was being let for the first time but there is no doubt that demesne still in hand, and hence only nominally valued, in 1535, had in the case of a very large number of monasteries been substantially reduced by 1538–9. Evidence about entry fines for leases is not extensive, but there is enough to indicate that laymen were willing to 'buy' leases of monastic land in the later 1530s as never before, and the appearance of large numbers of gentlemen in 1538 is very noticeable.[2] The effect of these

[2] *Ag. Hist.* IV, 327–9.

late monastic leases on the value of the monastic estates can hardly be exaggerated. It prompts the reflection that had the Dissolution been carried through in 1536 the Crown would have retained a good deal more opportunity for 'improving' the immediate yield.

The reference to repairs to monastic buildings at Cockersand has many echoes elsewhere. Whether moved by bravado or optimism, or indeed until well into 1538 by the absence of any real threat of dissolution, many of the governors both of the wealthy and even of the less wealthy houses were rebuilding and extending and in some cases very handsomely embellishing their fabric. They may even have been counselled by Cromwell's Visitors to put in hand necessary and overdue repairs. Many of the more substantial fines for leases almost certainly went in paying for building materials and labour, others towards the settlement of old debts, but many other uses could be found for ready cash. Many governors were later accused of selling off stock and thus 'wasting' the houses' resources but a good deal of this – perhaps excepting last-minute sales before dissolution – will have been a corollary to the letting of demesne. Exact information about the amount of cash thus realized is virtually non-existent, and what the Crown's officers were unable to discover is hardly likely to be revealed to historians. There were heads of religious houses who later assured Cromwell that they had sold no movable goods and made no grants under convent seal 'against the dissolution' and indeed one is led to wonder whether the prior of Bath would have regarded stock and land leases of his demesne made in, say, late 1537 as coming within the category of preparing for the end. He, at least, had been making such leases since the late 1520s (Doc. 2) and possibly even earlier. Would he not have claimed, and with some justification, that he was merely taking advantage of a fairly sudden and unprecedented lay demand for land? Hence the difficulty facing the government in putting any sort of brake on this eroding of its potential resources.

Perhaps the more reprehensible aspect of late conventual grants, at least from the point of view of the Crown as the ultimate loser by them, was the multiplication of what were called pensions or annuities to laymen or, what amounted virtually to the same thing, the creation of lay offices. It is rarely possible to discover the exact circumstances of such grants, but we have the dates for large numbers of them and these point once again to 1537 and 1538. Some may have been genuine annuities in respect of which lump sums had been paid by the recipients, but one would expect such a fact to be mentioned either in the text of the grant or indeed by the recipient when he eventually placed his claim for confirmation before the court of Augmentations. But no such evidence appears and it seems likely that in 1537 and 1538 such grants were normally made, much more so than the leases, in return for or in expectation of services to the monastery. In the more notorious cases they were undoubtedly given by heads of houses with, or more likely without, the consent of the convent, to their lay friends and relations. Why William Blake, yeoman, in May 1537, should have received an annuity for life of forty shillings from the prior of Newstead, Nottinghamshire, is not revealed in the indenture which he later carried to London (Doc. 16) nor is any reason given why in March 1538 Richard Standish, gentleman, should have been given for life the office of bailiff and surveyor of the lands of Ulverscroft Priory (*ibid.*), an office which had not existed, according to the *Valor*, in 1535. Individually such grants are not greatly significant but taken together – even for one house – they amount to a substantial, although terminable, charge on monastic revenues. Gabriel Donne, the last abbot of Buckfast in Devon, is notorious chiefly for the circumstances in which, a friend of Cromwell's, he was appointed in 1536, but his real achievement, ironically, was not that he ensured the abbey's eventual surrender but that in the two years preceding February 25, 1539 he charged the abbey revenues with new fees and annuities (seventeen of the latter) totalling nearly £70. This was in addition to fees of £4 odd agreed to as deductions by the *Valor* commissioners. Moreover, John Southcote, a local lawyer, continued to receive his old fee of 53s 4d as the abbey's understeward but on November 12, 1537 the appointment was renewed, for their lives, to John and his son Thomas.[3] Many of the yeomen farmers who, up and down the country, were employed by the monks as manorial bailiffs and collectors of rents and were in receipt of small fees now followed the lead of the gentlemen who held the higher monastic administrative offices and obtained written contracts under conventual seals.

It is not difficult to explain the eagerness with which laymen at all social levels accepted and no doubt solicited such fees. Men like Gabriel Donne had no long-term interest in the resources of their cures, but in general the grants of fees cause one to ponder just what, at any given time, were the real expectations of the majority of the heads of the larger houses who, we may believe, given a free choice would have preferred to carry on indefinitely. At all times, of course, the support of his lay neighbours was worth some sacrifice to a governor and indeed the more eminent local gentlemen expected to be on the monastic pay-roll, but it should be possible by a careful analysis of all the surviving evidence, to detect the approximate moment at which a particular abbot or prior or abbess saw dissolution by the Crown as a distinct possibility and either began desperately to build up vested interests in the continuance of his or her house, or to secure friends who would ensure the best possible

---

[3] J. A. Youings, *Devon Monastic Lands: Particulars for Grants, 1536–58*, Devon and Cornwall Record Society, New Ser., 1 (1955), pp. 137–8. See also Haigh, *Lancashire Monasteries*, p. 109 about similar arrangements at Cockersand.

terms for the governor and, if he or she cared for them and had not fallen out with them too badly, his or her community. The texts of the conventual grants need to be looked at carefully to see whether they contain a clause nullifying them if the house should not be dissolved, implying thereby that the governor's main concern was how to subsist in the event of dissolution.[4] Only a clause nullifying the grant if the house fell would seem to indicate a determined bid for survival, but the author knows of no instance of such a clause. In the last analysis it will probably emerge that the religious turned to laymen for help in assisting their passage into the world rather than for help in averting the crisis itself. By and large, when the time came, their lay friends did not let them down. The moment of truth could be at any time in late 1537, 1538, and even early 1539, for the last phase of the Dissolution itself was long-drawn-out and at no point did all remaining houses feel equally vulnerable. Some were still seriously hoping for survival quite late in 1539. It is, then, from their actions nearer home as well as from what survive of their letters to Cromwell that we must attempt to discover the reaction of the last of the Henrician monks and nuns to the possibility of dissolution.

Two points remain to be made before we return to the story of the Dissolution. The first is that for all the later expressions of official disapproval of the diversion of monastic resources into lay hands by the religious, at the time when the late conventual grants were being made there was a great deal of active and semi-official encouragement. Cromwell himself was almost certainly by far the greatest single recipient of grants, having been enjoying them regularly and in ever-increasing number at least since 1531 (Doc. 4b). But he also devoted a great deal of time and energy to obtaining from the monasteries leases, fees, and annuities for his many friends and associates. He even expected to be consulted about the normal complement of lay officers, as is clear from his correspondence with the newly-founded, or refounded, Chertsey Abbey at Bisham, Berkshire, in December 1537.[5] Here, as indeed on a number of other occasions, he found himself up against sturdy resistance. The abbot wished to choose his own friends among his neighbours. Cromwell's papers abound in letters of all kinds, those gratuitously offering him fees, those agreeing to his suggestions, and those informing him that the lease or the office he had asked for, for one of his friends, was not available or had already been granted to another. There are even somewhat transparent pleas, accompanied by supporting statements,

---

[4] For example, on 10 October 1538 the abbot of St Werburgh's, Chester, leased the abbey's parsonage of Sutton in Wirral for a substantial term, on condition that if the house should not be dissolved then the lease would be void: PRO, Exch., Augmentation Office, Misc. Books (E 315), 397, fo. 42.

[5] *LP* XII ii, 1267.

that the land in question was an essential part of the abbey's own farm and could not be spared. Much might be learned about Cromwell's personal standing at any particular moment from a careful charting of his successes and failures in those matters, for the religious were by no means ill-informed about the situation at Court. However, here was the minister who many think was single-minded in his endeavours to augment the royal resources, deliberately seeking to enable considerable numbers of laymen to anticipate, in the short run, the Crown's own depredations. It again raises the question as to how far, at any rate until the latter part of 1538, Cromwell himself really thought in terms of wholesale dissolution. Or was he preparing the way for the final outcome by making it difficult for influential laymen to object to the Crown itself completing the process of secularization? A third possibility is that in general he disapproved of these charges, but having enjoyed the fruits of the system since the early days of his official career, he did not choose to apply his own rules to himself and those towards whom he felt some obligation. In fact there is no evidence that he ever tried to stop such grants being made or that, in so far as he was responsible for the policy and practice of the court of Augmentations, he ever took steps to undo them. In the long run, and assuming that the property was retained in its ownership, the Crown could look forward to the eventual enjoyment of something much nearer the gross annual revenue, but in the short run leasehold rents were pegged for many decades, and the immediate proceeds, in the form of fines, of this process of partial capitalization had in most cases been placed beyond the reach of the Crown.

This leads to the second point, which should perhaps be introduced with a question. Why were laymen so ready to acquire a share of monastic resources, more especially leases for which they paid substantial fines? Was it not dangerous and risky to meddle in monastic lands? Up to a point, of course, they may have been persuaded that there would be no further suppression by the Crown, or they may have been prepared to gamble. The real point, however, is surely one of chronology. The act of 1536 had provided a clear undertaking, within certain limits, that the government would honour all properly authenticated conventual grants (Doc. 10, section III), and by now what had been promised had already been performed, and indeed generously so. By the middle of 1537 every part of the country had had some experience of the effect of dissolution on existing tenancies. Some laymen, indeed, had found it advisable to have their indentures confirmed and enrolled by the court of Augmentations, but there is no substance whatever, in respect either of 1536–7 or of 1538–9, in Savine's statement that large numbers of monastic tenants waited anxiously for their tenures to be renewed and that the price of security was an increase in rent.[6] There was little need for

[6] Savine, *English Monasteries*, p. 54.

anyone with a legitimate interest to be nervous, and the news will very quickly have spread that the Crown was taking over the monastic lands 'in so ample a manner as the late abbots . . . [etc.]', with all their liabilities and encumbrances. This knowledge – and it had also been provided for in the act that any further transfer of ownership would be made on the same terms – must have been a great encouragement to prospective monastic leaseholders in 1537–8. Even the fact that by now some portions of the freehold of the Crown's new estate had already been disposed of no doubt served as an added incentive to the land-hungry to obtain possession of land still in monastic hands with the hope of later being able to purchase. The knowledge that all but a few conventual grants would be honoured by the Crown must also have served to render pointless any attempts by the religious to use their convent seals to build up vested interests in the *status quo*.

But if laymen with an interest in monastic lands had by 1537–8 no reason to fear and even good reason to welcome a renewed attack by the Crown on the monasteries, the process by which some at least of the religious were brought to regard the Dissolution as something to contemplate at least with equanimity, if not with relish, was somewhat more delayed. An unknown, but probably substantial, number of men and some women had already left the cloister, especially in 1535–6 (Doc. 6), quite apart from those from the smaller houses dissolved in 1536–7 who did not accept transfer to other houses. The great majority of those still in religion in 1537 probably wanted to stay. If they thought or talked about the possibility of dispersal many of them will have known what had happened at Furness in Lancashire in the spring and early summer. Here, for the first time, a large and economically flourishing community had been dispersed and, apparently because of a shortage of available accommodation, without even the option of transfer to another house.[7] Most of them had been given capacities, that is licences to become secular priests, but as all must have realized, the supply of such men was already outstripping the demand for their services. For nuns to be faced with a similar prospect was daunting indeed. As yet there was no precedent for paying pensions to the dispossessed rank and file. That came, suddenly and, as it emerged, decisively, at the very end of 1537. The dissolution in November of Lewes Priory, in Sussex, was, as will emerge, a landmark in many respects, not least in its consequences for all, or nearly all, the remaining men and women religious, for at Lewes the entire community received pensions. The same thing happened at Abingdon in February 1538, and at all the houses which surrendered thereafter.[8] At the risk of crediting all concerned with only base and material motives, may it not be reasonable to suggest that when, by the

[7] Haigh, *Lancashire Monasteries*, pp. 104–5.
[8] *LP* XII ii, 1101(2), XIII i, p. 583.

late spring of 1538 the practice had become established of providing pensions for every member of a dispersed community there was no longer any reason for anyone to fear the consequences of the Dissolution? As John Onley well understood, people resist change largely through fear of the unknown.

The year 1537 which brought in many respects a return to normality, also then saw the beginning of what may be called the last phase of monastic history, the period of intense lay encroachment into the monastic economy. It also saw – and this is why it is so difficult to make a coherent story of the Dissolution – the first surrender of a large monastic house, that of Furness, and before the year was out, the beginning of what was to become a continuous chain of events. So far three distinct processes of suppression have been noted, voluntary surrender by the monastery itself, parliamentary dissolution, and forfeiture by the attainder of governors. The last stages of the Dissolution, occupying the years 1538 and 1539, with a few months' extension either end, brought dissolution by means of what have been aptly described as 'induced' surrenders. For this there was at least some precedent in that, as already noted, most of the early voluntary surrenders were occasioned by the visit of government agents. It is also possible to point to a number of surrenders, even in 1538–9, which proceeded in fact, as all were made to appear officially, from the initiative of all or some members of the communities concerned. Even in such cases the actual moment of surrender had to coincide with the presence of royal agents authorized to take possession. It is worth taking a close look at what happened at Furness in Lancashire. In the remote north-west of England in March 1537, Whalley Abbey, way inland from Furness, had already been dissolved as a result of the attainder of its abbot, and the king's commissioners for the pacification of the North, led by the earl of Sussex, were intent upon obtaining a similar end for Furness. They failed to find sufficient incriminating evidence, but the abbot, Roger Pyle, either did not fully understand the situation or lacked hope or heart for the future of his community, one which was indeed deeply divided. In the course of an interrogation by Sussex at Whalley on April 5th, abbot Pyle of Furness agreed to surrender his house to the king, to whose ancestors, as dukes of Lancaster, the abbey owed its foundation. The abbot signed a simple and informal conveyance in which he admitted 'the misorder and evil lives, both unto God and our Prince' of the abbey. This document was countersigned by Sussex and a number of other gentlemen present, and also, on his arrival the same evening, by Sir Anthony Fitzherbert, one of the king's judges. The following day Fitzherbert drafted a more formal instrument, a copy of which, dated April 9th, was sealed with the convent seal and signed not only by the abbot but also by the prior and no less than twenty-eight monks, as well as by Sussex, Fitzherbert and the other commissioners.

Thus, by a simple deed of gift the abbey and all its possessions were transferred to the Crown, without act of parliament or any sort of inquisition or formal escheat. Even Fitzherbert was apparently satisfied that the present members of the community could surrender for all time their corporate rights, although months later the monks claimed that they had been led to submit 'by a politic compulsion'.[9] It can hardly be doubted that the motives of the Crown's agents at this particular juncture were purely political, the anxiety to be rid of a potential source of disaffection. The substantial augmentation of the Crown's resources – the net annual income of Furness Abbey had been conservatively assessed in 1535 at over £800 – was merely accidental, and the failure to provide any alternative or additional means of subsistence for the monks other than licences to become secular priests places the dissolution of this large abbey in a class by itself.[10] It was certainly not a 'voluntary' surrender by a decayed and dwindling community, nor does it fit into the category of a parliamentary dissolution, or of a forfeiture by the attainder of its governor. However, except for the treatment of the monks, it formed an invaluable precedent for that process which was to become the normal pattern during the last, and numerically most important, phase of the Dissolution. Procedurally it linked the last and most important stage of the Dissolution with the appropriations of Cardinal Wolsey.

The cost of restoring peace and order in the North was no doubt considerable but any general attack on monastic resources in the months which followed the rebellions of 1536 would have been suicidal. That those communities which could be shown to have been actively involved in the risings should be dealt with very drastically was expected but that the political guilt of the few should involve the rest was an idea which few contemporaries would have found acceptable, and one to which neither Cromwell nor indeed any astute politician of the time would have subscribed. It was not until another eighteen months had elapsed, not, that is, until the latter part of 1538, that the Crown once more embarked on a planned campaign of dissolution. But there did begin, at the very end of 1537, a series of territorially isolated 'induced' surrenders the circumstances of which merit detailed inquiry.

Cromwell's ability, if not his determination, to secure the former monastic lands as a permanent and irreduceable part of the Crown's resources has usually been exaggerated. Disposal by the Crown took place from the very beginning. Between May 1st and October 1st, 1536

---

[9] *LP* XII i, 832 (printed in Wright, *Letters*, pp. 151–2), 840, 880, and 903. See also Knowles, *RO* III, 332–3.

[10] cf. Haigh, pp. 86–101, where the attack on Whalley and Furness is interpreted as a deliberate campaign to acquire monastic property for the Crown.

there had been fifteen separate grants by royal letters patent of substantial portions of the lands of the smaller monasteries. Between
October 1, 1536 and October 1, 1537 there were twenty-five. These were
very largely either gifts, or grants in exchange for other lands, to members of the king's Council, men whose natural expectation was to share
in the king's good fortune. So far Cromwell himself had not participated,
but on October 1, 1537 he was given the site, buildings and estates of the
late priory of Michelham in Sussex, valued at just over £170.[11] This
may well have shown the way to even better things in the same county,
for himself and his family. At Lewes there was the wealthy Cluniac
priory with its daughter-house at Castle Acre in Norfolk. Together they
had revenues of over £1,000 a year. By the beginning of November
Cromwell and the duke of Norfolk, a strange partnership some may
think, had brought the king to the point of agreeing to let them have the
two priories between them.[12] But first the communities had to be persuaded to surrender. How this was achieved is not at all clear. The
matter was handled by Harry Polsted, one of Cromwell's personal staff.
Later the prior of Lewes claimed that the duke had promised him all the
movable goods of the house and half the money owing to it. The community was not a happy one and there had been considerable disorder
there for some time.[13] A factor which may well have weighed heavily
with the monks was that at the surrender of Lewes, and, as already
indicated, for the first time, provision was made for the payment of
pensions not only to the governor but to each member of the community. The two deeds of surrender were dated November 16th and 22nd.
Within a month Norfolk's grant of Castle Acre was about to pass the
Great Seal but it was mid-February 1538 before the signed bill authorizing the grant to the Lord Privy Seal reached the Lord Chancellor's
office.[14] Cromwell's total grant on this occasion, which included not only
the site of Lewes Priory but lands and 'spiritual' revenues as far afield as
Halifax in Yorkshire and Berrynarber in Devon, was valued at £527 odd.
By early March Harry Polsted was busy making leases and selling off
part of the property at 21 years' purchase, and later that month Cromwell's Italian demolition expert was tearing down the priory church.
Norfolk, too, was seeking purchasers for part of his newly acquired

---

[11] *LP* xii ii, 1008, g. 3. An annual rent of £71 odd was reserved but the
remaining £100 a year was a free gift. The priory had been dissolved in 1536.

[12] *ibid.*, 1030. On December 1, 1537, in anticipation of the impending shareout,
Norfolk undertook to hand over to Cromwell a manor in Sussex and property at
Lewes: PRO, State Papers Domestic (SP 1), 126, p. 212a, calendared in *LP* xii
ii, 1154. The chronological significance of this joint enterprise of Cromwell and
Norfolk seems not to have been noticed hitherto.

[13] *ibid.*, 1062 and Knowles, *RO* iii, 350.

[14] *ibid.*, 1101, 1119, 1311, g. 30; and xiii i, 384, g. 74. The dates inserted in
the letters patent were those on which the warrants reached the Chancellor.

E

estate. He claimed that he was in financial difficulties, was dismayed to find the land at Castle Acre already very largely let by the monks for long terms, and begged Cromwell to find him, as promised, someone who would take the manor of West Walton in Norfolk, late of Lewes, at 40 years' purchase.[15] Where the king's two leading servants had shown the way, others would expect to follow.

Shortly before Christmas John Hussey, Lord Lisle's agent in London, was able to report that the abbey of Warden in Bedfordshire had also surrendered, and others, he understood, were about to go, among which he named, quite incorrectly, as it happened, Ramsey and St Albans. 'It is thought most will go down by consent of their abbots and priors,' he said, and added, 'so I trust something will fall to your lordship.'[16] By that he did not necessarily mean that *all abbeys* would soon be suppressed, but that some form of *voluntary* surrender of selected houses might be expected. John Uvedale, secretary of the reconstituted Council of the North, writing to Cromwell from York on January 8th, was even more sanguine. He was persuaded, he wrote, that 'the Holy Word of God will in brief time hunt all manner [of] religious persons (as they have been called) out of their monasteries, cowls and cloisters'. When the time comes, he added, he would be glad if Cromwell could obtain for him a lease of the house, the demesnes, and the parsonage, of the nunnery of Marrick.[17] Such thoughts were no doubt occurring to many more gentlemen than those whose letters to Cromwell have survived, especially those nearest the centre of things. Titchfield Abbey in Hampshire surrendered, according to the date on the formal surrender document, just after Christmas, but there is no doubt that very considerable interest in the site and buildings had already been shown by one of Cromwell's closest associates, Thomas Wriothesley. The two commissioners who received the prior's surrender were in close touch with him, and indeed one of them, John Crayford, was already acting as Wriothesley's clerk of works at Titchfield on December 22nd when he warned him that the cost of converting the buildings into a residence would be at least 300 marks. The royal letters patent granting the site to Wriothesley were dated December 30th. They contain a note to the effect that the property had come to the king by virtue of a fine levied in the court of Common Pleas in November, and that the deed of surrender had been enrolled in Chancery on December 18th.[18] Clearly

---

[15] *LP* XIII i, 290–93, 421, 504, 554, 590, and 593.

[16] *LP* XII ii, 1209.

[17] *LP* XIII i, 49. Marrick was not dissolved until September 1539.

[18] The original deed of surrender has not survived but its text was in fact enrolled twice in Chancery, the first entry giving the date as December 28th, the second – no doubt in order to expedite Wriothesley's grant – putting it forward to December 18th. The second refers to an acknowledgement in the Chapter

the dates on the early surrender documents are not to be taken literally.

The significance of all these 'Christmas presents' by the king to the Cromwellian circle must not, however, be exaggerated. Their long-term value lay in the experience they provided of the comparative ease with which well-chosen communities might be persuaded to throw in their hand. By the beginning of 1538 Cromwell may well have been seriously envisaging a really massive acquisition of church property for the Crown. The first full year's accounts of the regional officers of the Court of Augmentations were by now reaching Westminster, and the Court's real potential as a financial agency was no doubt becoming clear. But as yet any systematic scheme of suppression was out of the question, and indeed there is still no evidence of any great financial stringency, real or in prospect. There were not even any plans for calling Parliament in the near future – if, indeed, such a move was to be regarded as a necessary prerequisite to a further attack on the wealth of the Church.

The first eight months of 1538 did, however, see the surrender to the Crown, with all their property, of some thirty-five monasteries, as well as the attainder of the abbots of Lenton and Woburn. Muchelney Abbey in Somerset surrendered to Dr Thomas Legh, an experienced visitor of monasteries, in the early part of January. It was seriously in debt, to the tune of some £400, charged with fees, annuities and pensions totalling nearly £44 and its net income was only about £450. According to Legh all the monks 'subscribed to the instrument of their submission and surrender, and sealed the same with their common seal, and delivered the same as their act to me to the use and pleasure of our sovereign lord the king . . . in the presence of divers knights and gentlemen'. There is no evidence that any attempt was made locally to save the priory although ten months later when the abbot of Athelney was under pressure to follow likewise he spoke of 'the country [being likely to be] undone [thereby] as it is about Muchelney'. Before the end of the month the site, buildings and the whole of the abbey's landed property had been granted by royal letters patent to Edward earl of Hertford.[19] Early in February Abingdon Abbey in Berkshire surrendered to Dr William Petre and Dr John Tregonwell. This house, too, was in debt but it is clear from the flurry of activity which followed, the Chancellor of the court of Augmentations himself taking charge of the surveying of the property, that there was some sort of scheme afoot for converting the

---

House at Titchfield by Crayford dated January 20, 1538, by virtue of a commission dated the previous day. However, the patent under the Great Seal was issued in time for it to have arrived in Hampshire, to be shown to the tenants, by January 2, 1538: *LP* XII ii, 1245, 1274, 1275, 1311, g. 40; and XIII i, 19.

[19] *LP* XIII i, 27, 42; ii, 744; and i, 190, g. 41.

abbey buildings into a royal residence.[20] That the plan fell through does not alter the fact that this new phase of surrenders was embarked upon not in accordance with any overall scheme but simply because various people in high places had a use for the property of certain houses known to be in a weak position to resist. The commissioners involved travelled country-wide. Legh had been sent to Muchelney quite specifically by Cromwell. His next successful operation was in early March at Holme Cultram in Cumberland,[21] and then in May at Woburn in Bedfordshire. Here he was in the company, for this rather special occasion, of John Williams, Master of the King's Jewels, and Dr William Petre, like Legh a distinguished lawyer and one of the clerks in Chancery. What took place at Woburn was not typical of what happened generally in 1538. Obviously sufficient irregularities had come to light to make the abbot's attainder on a charge of treason comparatively certain, but the judicial inquiries appear to have been carried out after the abbot and convent had made formal surrender.[22]

Legh also made an extensive visitation during the spring of 1538, as Cromwell's deputy, throughout the northern province, and it was probably as the result of information supplied by him that certain abbots received letters summoning them to attend upon Cromwell in London. John, abbot of Combermere in Cheshire, received such a letter in early May, in his case containing a command that he should come up in order to surrender his monastery to the king. He tried to delay matters by offering to resign (Doc. 17b) but, in spite of the friendship of bishop Rowland Lee, he was eventually prevailed upon to surrender his house, in the company of his prior and eleven monks, to Richard Layton on July 27th.

The ease with which surrenders of carefully chosen houses could be obtained must by now have been appreciated by the government, but still its plans went no further than the slow and laborious task of seeking out weaknesses where they were to be found. In or about March Cromwell addressed a circular to the heads of religious houses in various parts of the country – how comprehensive the list was we do not know – the gist of whose message was that no properly conducted community need fear the government's intentions. No idle rumours, or indeed news of the voluntary surrender of any house, need put them in fear of suppression or 'change of life'. He gave them the king's word that 'unless overtures had been made by the houses that have resigned he would not have received them'. The letter went on to refer to 'the wilful waste and spoil that has lately been made in many abbeys, as though the governors of them minded only their own dissolution'. This letter has been cited

---

[20] *LP* XIII i, 242, 332. See also Richardson, *Court of Augmentations*, pp. 288–93.
[21] *ibid.*, 434.
[22] *ibid.*, 955, 981. See also G. Scott Thomson, 'The dissolution of Woburn Abbey', *TRHS* Ser. 3, XVI (1933).

by Gasquet and others as the supreme manifestation of the early Tudor government's betrayal of the monks. But without for a moment suggesting that Cromwell and whoever else was privy to the drafting of this communication was really in what today might be called 'good faith', read against the situation in the spring of 1538 it is just the kind of government statement which might have been expected. Factually it was not very far from the truth. It was undoubtedly prompted by the reports pouring in from the government's agents or visitors up and down the country of a proliferation of new leases of property and sales of movable goods. Some effort obviously had to be made to call a halt to this widespread diversion of monastic resources, and although the government's concern was an indication of its own interest in conserving those resources, and although the contents of the letter alone are not proof that no immediate or decisive action, no wholesale dissolution, was yet in contemplation, in fact the next three months brought only thirteen, widely scattered, surrenders.[23]

By mid-1538 there is a good deal of evidence of initiative on the part of local interests. At Bordesley Abbey in Worcestershire in May a certain Thomas Evans was hard at work trying to procure the resignation of the abbot so as to make room for his replacement by the abbey cellarer who undertook, if elected, to surrender the abbey to the king (Doc. 17a). Evans undoubtedly coveted the abbey demesne. In July, having failed to dislodge the old abbot, Evans urged Cromwell to proceed with suppression at once since harvest was at hand and it would be convenient to sell the corn in the field. Evans, no doubt, was anxious to get possession before winter. In fact a deed of surrender was obtained about ten days later, and Evans eventually got what he wanted, namely a lease of the abbey site and home farm.[24] Few outright grants were being made, as yet, to men outside the immediate Court circle, but an analysis of Crown lessees might well be very instructive about the selection of religious houses to 'go down' during the middle and latter part of 1538.

In June and July Legh was busy again in the Midlands, moving, if the dates on the deeds of surrender are to be regarded as at least approximate, from Worcestershire to Nottinghamshire and Lincolnshire and back again to Worcestershire in late July. William Petre received the surrender of Welbeck Abbey in Nottinghamshire and Roche, Yorkshire, in June, and at the beginning of August was at Walsingham. The image of Our Lady had been removed to London in mid-July, thereby

---

[23] *LP* XIII i, 573, Knowles, *RO* III, 353, n. 5, and F. A. Gasquet, *Henry VIII and the Dissolution of the Monasteries*, 1888 edn., II, 279–82. Richard Layton had busied himself scotching rumours of wholesale suppression in Norfolk in January 1538: *LP* XIII, i, 102.

[24] *LP* XIII i, 1073, 1177, 1343, 1401, 1433, 1505; XIV i, 1355, p. 610.

depriving the house of a very substantial source of revenue but the prior had been hopeful of having the community changed into a college of secular priests. Little more than a week later he wrote almost cheerfully to Cromwell, certainly with perfect resignation, thanking him for his 'labour' on their behalf and asking for the parsonage of Walsingham for himself. It was worth, he said, less than £30. He had heard that the commissioners had assigned him a pension of £100 and hoped that the necessary documents, together with their 'capacities' to become secular priests, would not be long delayed.[25]

Whatever informal pressures had been at work the actual surrenders were made with due formality, and in the presence, as at Muchelney, of a gathering of local knights and gentlemen, friends, fee'd men, and tenants, of the monks. As in most contemporary conveyances of property the donee was represented by his accredited attorneys. Those who received the surrender on the king's behalf had to be provided with the necessary authority. This now took the form of a commission under the king's privy seal. Only a mere handful of these has survived, and the earliest of these is that prepared for Dr Richard Layton and four other men in February 1539 (Doc. 18). It remains among the state papers no doubt because, owing to a change of plan, it was never issued. We can only surmise that the commissioners of 1537–8 were issued with similar instructions. These were to obtain a sufficient 'writing under convent seal', to take possession of all movable goods and supervise their sale, to deliver certain goods and cash to the departing religious, and to assign appropriate pensions. The buildings, lands, bells, and lead were then to be placed in reliable custody and the remaining cash, together with plate, jewels and ornaments to be brought or sent to the Tower of London. Whether the names of the houses were always inserted before the sealing of the commission is uncertain: there is some evidence in Layton's commission of room being left blank but this may have been incidental when such commissions were being prepared, in advance, by the clerks at Westminster. In 1537 and the early part of 1538 commissions must have been issued in respect of single houses, as happened even later when isolated houses were being dealt with. But from the latter part of 1538 the commissions were usually wider, perhaps not even specifying the names of the houses, these being contained in confidential lists handed to the commissioners (Doc. 20 p. 180). The commissions were issued on the initiative of Thomas Cromwell and the three late ones which survive actually bear his signature.[26] In 1536 it should be

---

[25] *LP* XIII i, 1376; ii. 31, 86.

[26] For the full text of the commission dated August 1539 to take the surrender of Haughmond Abbey, Cheshire see *Deputy Keeper of the Public Records, Eighth Report of*, 1847, Appdx II, 3, and for a calendar of all surviving deeds of surrender see *ibid.*, pp. 6–51.

recalled, the commissioners sent to the houses scheduled for dissolution under the act of that year were issued by the Court of Augmentations, but these later commissioners had no statutory authority. Although there can have been few houses where their arrival was totally unexpected, they had to be ready to deal with varying degrees of obstinacy on the part of the monks as well as their governors. At Vale Royal in Cheshire in 1538 the text of the commission carried by Thomas Holcroft evidently made reference both to the fact that Cromwell was the abbey's chief steward and to the house being of the king's foundation. This latter was probably inserted whenever appropriate. Nevertheless, wrote the abbot on 9 September, 'We never consented to surrender and never will unless the king commands it, which I do not perceive in Mr Holcroft's commission that he does.' This the abbot wrote from Lichfield on his way up to London, but the deed whereby he himself, the prior and thirteen others surrendered their possessions to the king is dated 7 September and it has therefore been concluded that his signature was forged in his absence. It is quite possible, however, that the deed of surrender was for some reason antedated. Holcroft at any rate covered himself by sending to London, in the form of questions to be put to the abbot, his own account of what had transpired, the implication being that there had been disagreement, after he and the abbot 'were concluded for the surrender', about the disposal of stock, the despatch of the monks (who the abbot said 'were but knaves') and the granting of an ante-dated lease.[27] Clearly Vale Royal was living up to its reputation as a somewhat obstinate community.

Apart from any preliminary 'softening up', the houses were now dealt with in one operation, not two as in 1536–7. Hence the inventories of movables were prepared with a view to immediate sales. These inventories, with their echoes of the auction-room, their stark details of vestments and church ornaments sold to laymen (Doc. 22), of all the records of the Dissolution still after four centuries have the power to shock, and the story, which there is no reason to disbelieve, of the monks of Bisham selling their own habits in an adjoining room only serves to heighten the tragedy.[28] But it must be remembered that all this was often the climax to weeks and even months of uncertainty and like most climaxes in human affairs it could induce, in all concerned, a feeling of release and almost of gaiety.

The deeds of surrender, with their enrolments on the dorse of the Close Rolls in the court of Chancery, survive in abundance. They formed, of course, the Crown's title deeds to the property of all the

[27] *LP* XIII ii, 297, 314–15, and Knowles, *RO* III, 354. The abbot's letter is in Wright, *Letters*, pp. 244–5 and also in Dugdale, *Monasticon Anglicanum* (1815 edn.) v. 702.

[28] *LP* XIII i, 1239.

religious houses except those suppressed by attainder or by act of
parliament. Very few indeed have been printed in *extenso* and as a class
they have never been systematically studied. They would almost certainly repay the kind of diplomatic and palaeographical analysis which
medieval scholars devote to early charters. As already indicated, comparison with other evidence throws doubt on the accuracy of their
dating though this was a technical point of little relevance to their
validity. The best known, and most often quoted, are those which
incorporate elaborate confessions of moral guilt, or of mere mismanage-
ment, by the monks, confessions which no doubt gave great satisfaction
to the government but were regarded by its lawyers as more or less
irrelevant. Such was the well-known confession, dated March 1, 1538,
of the prior and canons of St Andrew's, Northampton, drawn up for
them by one of the commissioners, Robert Southwell, Attorney of the
court of Augmentations. He had arrived there hot from a conveyancing
tangle with which he had had to contend at West Acre Priory in Norfolk
where the prior had anticipated the Crown by conveying some of his
estates to 'gentlemen of the country' and their wives. At Northampton
he sought similar 'occasions' for suppression, and the confession of the
monks regarding 'the enormities of their past living' was the best he
could manage. He supposed that the situation at Northampton was
typical of that obtaining elsewhere and no doubt saw his literary efforts
as a useful exemplar. At his instigation the canons appealed to the king,
as the undoubted founder of the house, 'graciously to accept our free
gifts, without coercion, persuasion or procurement of any creature living
other than of our voluntary free will, of all such possessions, right, title
or interest as we the said prior and convent hath or ever had . . . in or to
[his] said monastery of Northampton'. No wonder the more astute of the
Crown's lawyers saw to it that such a barbaric document was covered
by a straightforward feoffment, duly enrolled in Chancery.[29] The only
other monastic 'confession' extant is that of the abbot and convent of
Bittlesden in Berkshire dated September 25, 1538 and this is to be
explained by the fact that the royal commissioner was Dr John London
whose main energies in 1538 were devoted to obtaining the surrender of
houses of friars under somewhat different circumstances.[30] 'Confessions'

---

[29] For the full text of the Northampton 'confession' see J. R. Tanner, *Tudor
Constitutional Documents*, 1922, pp. 89–93, and for Southwell's reports to
Cromwell and the more conventional surrender document, *LP* xiii i, 86, 101–2,
404, and 407 (which is also in Wright, pp. 171–3).

[30] *LP* xiii ii, 421. The text of the Bittlesden 'confession' is printed in Rymer's
Foedera, xiv, 610–11, and has recently appeared in the more accessible *Dissolution
of the Monasteries* by G. W. O. Woodward, pp. 118–19. It should not be regarded
as typical. Dr London was a little out of touch with current practice, or so it
would seem from his statement in October 1538 (*LP* xiii ii, 767) that he was
following the procedure, where the king was not the founder, of obtaining a

of some kind were *de rigeur* where the friaries were concerned. But as
early as November 1537 when Harry Polsted was dealing with the surrender of Lewes Priory he wrote to Cromwell that, 'as concerning the
preamble of the deed', it had now been 'fully resolved that there [should]
be no such preamble'.[31]

In fact although government propaganda never allowed the point to
be lost sight of that the whole process of the Dissolution was directed
towards the transfer of monastic property into the hands of those better
fitted to make use of it, the actual conveyances were the work of lawyers
rather than of politicians. With minor verbal variations they were drawn
up (Doc. 21) in the form of simple conveyances of freehold property,
basically deeds of gift or feoffments, with clauses of warranty, etc., but
with a good deal of labouring of the fact that the grant had been made
voluntarily, and that the conveyance was made quite simply to the king
and his heirs and successors. No attempt was made to name the landed
property involved beyond setting down a list of counties in which the
site, precincts, manors, etc., were situated. There was, however, enough
of such detail, including the dating clauses, in the text of the deeds to
preclude their having been drawn up in bulk at Westminster, complete
except for the seals and signatures. The 'habendum' clause of course
contained no reference to the grantee's tenurial obligations but did
endow the king, his heirs and assigns with all the rights of the monastery,
however acquired. There followed a clause placing in the king's hands
plenary powers to dispose of the property at will, or at any rate preclud-
ing the governor and convent from raising any objection to his doing
what they themselves had hitherto been able to do only with his licence.
It was this somewhat anomalous situation which no doubt suggested to
the lawyers who devised the form of these deeds of surrender that they
should resemble quitclaims, instruments used when the grantee already
enjoyed some legal interest in the property. No drafts or exemplars are
known to have survived but there must have been some sort of master-
copy and presumably others were carried by those who acted as clerks
for the commissioners. Unlike the more informal 'confessions', the
deeds of surrender proper contained no reference to the monks' change
of habit or to the provision of pensions. The latter were usually set out,
on the authority of the commissioners, on separate sheets, the names
usually tallying with those inserted in the margin of the deeds. There is
no reason for doubting that all such deeds of surrender originally had
appended to them authentic impressions of the conventual seals, but

---

'feoffment' as well as a 'deed of surrender', presumably meaning by the latter
something more like a confession of guilt. It is possible that many more confessions were placed on record, but one would have expected such documents
to have survived owing to their value to the government as propaganda.

[31] BM Cott. MS Cleop. E IV, fo. 233, calendared in LP XII ii, 1062.

the extent to which the list of names of the religious were, or were intended to look like, genuine signatures is a problem which still awaits the attention of palaeographers.

The commissioner whose name appeared on the deed of surrender, acknowledging its legal validity, was always a lawyer of some standing, usually a Clerk or Master in Chancery. In the absence of most of the original commissions it is not a simple task to discover the names of the other commissioners. But from surviving letters to Cromwell, from the accounts of their disposal of the movables (Doc. 22) and from such miscellaneous sources as the accounts of Sir John Williams, Master of the King's Jewels,[32] most of the commissioners' names can be recovered. There were usually four or five named, but, as in the case of the discarded Lincolnshire commission of 1539 (Doc. 18), not all were required to be present. They more often than not included one or more of that select group of well-tried government agents and civil lawyers, Dr Richard Layton, Dr Thomas Legh, Dr John London, Dr John Tregonwell, and Dr William Petre. The commissioners also included one and sometimes two of the officers, central or local, of the Court of Augmentations. But as a body they were responsible quite clearly to Cromwell himself. Their assignment of pensions was subject to Cromwell's personal scrutiny – his signature appears on most of their lists – before these passed to the court of Augmentations for the necessary patents to be issued. This is a fine example of the propensity, recognized by Professor Elton, of this energetic chief minister to reserve to himself what he saw as vital controls, if necessary setting aside the machinery he himself had erected.[33]

The duties of the commissioners were normally confined to those of formally receiving the surrenders, dealing with movable goods and the necessary clearing up of debts, and the making of cash payments to the departing religious and their servants. But in some instances they proceeded, as in 1536, to make new surveys of the monastic lands, and by July 1538 their somewhat amateurish efforts had moved Sir Richard Rich, Chancellor and chief officer of the court of Augmentations, to write somewhat bluntly to Cromwell. Should he, he asked, send officers of the Augmentations to survey St Augustine's at Canterbury or would those Cromwell had appointed for the dissolution do it? What answer, if any, he received we do not know, but at the end of the month he wrote to his own officers in Worcester inquiring by what authority the late

[32] *Sir John Williams's Account of Monastic Treasures*, ed. W. B. Turnbull, Abbotsford Club, 1836.

[33] G. R. Elton, *Tudor Revolution*, p. 215. It has been suggested (S. E. Lehmberg, 'Supremacy and Vicegerency', *EHR* LXXXI (1966), p. 235) that in supervising the Dissolution Cromwell was exercising powers which he possessed as the king's deputy as supreme head of the Church in England, but such powers would appear to be quite irrelevant to his relationship with the court of Augmentations.

monastery of Bordesley had been defaced and pulled down and the materials sold, and instructing all concerned to wait upon him in London. Such stone and glass as remained was to be offered to Sir George Throckmorton.[34] The date of these altercations should be noted. Until mid-1538 the commissioners had proceeded in a leisurely fashion and, no doubt beset by suitors, had cast themselves in the role of temporary landlords. Within a very few months they were regularly moving on to their next assignment much too quickly to have time to accomplish more than the sketchiest of arrangements for the sale of movables and the temporary custody of buildings and demesne (Doc. 20, a–d). By 1539, and probably earlier in some cases, virtually the whole clearing-up operation was normally handled by the Augmentations men *ex officio*, though in many cases their dual identity as both commissioners and civil servants must have gone far to make the takeover as smooth as possible for everybody concerned, including local people eager to partake in whatever was on offer. At St Osyth's Abbey, Essex, however, which was dissolved at the end of July 1539 in what appears to have been an isolated operation – apart from those of some Lincolnshire houses there are no other deeds of surrender between May 1st and mid-August 1539 – the commissioners stayed on to see most of the business through (Doc. 22).

Two other quite separate campaigns were carried out in 1538, and in their objectives both must be clearly distinguished from the Dissolution proper. The first in point of time was the visitation of the houses of friars. This resulted in their total surrender and although it is easy, and tempting, to believe that this was the real objective, nevertheless one cannot help feeling that, through the extraordinarily successful tactics of Dr Ingworth, the surrender of the friars just happened, and certainly without the exercise of direct pressure by the government. Except for the Gilbertines they were the only religious order or orders dealt with as a self-contained operation. The friars had, of course, long attracted the attention of the government, owing to their influence as preachers. As early as April 1534 there had been a commission to visit them, but only for the purpose of separating the compliant from the dangerous. The staunch resistance put up then by a mere handful is more properly a part of the religious and political history of the period, and it did not result in widespread dispersal. The buildings of the Greenwich Observant Friars who were dispersed in 1534 were in fact given to the less troublesome Friars Minor.[35] However, on February 6, 1538 Richard Ingworth, a former prior provincial of the Dominicans but now bishop of Dover, was

[34] *LP* XIII i, 1465, 1505. Rich's outburst is odd, however, considering the number of his own staff who were regularly named as commissioners. On this point see Elton, p. 217.

[35] Knowles, *RO* III, 206–11.

commissioned to visit all four orders of friars.[36] His instructions were far from precise and he had no authority to dissolve out of hand. But by applying to each house certain pressures to reform he obtained surrender after surrender, if not on his first, at least on his second visit. Exactly what his demands were is not clear but the friars apparently found them, under present conditions, worse than dispersal. By early May Ingworth's successes were being noted at Westminster and he secured authority, where surrender had taken place, to place the friars' meagre property into safe custody and to make inventories of their few possessions.[37] A great deal of Ingworth's success was probably due to the support he received from the local inhabitants who, as far as can be judged from surviving records, made no effort to protect the friars. For example, he was first at Gloucester in late May and his return in late July led to a wholesale surrender of all four houses. Among the state papers is a record of the proceedings, signed by local witnesses (Doc. 19a) and no doubt obtained by Ingworth on account of his continued uneasiness about his lack of authority. His debt to Alderman Bell is very obvious (Doc. 19b), as also is the fact that the buildings of the Gloucester friaries were in better condition than was usually the case – for the most part Ingworth reported only ruins – and this made them, for all their limited area, all the more valuable to the acquisitive citizens of Gloucester. A few houses of friars surrendered to other agents of Thomas Cromwell, but Ingworth dealt with the great majority, completing his task in little more than twelve months.

The best of the friars had gone long before Ingworth's arrival, and for those who were left, 'little more than a rump' as Professor Knowles describes them, impoverished both materially and spiritually and abandoned by laymen, the final but logical indignity was that they received no pensions. The logic was inescapable. They owned no property, enjoyed no regular income, and, although the Crown was able to lease or sell their urban sites, officially they were losing nothing and had no claim to compensation. Their only hope was to find employment as secular priests. Capacities were forthcoming but the secular world offered little welcome. Almost the last we hear of Ingworth is a letter of 18 March 1539 to Cromwell (Doc. 38) reporting that in the diocese of York the former friars were forbidden, on the bishop's own order, to say mass in any parish church unless they had their letters of orders as well as their capacities. The bishop of Rome's capacities, added the former friar somewhat tartly, were never thus disregarded.

The second of the independent operations of 1538 was the dismantling of the shrines. This, too, had no statutory basis but followed naturally from the guarded discouragement given to the country in the Ten

Articles and Cromwell's Injunctions of 1536, followed up by the less restrained Injunctions of 1538, to the offering of money and other valuables at places of pilgrimage. There can be little doubt of the government's acquisitive instincts regarding the immense haul of gold, silver and precious stones. Although in some cases the proceeds were disappointing, the stories of wagonloads of treasure from the shrine of St Thomas at Canterbury are no exaggeration. But the more serious loss to the religious houses who possessed such means of attracting popular devotion was in the cutting off of so substantial a part of their regular cash income. At Walsingham in Norfolk in 1535 the *Valor* commissioners had assessed the offerings in the chapel of the Blessed Virgin Mary at £250 a year or almost forty *per cent* of the priory's total income (Doc. 4a). Walsingham surrendered shortly after losing its shrine but Bury St Edmunds and St Augustine's at Canterbury survived their losses for over twelve months. The dismantling of the shrines did not make surrender inevitable but it undoubtedly dealt the houses concerned a blow which contributed greatly to their weakening resistance.

By the early autumn of 1538 the pace had quickened. In September William Petre was in Lincolnshire and Nottinghamshire, where, in the course of just over two weeks, he received the surrender of nine Gilbertine houses, including Sempringham itself, each of the deeds of surrender carrying the seal not only of the priory but also of the Grand Master of the Order, Robert Holgate, who barely two years earlier had obtained for his order complete exemption from parliamentary suppression. Like all the small houses which were given formal exemption from the act of 1536, these Gilbertine convents followed the normal course and surrendered by deed of gift.[38] On 3 October, John Freeman, Augmentations Receiver for Lincolnshire, furnished Cromwell with a summary of the proceeds, namely revenues of £1,407. Out of this there had to be allowed £574 6s 8d in pensions but, Freeman added, there were many benefices, and as these became vacant they could be bestowed on the former religious and pensions saved accordingly. In addition he put the value of goods, sold and unsold, at £4,729 3s. Freeman added a suggestion that when Cromwell was sending commissions to any one house in a shire he might as well send to all remaining houses in that shire, 'for they are in a readiness to surrender without any[one] coming, and that doth appear by their acts, for they are in a customed sort of all spoil and bribery, as well the great houses as small, of all the religious houses in England, for they leave neither demesnes unlet nor honest stuff in their houses, but also [di]minisheth the great part of their stock and store. Therefore they would be taken betime.'[39] Cromwell needed no such advice, although the cumulative effect of many such reports of

---

[38] *ibid.*, ii, 375, 411, 423, 432, 440, 449, 470, 517, 529.
[39] *ibid.*, 528.

leasing by the religious and of other forms of 'waste' of their goods may well have indicated how great was the need to proceed with more despatch, before everything was reduced to basic rents. Be that as it may, by Michaelmas Dr Thomas Legh was already engaged in something of a grand sweep in Staffordshire where he dealt with eight houses between mid-September and mid-October, with excursions also into Northamptonshire, Warwickshire and Derbyshire – a total 'bag' of twenty-one separate monasteries in just over two months.

Thomas Legh's great sweep in the Midlands in the autumn of 1538 marked in fact the beginning of a new phase, the implementing of plans which must have been laid not later than the end of August. Now, at last, and possibly for the first time since the early months of 1536, the course of the Dissolution was to be mapped on government initiative alone. For this there were now more cogent reasons than the reports about the dissipation of monastic resources. The latter part of 1538 brought a renewal, and in a more intense form, of the old anxieties about a possible invasion from the continent of Europe. Now and for many months to come the Crown was faced with very heavy expenditure, principally for the putting into a state of readiness of the coastal defences. Cash was an urgent necessity, and if ever there was a moment when Cromwell knew that he must proceed to exploit the possibilities of dissolution to the utmost it was in the weeks following the meeting between the king of France and the Emperor, at Nice, in June 1538. In fact it took the whole of 1539 and part of 1540 to complete the annexation of every single religious house in the country.[40] But the time for selecting which houses to dissolve was past, and now, as the months went by, it was a question of clearing things up as expeditiously as possible and only leaving for the time being those houses where the commissioners, now bent on territorial coverage, came up against stiff opposition.

One of the best documented 'clean sweeps' was that embarked upon in the early months of 1539 by Dr John Tregonwell and Dr William Petre. They probably received their commission in the previous December, for Tregonwell had apparently been at Shaftesbury Abbey in Dorset before Christmas, a visit which Sir Thomas Arundell felt had resulted in a stiffening of the attitude of the nuns.[41] Their objectives appear to have been to clear all the remaining religious houses in Dorset, Somerset, Devon, Cornwall and at least parts of Wiltshire, all, that is, except the great abbey of Glastonbury. It is just possible that they ventured to invite the abbot of the latter to surrender but no echo of

---

[40] The comparative slowness with which the operation still continued may well confirm the view of F. C. Dietz (*English Government Finance*, p. 143), supported by W. C. Richardson (*Court of Augmentations*, p. 354, n. 82) that until 1540 there was no real financial crisis.

[41] *LP* XIII ii, 1092.

their reception has come down to us. Even without Glastonbury the list of houses assigned to the commissioners was formidable. In less than four months they visited over forty separate religious houses. The dates on the deeds of surrender in fact tally remarkably well with the evidence in the commissioners' letters to Cromwell (Docs. 20 and 21). By mid-January they were dealing successfully with three houses in Wiltshire but left Malmesbury alone for the moment as the abbot was in London.[42] On 20–21 January they took possession of Lacock and on 23 January they were at Keynsham in Somerset. Their next call was at the Carthusian priory of Hinton (Doc. 20a). This was a house which had enjoyed a considerable spiritual reputation – as indeed did most of its order – and the last prior, Edmund Horde, was a man of some literary distinction. His first response to the commissioners' overtures was to decline voluntarily to surrender his house. Next morning they found him even more resolved and all but three of the convent equally so. One of them, Nicholas Baland, was brave enough to deny the king's supremacy but the rest prudently stated that he was mentally unstable. The commissioners decided not to press the matter and departed for Bath where the priory surrendered, apparently without protest. They then proceeded without meeting any further resistance across Somerset and into Devon. Including St John's Hospital at Exeter they dealt with nine houses in just over two weeks. In order to forestall further 'waste' of monastic resources, including new leases, they then divided (Doc. 20b), with the result that they took the surrenders of the eight remaining houses in Devon and Cornwall in exactly two weeks and were reunited on the Dorset border by 8 March. In view of the distances travelled on what were certainly appalling roads – and in mid-winter – it was a remarkable physical achievement. They can have given scant attention to the sale of goods but they found time to take possession of enormous quantities of plate, not only in the monastic houses they visited but also at the cathedral churches of Wells, Exeter and Salisbury.[43] None of them was an officer of the court of Augmentations, and they were possibly instructed to leave all the clearing up to the professionals. It is perhaps significant that no inventories of movables are extant for these west country houses, only the barest details about sales being available in the local Receiver's Accounts for 1538–9. They did, however, meticulously assign pensions, including £6 13s 4d a year to Nicholas Baland of Hinton.[44] Their return to Somerset brought them once more up against resistance

[42] *ibid.*, XIV i, 78. Malmesbury did not surrender until the following Autumn: *ibid.*, ii, 687.

[43] Turnbull, *Monastic Treasures*, pp. 23–4. On or before May 2nd the commissioners for the western counties delivered at the Tower of London over 45 thousand ounces – about 1½ tons – of plate, gold, gilt, parcel gilt, and white.

[44] *LP* xv, p. 543.

(Doc. 20c). The prior of Montacute was obstinate and the commissioners suspected him of being in league with the abbot of Bruton. Apparently helpless, they could only report the situation to Cromwell and await further instructions. Dividing forces once again, they proceeded to obtain the submission of ten further houses in Dorset and Wiltshire (Doc. 20d).

The prior of Montacute eventually gave in on or about March 20th but by what means he was persuaded to surrender is nowhere recorded. He was appointed a pension of £80 a year, together with a house in East Chinnock in Dorset which he had built himself.[45] But some light is thrown on what happened in the end at Hinton by a letter written on February 10th, a few days after the commissioners' first visit, by prior Horde to his brother Alan, a Middle Temple lawyer. Alan had apparently admonished his brother for his obstinacy, to which he received a very frank reply (Doc. 20e). Of sterner metal than some of his contemporaries, Edmund Horde was in the end no hero. He and sixteen of his convent signed a deed of surrender on March 31st. It is true that the commissioners' passage through Somerset was not quite as easy as their rapid peregrination of Devon and Cornwall, but the clashes they were involved in were of words only and hardly even of wills. It should be noted that, although obviously anxious to impress Cromwell, at no time do they give any indication in their reports that they had subjected the monks to any rough handling. Their wisdom in moving on and leaving awkward customers to become isolated and more than ever vulnerable to secular pressures resulted in almost complete success.

In 1539, apart from the quite incomparable heroism, or, as some would call it, obstinacy, of the abbots of Reading, Glastonbury and Colchester, some of the stiffest of such other resistance as was encountered came from the women. The abbess of Godstow, having refused to surrender to Dr London in November 1538, earned for her community a whole year's grace.[46] The commissioners in the west parts found the abbess of Amesbury quite adamant in her refusal to do their bidding. Her words, if accurately reported by the commissioners (Doc. 20d), must be interpreted as meaning that she herself would retire from her office, if called upon to do so by the king, but would not surrender her house. She was marginally more successful than the abbot of Combermere (Doc. 17b), and by her stand the dissolution of the house was delayed for eight months, scant respite perhaps, but no doubt her nuns were thus enabled to make more leisurely arrangements for their retirement. She herself resigned, leaving her house to be surrendered by her successor, and received no pension. The abbess of Wilton was rather more co-operative, but she had already made her preparations and with

---

[45] *LP* xiv i, 575.
[46] *ibid.*, ii, 539. See also Knowles, *RO* iii, 355–6.

a pension of £100 and a house at Fovant with orchards, gardens, and
three acres of meadow and pasture, and a weekly load of wood, she was
assured of being able to continue in the comfort to which she had been
accustomed. Her thirty-two sisters were granted pensions of £172 a year
between them, a total charge on the abbey's net income of some 45 per
cent.[47] The official statement prepared in the early summer of 1539 by
one of the Crown's public relations officers which declared that religious
persons who had surrendered had been given 'pensions proportionate
to the revenues of their houses' was, for all its obvious concern to
'whitewash' the Henrician regime, in this particular instance by no
means overstating the facts. A few months earlier, in late January 1539,
Castillon, the French ambassador, had reported that the king, ignoring
the displeasure of the nobility, 'whose daughters and kinswomen possessed' the remaining nunneries, had now ordered all the nuns to return
to their families, with permission to marry. 'It is thought,' he wrote,
with singularly ill-informed optimism, 'the disaffected on this account
will be sufficient to give battle.'[48] He was, of course, right about the
aristocratic connections of the nuns but wrong about their lordships'
likely reaction when such reasonable, if not generous, provision had
been made for their womenfolk.

Castillon was also misinformed about the marriage prospects of
former nuns, or perhaps he was not yet aware that Henry was moving,
in the spring of 1539, into a position of strict Catholic orthodoxy. The
parliament which sat between April 28th and June 28th not only provided,
in the Act of Six Articles, an absolute prohibition on the marriage of
priests but also added another statute (Doc. 39) which, although enabling 'such as were religious persons' to purchase land, to sue and be
sued, and in every other way to live in the world 'as if they had never
been professed nor entered into religion', nevertheless precluded from
marriage any who had been professed at the age of twenty-one or over,
unless it could be proved that they had been in some way coerced into
making their vows. Not until Edward VI's reign were these matrimonial
prohibitions removed.[49]

The first session of the 1539 parliament was also called upon to settle
a problem which had vexed lawyers throughout the period of the
'induced' surrenders and indeed earlier still and with regard to all surrenders of religious houses for which there was no statutory authority,
namely the legal validity of the king's title to the property. As already
indicated, a large number of religious houses had surrendered their
corporate ownership to the king, his heirs, and successors, by means of
a simple feoffment or deed of gift. At the surrender of Lewes Priory in

[47] *ibid.*, i, 597, *VE* II, 111–12, *VCH Wilts* III, 240, 255, and *Ag. Hist.* IV. 327.
[48] *LP* XIV i, 402, p. 155; 144, p. 53.
[49] Knowles, *RO* III, 413.

November 1537 Cromwell's man, Harry Polsted, also arranged for the levying of a final concord.[50] This was a form of action in the court of Common Pleas, highly technical but used a great deal in contemporary conveyancing to obtain a written record which the court would uphold. This required the attendance of a legal officer of the Crown to 'take knowledge of' or 'acknowledge' the details in the presence of the parties or their agents. This precaution seems to have become the normal practice in the early surrenders. In January 1538 when Dr Thomas Legh had obtained the deed of surrender at Muchelney, Somerset, in the presence of many local gentlemen, he proceeded, as he was himself a civil (i.e. canon) lawyer, to conduct the abbot to the house nearby of no less a person than the Lord Chief Justice, Sir John Fitzjames, who took the necessary 'note' for the levying of a fine. Although the records of the court of Common Pleas have not been thoroughly searched, it seems fairly clear from the collections of 'Feet of Fines' in print that such a course was not generally followed after about the middle of 1538.[51] Audley, the Lord Chancellor, always had misgivings about the utility of a fine and recovery (another legal fiction), which often could not be executed until the beginning of a new law term. In December 1537, when consulted about Titchfield, he said, 'If the house be dissolved before the execution it is as if a man died before executing a deed.' At West Acre Priory, Norfolk, in January 1538, the commissioners, following legal advice, delayed dispersing the community until the first day of the law term. Such a procedure, as Audley well understood, if generally followed, would have resulted in very inconvenient delays. He preferred to rely on a simple deed of gift, acknowledged before a judge and enrolled in one of the courts, a procedure which resulted in the enrolment of most, if not all, of the deeds of surrender in the court of Chancery, on the dorse of the Close Rolls.[52]

But the lawyers were clearly still not entirely happy. As already indicated there was a longstanding statutory obligation on the Crown, if the property was to be freely alienable, to arrange for the holding of local inquests. No doubt for the same reasons that these were avoided by resort to statute in the case of Christ Church, Aldgate, in 1532, none were held in 1536–40. The omission had been covered as far as the property of the smaller houses was concerned by the statute of 1536 (Doc. 10, section VII). There remained this element of weakness in the king's title to the property of the larger houses. The misgivings of the

---

[50] *LP* XII ii, 1062.

[51] For the text of such a fine see Williams, *English Hist. Docs.* v. 781. It should be recognized that the numerical details contained in such a document were not necessarily accurate.

[52] For Audley's opinion see BM Cott. MS. Cleop. E IV, fos 195–8, calendared in *LP* XII ii, 1153. See also *LP* XIII i, 86 and 101 for what happened at West Acre Priory.

lawyers no doubt increased as more and more of their clients laid out considerable sums of money on purchases of the former monastic lands from a king whose very right to make the grants might at some future date be questioned. Such would appear to have been the background to the statute of 1539 (Doc. 23) which has so often been mistakenly regarded as a second act authorizing the dissolution of monasteries. But after reciting that many abbots, etc., 'by their sufficient writings of record under their convent and common seals' have voluntarily surrendered their lands and possessions to the king, his heirs and successors, the act proceeds to declare that the king shall 'have, hold, possess, and enjoy them . . . in as large and ample a manner and form as the late abbots, [etc.]'. Section II extended the same security of title to the king in all monasteries 'which hereafter shall happen to be dissolved, renounced, relinquished, forfeited, [etc.]', and sections III and XII gave statutory sanction to the authority which the court of Augmentations had long been exercising in respect of surrendered monastic lands.

Several sections of the act refined in certain details, though not in basic principles, the provisions in the act of 1536 regarding the position of existing tenancies and other interests in the former monastic lands created by the religious. These were confirmed in general terms (section IV) but there followed, as in 1536, a degree of exception for grants and leases made within a year of dissolution. On the whole, like those in the act of 1536 which they followed in principle, these favoured the tenants. The leases declared void were only those (section V) of land not normally leased and those granted in reversion. 'Old rents' were defined as those appertaining during the last twenty years, and for this purpose the operative date was the first day of the present parliament. But even late leases in reversion could be confirmed (section IX) for terms of up to twenty-one years. All leases for lives seem to have been countenanced too (section X), provided that the lessees were already in occupation at the time of the making of the lease, either as life tenants or tenants for years, and that their term had not expired. There was also special mention (section X) of customary copyholdings for lives. Leases for years were less favoured, but this act, like that of 1536, did nothing to upset any arrangement more than a year old, including long leases for years, whatever rent had been reserved.[53] There was a very mildly-worded cancellation (section VI) of any outright grants by the monks, but again only of those made within the past year, without licence, of land in which the king had a particular proprietory interest. Recent sales of wood by the monks were also called in but provision was made for compensation for the purchasers (sections V and XIII). Sections VII and VIII applied all that had preceded to monastic lands still to be surrendered. A very long section

[53] See *supra*, pp. 43–4.

(XVI) dealt with a variety of 'ambiguities, doubts and questions' which had arisen thanks to insufficient drafting of letters patent and indentures under the Great Seal and the seal of the courts of the duchy of Lancaster and of Augmentations and to the failure to hold inquests. All such conveyances made since the first day of the parliament of 1536, and to be made during the coming three years, were declared to be 'good, effectual and available in the law of this realm in all respects, purposes, constructions and intents against his majesty, his heirs and successors . . .', and all existing rights in the property so granted were protected, except any which might be claimed by the Crown, by the former governors, or by founders. This last clause leaves little doubt as to the initiators of the statute of 1539. It was intended to serve the interests, not, as is usually assumed, of the king and his heirs, but of an army of tenants, and of a still fairly small but significant number of grantees of monastic lands. The interest of the latter, where conflict may be seen to have existed, gave way to that of the former, but, as already indicated, many of the more recent monastic tenants were knights and gentlemen. And if further proof be needed it can be found in section XVII which was an attempt to confirm the title both of the king as immediate successor of the religious and of all his subjects who acquired their title from him, both in their right to enjoy, and their freedom from, parochial tithes. Laymen were determined in this respect, as in all others, to inherit to the full the landed rights of the monks.[54]

This same first parliament of 1539 gave statutory form to a project whose echoes were first heard in Wolsey's time, when it won a measure of approval from the Pope. This was the diversion of some of the revenues of the monastic orders to the endowment of new or reconstituted bishoprics. There had been considerable support, both clerical and lay, but largely from interested parties, for such a scheme, and indeed there were still some supporters, even late in 1539, for the idea of 'altering' some of the

[54] For the more usual interpretation of the act see Knowles, *RO* III, 358, and Dickens, *English Reformation*, p. 143. But with these may be compared Woodward, *Dissolution of the Monasteries*, p. 101. There still remained loose ends. An act of 1540 (32 Henry VIII, c. 20) provided for the vesting in the Crown of all the 'franchises and temporal jurisdictions' of the monasteries (cf. Doc. 5, section 11). These were declared to be 'revived' and were placed under the court of Augmentations. They would appear to have been covered by the act of 1539 but no doubt some extra thunder was thought to be needed to prevent neighbouring authorities, particularly in the towns, from assuming that with the Dissolution monastic liberties had simply been extinguished. In London the old immunity of the inhabitants of the Black Friars' precinct from city jurisdiction made possible, in the reign of Queen Elizabeth, the establishment there of a theatre of which Shakespeare was the lessee. Not until 1608 did the city buy from James I a charter extending its authority over both the Black and the White Friars. Other former monastic enclaves, notably Clerkenwell and the London Charterhouse, were never absorbed: E. Jeffries Davis, 'The Transformation of London', *Tudor Studies*, ed. R. W. Seton-Watson, 1924, pp. 299–300.

monasteries into colleges of secular priests. This was in fact what happened at the small Benedictine abbey of Burton on Trent and at Thornton Priory in Lincolnshire. Both were among the churches selected as possible cathedrals but were rejected as territorially inconvenient. As colleges neither survived until the end of the 1540s.[55] Within limits the scheme for establishing new bishoprics did go forward. The act (31 Henry VIII, c. 9), which authorized the king to erect new sees by letters patent, to provide them with the necessary endowments, and to give to the new secular cathedrals their statutes, was, as far as its enacting clauses went, extremely short. But it was provided with a preamble, said to have been supplied by the king himself, which contains the most extraordinary collection of largely irrelevant jargon: 'Forasmuch as it is not unknown the slothful and ungodly life which hath been used among all those sorts which have born the name of religious folk, and to the intent that from henceforth many of them might be turned to better use as hereafter shall follow, whereby God's word might the better be set forth, children brought up in learning, clerks nourished in the universities, old servants decayed to have livings, almshouses for poor folk to be sustained in, Readers of Greek, Hebrew and Latin to have good stipends, daily alms to be administered, mending of highways, exhibition of ministers of the Church . . .' The new bishoprics quite clearly suggested themselves to the king as a universal remedy for all the ills which beset the realm.[56]

In fact a good deal of thought went into the execution of the plan, though not, it may be thought, resulting in the best possible outcome. There is some evidence that Henry himself would have added very substantially to the number of existing sees but that Cromwell exercised a restraining hand on too extensive a diversion of the new resources of the Crown. However, Cromwell's scheme for Canterbury was criticized by Cranmer on the grounds that there was too generous provision for the stipends of prebendaries. Eventually eight existing cathedral churches which had supported communities of monks or canons were re-established as secular cathedrals, namely Canterbury, Rochester, Winchester, Ely, Norwich, Worcester, Durham and Carlisle. To these were added six former abbeys whose churches now became, for the first time, cathedrals or centres of new sees. These were Westminster, Gloucester, Peterborough, Chester, Oxford and Bristol, but within ten years Westminster became a mere secular college. Altogether monastic revenues of nearly £20,000 a year were involved but, assuming that the monastic cathedral churches would have had to be provided for in any

---

[55] D. Knowles and R. N. Hadcock, *Medieval Religious Houses*, 1953, pp. 61, 156, 343.

[56] *Statutes*, III, 728. There is a distinctly 'commonwealth' air to this preamble: an idea the author owes to a suggestion made by Professor Elton.

case, the net gain to the Church – and the net loss to the Crown – of the whole project was rather over £5,000.[57]

The king's expressed concern to see 'children brought up in learning' did not lead him to set aside any substantial part of the former monastic resources for the founding of new schools. The net loss to education brought about by the Dissolution has often been miscalculated owing to an exaggeration of the amount of teaching undertaken on the eve of the Dissolution by the monks. Even allowing for the great reluctance of the *Valor* commissioners of 1535 to allow deductions on account of money which the monks were required by the terms of gifts to spend on education, and indeed, where they allowed anything at all, confining it to food and clothing rather than the maintenance of schoolmasters, the evidence of a monastic contribution to education is very slight indeed. Perhaps because of this Thomas Starkey's was a lone voice (Doc. 14). Most of Henry's own contemporaries paid little more than lip-service to the idea that part of the monastic property should be set aside by the Crown for the endowment of schools. One or two somewhat half-hearted attempts were actually made to save certain of the monasteries and turn them into educational institutions. Such a plea by the abbot and convent of Evesham, probably in 1538, had little more chance of success than that, in August 1539, on behalf of Winchcombe, whose abbot still nourished the hope that the merit he claimed for his house might save it from suppression.[58] The fact is that the pressure of the educationalists on the government was not nearly great enough. Steps were indeed taken to provide for the continuance of existing regular payments in support of schoolmasters but these were honoured because and only in so far as they were authentic charges on monastic revenues, and one suspects that no officer of the court of Augmentations would have felt obliged to ensure that those in receipt of such payments were more than simply alive. Whether such men continued to perform their professional duties is a subject which calls for investigation. Similarly, where provision was made for teaching in the 'altered' cathedrals this only perpetuated existing arrangements.[59] At the risk of appearing to defend the

[57] Knowles, *RO* III, 358–9, 389–92. See also Scarisbrick, *Henry VIII*, pp. 513–14.

[58] *LP* XIII ii, 866; XIV ii, 58.

[59] Simon, *Education and Society in Tudor England*, p. 186. Recent investigations in the west Midlands have shown that at Evesham, the only place in the area where a monastery had maintained a school for children other than novices and paupers, the local Augmentations officers not only continued to pay the last monastic schoolmaster's salary but also that of a successor. At Bruton and Winchcombe, however, the monastic schoolmasters were awarded pensions and accommodation for life but were in fact discharged from any obligation to provide free tuition: N. I. Orme, 'Schools and Education in Gloucestershire and the neighbouring counties', unpublished D.Phil. thesis, Oxford, 1968, pp.

Crown's failure to do more to endow educational establishments it should, perhaps, be pointed out that many laymen besides Henry shrank from placing such a powerful weapon in the hands of the Church, and that it was open to wealthy citizens to purchase the former monastic lands and found, as many of them did, entirely new and lay schools. Had more laymen followed the example set by the wealthy London Mercers, then indeed Henry VIII might well have earned a reputation as a ruler who obtained schools for the nation's children at the expense of those best able to find the money for their endowment.[60]

The same principle of providing compensation only for existing interests was applied to those cases where monastic churches had served in part as parish churches. In quite a number of cases the churches were handed over to the parishioners as free gifts, though without any endowment, and one suspects that this degree of generosity was justified in official eyes because, on the whole, grantees of monastic property were not required to pay for buildings.[61] In other cases churches were actually sold to parishioners for cash, again an extension of the policy followed wherever possible by the officers of the court of Augmentations, presumably with the general approval of the king and his ministers, of accommodating local people wherever possible and of considering sympathetically their claims to occupy land and buildings vacated by the religious.

The parliamentary session of April–June 1539 in fact brought a temporary halt to further suppression. Not until July did operations recommence when Dr London took the delayed surrenders (Doc. 18) of five houses in Lincolnshire and two in Nottinghamshire.[62] Meanwhile government propagandists were still declaring that some houses, 'in respect of the places they stand in', the king would not dissolve. On July 19th, supervised by no less a lawyer than the Master of the Rolls, Christopher Hales, Christchurch Priory, Canterbury, conveyed to the king its manor of Merstham in Surrey. At the same time, however, the recent act was being referred to as the king's authority for receiving voluntary surrenders, and critics of the king were asked 'what fault can be found if lands and goods held by the king's authority are returned

---

99–100, 206–7, 225–6. One looks forward to the publication of Dr Orme's findings over a wider area.

[60] However the Mercers reserved the right to give preference in the allocating of the twenty-five free places in their school to the children of freemen of the Company: Sir John Watney, *The Hospital of St Thomas of Acon*, 1906, pp. 128–32, 144. For a notable example of an educational foundation by a wealthy individual grantee of monastic lands see M. E. James, *Change and Continuity in the Tudor North: the rise of Thomas, first Lord Wharton*, Borthwick Papers, 27, York, 1965, pp. 42–4.

[61] See *infra*, p. 124.

[62] *LP* XIV i, 1222–1313 *passim*, and 1321.

again by the assent of the realm?'[63] By the latter part of August steps were being taken to mop up the dozen or so small houses which, although allowed to escape dissolution in 1536-7, had never received patents of exemption and could therefore be dissolved by authority of the act of 1536. For them there are no deeds of surrender, and the dates of their dissolution can be traced only in the relevant Receivers' accounts of the court of Augmentations.

By the early autumn plans were laid for the final onslaught. This took the form of three main territorial sweeps for which no commissions have survived but the course of which are clearly traceable from the deeds of surrender. There were also a number of separate commissions for individual houses such as that issued on August 24th to Rowland Lee, bishop of Chester, and Sir William Sulyard, president and member respectively of the Council in the marches of Wales, to take the surrender of the monastery of Haughmond, Shropshire. They completed their task little more than a fortnight later.[64] Although the last deed of surrender, that for Waltham Abbey in Essex, was dated March 23, 1540, arrangements for the final phase must have been complete well before the end of 1539. In fact the surrender of Waltham, as well as those of Thetford Priory in Suffolk (16 Feb.) and Leeds Priory, Kent (18 March), must have been delayed for some reason. To all intents and purposes the surrender of Evesham Abbey, Worcestershire, on January 27, 1540 (Doc. 24) really brought the great final sweep of the autumn and winter of 1539-40 to an end. In all there were some thirty commissioners named for this final phase, most of whom will have been active for at least part of the time. They operated in three main groups, dealing respectively with the western counties (Herefordshire, Worcestershire, Wiltshire, Gloucestershire and Hampshire), Yorkshire and the North, and the eastern counties, including Bedfordshire. A small group also dealt with Oxfordshire, and Syon Abbey and St Albans were covered separately. Over eighty houses, most of them very wealthy, fell to the king in the three months ending on January 27th.[65] Of the thirty or so commissioners, twelve were officers of the court of Augmentations and most of the remainder were experienced lawyers and royal servants like Petre, London, Layton, Legh and Tregonwell. There are few echoes of the passage of the commissioners among the state papers other than the occasional letter reporting progress and the requests for instructions and clarification. It is perhaps worth noting that in November the commissioners then at Bury St Edmunds sought guidance direct from the king himself but also wrote a covering letter to Cromwell. From Ramsey a week or so later one of the commissioners, Philip Paris,

---

[63] *ibid.*, 402, pp. 155 and 1286.
[64] *ibid.*, ii, 78, 140.
[65] *LP* xiv ii and xv, *passim*.

wrote of certain difficulties encountered in the assigning of pensions.[66] But for the most part their progress would appear to have been even smoother than that of Petre and Tregonwell in the western counties earlier in the year.[67]

There remained the really hard core. Typical of the government's approach over the last two years the really recalcitrant houses were left until they were isolated. At Glastonbury in Somerset a special body of commissioners arrived in September. They can have had little expectation of an easy victory, but the abbot's own hope of saving his ancient house was suicidal. He was utterly isolated, from Rome, from his fellow abbots, now all comfortably settled with or expectant of pensions, and from neighbouring laymen, all of whom knew that as his tenants they would be secure, as his officers their fees would be confirmed, as corrodians or annuitants they would be looked after, and that some of his lands would become available for purchase. A charge was brought against the abbot, probably well-founded but none the less with deliberate intent to obtain a colourable case for attainder. It was indeed, as Professor Knowles points out, ironic that the charge was that of robbing his own abbey church, that is of concealing its treasures from the king's officers.[68] Perhaps someone one day will be able to construct from the extensive documents sufficient proof to exculpate at least the government's agents, Richard Pollard, William Petre, and John lord Russell. None of them, incidentally, was an officer of the court of Augmentations, Pollard and Petre being lawyers and Russell the recently appointed President of the Council of the West. It can be safely assumed that the abbot had been given the chance of surrendering 'voluntarily' but had refused. Approaches had been made to the abbot of St John's, Colchester, as early as November 1538 but without success. In vain, however, did he declare on that occasion that 'the king shall never have my house but against my will and against my heart, for I know by my learning that he cannot take it by right and law'.[69] We may admire his courage but hardly his learning for before many months had passed dozens of deeds of surrender, their legality placed beyond all doubt by the king in his parliament, had proved him mistaken.

[66] *LP* xiv ii, 475–6, 584.

[67] There exist, in draft form, some instructions to commissioners which provide, *inter alia*, for the taking over of 'obstinate' houses by force, followed by the imprisonment of unco-operative monks and nuns: PRO, Exch., Treasurer's Remembrancer, Misc. Books (E 36), 116, calendared in *LP* xiv i, 1189. It is unlikely that such instructions were ever issued and in any case they appear to depend upon the passage of an act entitled 'for the alteration of ecclesiastical tenures at the king's pleasure'. It seems possible that the act enabling the king to erect new bishoprics is all that survived of a much more comprehensive measure.

[68] Knowles, *RO* iii, 381.

[69] *ibid.*, 377, and *LP* xiii ii, 764, 887.

The regular religious life in England and Wales was not entirely extinguished, even in 1540. The parliament of April to July of that year passed an act (32 Henry VIII, c. 24) dissolving the order of St John of Jerusalem and vesting its property in the Crown, and in 1545 the remaining conventual hospitals were dissolved, also by statute (37 Henry VIII, c. 4).[70] The government of Henry VIII, no longer dominated by Thomas Cromwell, now automatically resorted to acts of parliament as the most convenient way of acquiring the property of the Church. Inevitably it was in statutory form that Mary I, in the course of repealing most of the Henrician church settlement, confirmed the ownership of the former monastic lands in lay possession (1 & 2 Philip and Mary, c. 8), and that Elizabeth dissolved the Marian foundations (1 Elizabeth, c. 24).[71] As far as the responsibilities of the court of Augmentations were concerned, the process of secularization was only complete when Edward VI's first parliament secured for the king the property of the chantry chapels and religious guilds.

[70] *Statutes*, III, 778–81, 988–93.
[71] *ibid.*, IV, 251–2, 397–8.

4

The Court of Augmentations takes Charge

'. . . as concerning my affairs I find my lord Chancellor as good to me as any man can wish, but the search from auditor to auditor, from clerk to clerk of Augmentations, and daily attendance, passeth the bishop of Rome's feigned purgatory, for it lighteth the purse, wearieth the legs, distempereth the body, for when upon promise the suitor thinketh him most sure he is furtherest from his desire, yet hope assuageth great part of his pains and labour.' Thomas Warley to Lord Lisle, 17 February 1540.[1]

The act establishing the court of Augmentations (Doc. 25) although separated by only a few weeks from that dissolving the lesser monasteries (Doc. 10), and like the latter first presented as a bill in the Lords, was an altogether more professional piece of parliamentary drafting. By and large its provisions proved remarkably workable, and each of its many sections repays careful study. More than any other evidence its contents would appear to argue the existence at this juncture of plans not only to proceed with the confiscation of all religious houses and their property but also to retain the greater part towards the permanent augmentation of the Crown's resources. However, the new department was not conceived on extravagant lines. Its initial personnel numbered no more than was required to take charge of the property of the smaller monasteries, even allowing for some degree of exemption from the act. It was also capable of indefinite expansion, downwards and sideways, or indeed of contraction, should circumstances require. The strength of the court of Augmentations lay not only in its adaptability but, as a working government department, in its independence. It was, of course, closely linked with the Privy Council through its chief officer or Chancellor, who was *ex officio* a member of that body, and was subject at all times to that body's instructions and influence. There was also, during the first four years of the court's existence, the personal intervention in its affairs of

[1] PRO State Papers Domestic, Henry VIII (SP 3), 8, p. 42.

Thomas Cromwell.[2] But in its day to day workings the new court was able to remain much more detached and self-contained than can ever have been the case with the office of General Surveyors. Any encroachment on its preserves by the Exchequer was firmly precluded by the terms of the act (section XXII).

The court's central officers numbered four, a Chancellor, a Treasurer, an Attorney and a Solicitor, with a Clerk, an Usher, and, to begin with, one Messenger. Except for the addition of a Solicitor this followed the long-established pattern of the Duchy of Lancaster. Of the big four only the Chancellor and Treasurer – if one is to judge by their salaries – were full-time, the two law officers being retained for their occasional services when required. Sir Richard Rich, the first Chancellor, received in fees and diets £300 a year, a basic income with which each of his successors had to be content. Sir Thomas Pope, the first Treasurer, was paid £120, but from 1540 his successor, Sir Edward North, was put on a level with the Chancellor. Neither the Attorney nor the Solicitor was ever paid a regular salary of as much as £100 a year. Richard Duke, the first Clerk, was appointed at a salary of £10 which was later increased to £40.[3]

But what really characterized the court of Augmentations was the appointment, provided for in outline in the act (section III), of local, that is regional, officers who between them covered the whole of England and Wales. It is always a risk to claim novelty for any development in the history of royal administration, and indeed there were precedents for the appointment of regional officers for Crown lands,[4] but the allocation of each English county and, in Wales, of each of the four dioceses, to the district or circuit of one of seventeen Particular Receivers and one of ten Auditors was an apportionment of continuing regional responsibility for which there is no known precedent. No time was lost in defining the regional limits and appointments to these posts were made, along with those to the central offices, in late April and early May 1536. The regional Receivers were, without exception, local men by birth and family, with homes within their districts, men who, however busy they may have been in the service of the Crown in London and elsewhere in

[2] For Cromwell's relations with the officers of the court of Augmentations and his part in the court's establishment see Elton, *Tudor Revolution*, pp. 203–19, and *supra*, p. 74. Like the Act of Dissolution of 1536 (Doc. 11), that establishing the court of Augmentations was introduced into the Lords. For an indication that the bill was framed by Audley and Rich, rather than by Cromwell, see *Wyatt Papers*, ed. Loades, p. 159.

[3] Richardson, *Court of Augmentations*, pp. 492–3.

[4] Regional officers responsible for certain Crown revenues had been appointed by Edward IV and the General Surveyors of Crown lands had appointed local officers for Woods: B. P. Wolffe, 'The management of the English royal estate under the Yorkist kings', *EHR* LXXI (1956), pp. 2, 4–5 and *The Crown Lands*, p. 47. See also Richardson, pp. 4, 277.

recent years, were known in and were themselves familiar with local society and local conditions. Most if not all of them will have been closely connected with the local religious communities and also have been involved in the 1535 survey of the revenues of the Church. The Auditors, on the whole, had fewer local connections.

The Receivers were appointed first and, except for Lincolnshire and Yorkshire, which formed the whole districts of John Freeman and Leonard Beckwith respectively, the other English districts comprised groups of up to three and even four counties. The Auditors, who were fewer in number, were appointed in most cases to one or two of the Receivers' districts but for no obvious reason two of them, Thomas Mildmay and William Cavendish, were given circuits which in each case included two complete districts and parts of two others, so that in the case of Bedfordshire, Essex, Herts., London, Middlesex and Kent, the county unit was bound to retain its identity, forming part of no self-contained region.[5] Indeed, as the records themselves make clear, for the entire history of the court of Augmentations and, as it became after 1554, the office of Augmentations in the court of Exchequer, the county unit everywhere retained its identity. It is an identity which is reflected even at the present day, when for practical purposes, not least the accessibility of their sources, most scholars working on the Dissolution and more particularly the administration and dispersal of monastic lands, find the county unit the most convenient basis on which to work.

There were, at least until 1547, certain exceptions to the exclusively local, that is county or even regional, responsibilities of the Receivers and Auditors. In 1536-7 and in subsequent years as the religious houses were dissolved or surrendered, the site, buildings, and the whole of the property of each house, wherever the latter might be situated, were placed under the charge of the Receiver and Auditor of the county, district and circuit in which the site of the former monastery lay. To this extent the old 'honorial' unit persisted and, in their accounts (Docs. 26, 27), the local officers unfailingly dealt with the property monastery by monastery, never for a moment losing sight of the identity of the former owners. To this extent the court of Augmentations followed the practice of the General Surveyors in continuing to recognize the identity of the individual estates – Warwick lands, Spencer lands, etc. – which had come into Crown hands. The difference lay in the fact that, above the manorial or equivalent level, all the property was the direct responsibility of the regional officers and not of officers appointed to deal with individual monastic estates. This in itself was a considerable economy,

[5] For a complete list of the regional officers, their districts and circuits, and the dates of their appointment, see Richardson, pp. 49–50, 55–6. One Receiver's district comprised the bishopric of Durham and the archdeaconry of Richmond, the latter including part of Yorkshire.

at least in personnel, but the really logical step was not taken until 1547 when, after the uniting of the courts of Augmentations and General Surveyors, the regional officers of the former took charge of all Crown lands within their territory, irrespective of the location of the former monastic owner.[6] This is clear in each of the accounts for 1546–7 (Doc. 26c) and the years that followed. For example, in 1558–9 John Aylworth, Particular Receiver for the four south western counties, included (Doc. 27b) among the revenues for which he was responsible, those from lands in the county of Devon which had formerly belonged to religious houses as far away as Pembrokeshire, Shropshire, Middlesex and Surrey. His predecessor until 1544, Sir Thomas Arundell, and Aylworth himself until 1546–7, had been responsible only for the revenues of monastic houses in the four counties, but this had involved him in collecting rents, etc., formerly appertaining to the little priory of Canonsleigh from as far afield as Gusford in Suffolk and Manningtree in Essex.[7]

There were, of course, other government agencies already dealing with the landed resources and revenues of the Crown, apart from the ancient Exchequer whose responsibilities in this field had become minimal ever since the Yorkist reorganization. These were the office of General Surveyors, which administered all lands which had hitherto come to the Crown by purchase, by exchange, or by process of attainder of the king's subjects, and the duchies of Lancaster and Cornwall, each with its own central staff and its local officers in those areas where the chief estates in each case lay. In the context of the royal finances as a whole the prestige of any one of these depended on how much revenue was at any time allocated to it, and there were those in government circles who were not averse to empire building on behalf of the duchy of Lancaster chamber in connection with the monastic lands. The act establishing the court of Augmentations laid down very clearly (Doc. 25, section xxiv) that all former monastic lands within the county palatine of Lancaster, or lands elsewhere appertaining to religious houses then being dissolved and which had been founded by the king's predecessors as dukes of Lancaster, might, if the king so wished, be assigned to the duchy's officers. This might be interpreted as an application on a limited scale of the principle of reversion to founders.[8] In the event the statutory arrangement was modified as the result of a conference between the chief officers of the two departments. All four of the lesser autonomous monasteries in Lancashire were annexed to the duchy, and Furness

---

[6] cf. Dietz, *English Government Finance*, p. 294; Elton, *Tudor Revolution*, pp. 166–7, 206–7; and Richardson, p. 277.

[7] PRO Special Collections, Ministers' Accounts (SC 6), Henry VIII, 597 (m. 68d) – 603.

[8] See *supra*, p. 40. In fact of the twenty-five houses whose foundation appertained to the earls and dukes of Lancaster none was actually situated in Lancashire: R. Somerville, *History of the duchy of Lancaster*, i (1953), 287.

Abbey, by a special arrangement made in 1540, was also handed over. The duchy gained no former monastic property outside Lancashire.[9] Cockersand Abbey was not dissolved until 1539 and by the act of that year (Doc. 23) all monastic property then being surrendered became the responsibility of the court of Augmentations. The only other house in Lancashire, Whalley, by the circumstances of its surrender, became the responsibility of the General Surveyors, to whom were also allocated the property of some dozen other former monasteries whose governors had been attainted, from Jervaulx, Sawley and Bridlington in the north to Glastonbury in Somerset and Colchester in Essex. The total net revenue involved, using the valuation of 1535, was just over £8,000.[10] Further portions of the former monastic lands came to the General Surveyors when, having been granted by the Crown to some of the more prominent early Tudor politicians, they returned to Crown possession as the result of the attainder of their owners. These included the very substantial grants of monastic estates which had been made to Thomas Cromwell himself before his fall in 1540. When the General Surveyors became united with the Augmentations in 1547 such property became, for practical purposes, reunited with the nearby estates of its former owners still in Crown hands, but as far as the formal records of administration were concerned such property was now firmly associated in the official mind with the name of its most recent owner. How far, in his pursuit of the later history of the property of the dissolved monasteries, should the historian of the Dissolution go? The answer of the Augmentations officers is unequivocal: once the property had left Crown hands it was no longer ex-monastic, but while it remained permanently in their charge its provenance was never for a moment lost sight of.

Once the court of Augmentations had taken charge of the property of the lesser monasteries dissolved in accordance with the act of 1536, a process completed by the early summer of 1537, there followed a period of some eighteen months during which its responsibilities were only marginally enlarged, especially if allowance is made for the permanent alienation of part of the property by the Crown. By the beginning of the new financial year at Michaelmas 1538 the surrenders were coming thick and fast and the accounts for 1538–9 include all or part of one year's revenue from the largest accumulation of property which the new court was ever to handle. By Michaelmas 1539 – or very soon afterwards – alienation was in full swing, and from then on each year saw further considerable reductions in overall responsibility, at least in so far as the

---

[9] For the working out of the division of responsibility with the Duchy see Somerville, pp. 288–92; Richardson, p. 215; and Elton, *Tudor Revolution*, pp. 208–11. See also the latter's *Tudor Constitution*, pp. 378–80, and for a slightly different reconstruction of the negotiations between the two bodies see Haigh, *Lancashire Monasteries*, pp. 38–41.

[10] Richardson, p. 275.

court's primary function was concerned, the collection of the revenue currently arising from the former monastic land in Crown hands.

Professor W. C. Richardson, the author of the only substantial history of the court of Augmentations, sees the work of the new government deparment very much from the standpoint of the central officers. This being so it is odd that he should ever have thought to divide their work into compartments. Convenient as his method is for purposes of historical analysis, he is perhaps unwise to attempt any clear distinction between the three functions, administrative, judicial, and financial, to which he devotes separate chapters. Careful reading of Professor Richardson's book shows how very unreal his distinctions are. The collecting of revenue naturally involved the court of Augmentations in judicial activity, and much of what he describes under the latter title really only amounted to the sorting out, by a tribunal composed of the central officers, of some of the many problems and uncertainties raised by the Dissolution. In so far as the surviving records enable one to see the whole picture it would appear that most of the so-called 'cases' brought before the court ended in some administrative action rather than in any sort of judicial decision and penalty. Very surprisingly Professor Richardson appears convinced that the court of Augmentations was conceived primarily as 'an administrative court and only secondarily [as] a financial one' and goes on to imply that it was only the logic of events that led to its importance as a financial agency.[11] To be fair one must admit that he is himself primarily concerned to view the court's activities in the context of the history of Tudor government and administration, that is he is more interested in the contribution of the court to national – that is, royal – finance than in how the money was collected. To those who are less interested in central government and more interested in the Dissolution and in the later history of monastic property and personnel, the function of the court appears as a composite and undifferentiated one of handling, on the Crown's behalf, this great accretion to its resources. No one these days will surely deny that the interests of the Crown lay in the extraction of the maximum profit compatible with the common law and the maintenance of internal public security. Even the preamble to the act establishing the court (Doc. 25), which for once is perfectly straightforward and businesslike without the usual heavy propaganda, sets out its objectives quite simply and clearly in these terms. The most superficial familiarity with the records, more particularly those concerned with the court's activities in the field, certainly engenders such a view.

The records accumulated by the court of Augmentations, even in its first decade, are daunting both in their variety and in their sheer physical bulk. It was perhaps characteristic of an administrative agency

[11] *ibid.*, p. 325, but cf. *ibid.*, p. 371.

conceived by Thomas Cromwell that it should be prolific of written record. There is much duplication. There are also maddening gaps and in places very considerable confusion, but the Dissolution and what followed is one of the best documented episodes in early modern English history.[12] In the first place the court's Keeper of Records took into his custody a great mass of monastic archives, not, regrettably, the literary manuscripts as such, but material essential for administrative continuity. These included some cartularies and registers of leases, but far more typical of the official collections in the Public Record Office are the thousands of title deeds and counterparts of conventual leases, together with large numbers of court rolls, accounts, and monastic rentals. From its inception, and in accordance with the statute by which it was created (Doc. 25, section VII), the court kept various series of registers in which were enrolled, that is copied, the full texts of outgoing instruments under its great seal. These included appointments to offices, both central and local, recognizances and bonds, leases and life grants of lands, and pensions to the former religious.[13] Also placed on record were decisions of the court necessitating some administrative or, more often, financial action for which the appropriate officer of the court, central or local, needed a warrant or authorization.

These last are to be found in what are undoubtedly the most valuable and indispensable of the hundreds of 'Miscellaneous Books' of the court, the registers of Decrees and Orders. These are in themselves splendid volumes, the first of them opening with several pages of most elaborate 'black and white' illumination. St George slaying a dragon in front of a defenceless female figure, with the motto 'Salus Juris Principi', is presumably no more than a reminder that the court began to operate on April 23, 1536. Henry himself is splendidly depicted, enthroned, holding orb and sceptre and supported by two of his ministers. Could they be Richard Rich and Thomas Pope or the former and his master, Thomas Cromwell? There follow, in very fine 'Chancery' script, the results of the court's deliberations, the majority of the earliest entries consisting only of a statement to the effect that a certain person appeared before the officers of the court and exhibited a grant, usually under conventual seal, of which the full text is given. This is followed by the formal confirmation by the court, with instructions, where appropriate, to the officer to make payment. It might, for example, be an order to pay a monastic annuity. In November 1541 (Doc. 16) William Blake,

---

[12] No attempt will be made here to deal with the archival arrangement of the records, which will serve only to confuse the non-specialist. See Richardson, pp. 484–91, and also E. Lewis and J. Conway Davies, *Records of the court of Augmentations relating to Wales and Monmouthshire*, 1954, pp. ix–xvi.

[13] Those for the reign of Henry VIII are calendared in *LP* XIII i, 1520; XIV i, 1355; XV, 1032; XVI, 1500; XVII, 1258; XVIII i, 982; XIX i, 1036; XX i, 1336; and XXI i, 1538.

yeoman, exhibited to the court his 'evidence' of the grant to him in
May 1537 by Newstead Priory, Nottinghamshire, of an annuity of £2 a
year out of its lands in Derbyshire. This was duly confirmed and payment ordered, with arrears. In a separate register is recorded the appearance on the same day of Richard Standish, gentleman, laying claim to
the office of bailiff and surveyor of the lands of Ulverscroft Priory,
Leicestershire, by a conventual grant of 1538. In the case of grants of
corrodies, whereby monasteries had contracted to provide board and
lodging for life, either on payment of a lump sum or as retirement
benefits for old servants (Doc. 29a), the officers of the court were faced
with the difficult task of commuting the benefits into a fixed annual cash
sum whereby the Crown's obligation could conveniently be discharged
by the appropriate local Receiver. Other entries concern the settlement,
again by the appropriate Augmentations Receiver, of some of the larger
monastic debts, such as those found in June 1537 to be due to William
and Alice Hale and John Mills of Southampton from the revenues late
of monasteries in Suffolk and Hampshire respectively (Doc. 30). By no
means all the conventual grants of fees and annuities honoured by the
Crown can be traced in the enrolment books. Unless many volumes have
been lost it seems likely that, although all grants should have been officially confirmed, men resorted to the court (and incurred the necessary
expense) only when they had failed to obtain satisfaction from the
regional officers. However, the enrolment of several dozen conventual
grants to Cromwell himself in October 1539 (Doc. 4b) would appear to
upset any simple explanation.

What one does not find in the books of Decrees and Orders are the
purely judicial verdicts of the court, those which relate to the civil cases
in which the officers were appealed to as adjudicators in disputes over
former monastic lands which had arisen not between the court or its
officers and lay interests but 'between party and party'. The statute had
made no provision for the bringing of civil actions before the court but
there is ample evidence that such were brought and dealt with.[14] The
court kept no plea rolls and all but one of its Appearance Books have
disappeared, but, fortunately for historians, it followed the practice of
Chancery and the other conciliar courts such as Star Chamber and the
court of Requests and required both plaintiff and defendant to submit
their cases in writing.[15] Suits began with a written deposition by the
plaintiff setting out, from his point of view, the facts of the case and the

---

[14] Professor Elton discovered evidence that the omission in the statute was put
right administratively, probably shortly after the passage of the act: *Tudor
Revolution*, pp. 207–8. The provision was embodied in statute in 1542.

[15] These 'Proceedings' are relatively unknown, except for those relating to the
twelve Welsh counties and to Monmouthshire calendared by Lewis and Davies,
ut supra.

extent of his alleged injury, ending with a request to the court to call the defendant to make appearance. The deposition having been accepted, the Chancellor or one of the other officers of the court instructed the Clerk to issue letters under the court's privy seal summoning the defendant to appear. This resulted in a written answer in which the defendant normally alleged malicious intent on the part of the plaintiff, set out his own case and asked for the case to be dismissed with costs against the plaintiff. This was often followed by a replication or further statement by the plaintiff and a rejoinder by the defendant. The documents which usually survive are the Clerk's engrossments or copies which were filed with the court's records. John Packington's plea concerning the rectorial tithes of Westwood, Worcestershire (Doc. 40), is typical of many, not least for the fact that it is not at all easy to decide whether or not his case was sound in law, and that no verdict is known. From the facts of the case, as set down in the deposition, answer, and replication, about which there were apparently no doubts, it would appear that the plaintiff was in a weak position in laying claim to income which his predecessor, the prioress, had never enjoyed, for if the woods in question were indeed part of the priory's demesne it seems unlikely that they would have been subject to tithe.

Professor Richardson states that the court had no jurisdiction over disputes arising concerning property which had been alienated, that is property of which the Crown no longer held the freehold. But Packington's case and many others of a similar nature would appear to upset such a contention, for which indeed Professor Richardson cites no evidence.[16] He also says that the court not only followed the procedure of the conciliar courts but reached its judgements in accordance with principles of equity rather than the common law. This is misleading and largely untrue. Some use of the court's discretion may well have been unavoidable when it was faced by disputes arising, like that at Westwood, out of the change of ownership, and for which the common law provided little or no guidance. Cases where, as a result of the Dissolution and subsequent alienation of property by the Crown, ownership of tithes and of tithable demesne formerly in monastic occupation was separated presented even greater difficulties. The relevant part of the act of 1539 (Doc. 23, section XVII), which merely provided for the preservation of the rights of the former owners, was clearly inadequate once dispersal of

16 *Op. cit.*, p. 371. There is evidence that some such limitation was contemplated: Elton, p. 207. The act of 1536 (Doc. 10) gave no precise guidance but in 1541 it was provided in 33 Henry VIII, c. 39, section XXXVIII that disputes concerning lands granted by the Crown in fee by letters patent on which was reserved any rent payable to the court of Augmentations (i.e. monastic lands) should be heard and determined by the Chancellor and Council of that court, with provision for compensation for grantees deprived of any part of their grant as the result of the court's decision: *Statutes*, III, pp. 887–8.

the property had begun and there had to be further legislation, especially about tithes.[17] The use of equity procedures, and of equity principles, when the latter were necessary, did not necessarily lead to any conflict with the common law courts. Most if not all of the court's central officers, though not of the bench, were by training common lawyers. The court was erected by force of statute not by the exercise of the king's prerogative, and there is no reason for thinking that any of the court's unpopularity in some quarters was due to its activities as a court of law. On occasion tenants and also new owners of former monastic lands entered into litigation against the Crown in the court. That they did so at all would suggest some expectation of redress and supports Professor Richardson's belief that by and large the central officers of the court of Augmentations dealt fairly with those who sought their help. But with only the depositions (of which only an unknown proportion has survived) our knowledge of the court's judicial activities must be limited.

Work still needs to be done on the use made by the Chancellor of the powers given to him in the act of 1536 (Doc. 25, section IX) to take bonds of the Particular Receivers and of all bailiffs and collectors of rent, implying, of course, that proceedings could be taken against any who did not fulfil their obligations. This was in fact the meaning of the first half of section X which went on to provide that if such cases should need a trial by jury they would be transferred to the court of King's Bench, any money resulting therefrom being firmly reserved for the Augmentations. Sections XI and XII also related to the recovery of debts by judicial process in the court itself, following the practice of the duchy of Lancaster. Section XIII provided for penalties to be levied on officers of the court found guilty of withholding or concealing the king's revenues. In practice, as we shall see, the accountants at every level had a very good run with their money.

Central to the work of the court, the permanent link between the regions and Westminster, and indeed epitomizing the essential function of the new department for the Augmentation of the Revenues of the King's Crown are the records of those responsible for collecting the revenues. There are three main series of accounts, and their interpretation, which is by no means as easy as it may first appear, provides at least some understanding of the way in which the new resources of the Crown were handled.

First there are the many hundreds of rolls containing the Ministers'

[17] An act of 1540, 32 Henry VIII, c. 7, made further and more elaborate provision for protecting the right of laymen to levy tithes: *Statutes*, III, pp. 751–3. The preamble explains that laymen could not sue for non-payment of tithe in the ecclesiastical courts and had no remedy at Common Law. There is, however, no specific reference to the court of Augmentations. It was, of course, only as the result of the dispersal of monastic property that laymen came to own, as well as lease, tithes and other 'spiritual' revenue.

Accounts. As is very clear from the *Valor Ecclesiasticus* (Doc. 4a), the property of the religious houses was comprised very largely of manors or collections of rents, most of them very well organized as a *rentier* estate and provided with salaried bailiffs or collectors of rents long accustomed to presenting annual accounts to the appropriate monastic officers, lay and clerical, and to paying over, or admitting liability for, the balance due, in cash or kind. At this level it was a very simple business, after the Dissolution, for the former monastic bailiffs, farmers etc. to present their accounts and pay over their balances to the appropriate Auditors and Receivers respectively, of the court of Augmentations. There was, indeed, no point in discontinuing the services of manorial bailiffs, many of whom in any case had been appointed for life and, as already indicated, had taken the precaution of obtaining indentures of appointment under convent seal. Their fees would have to be paid in any case, unless the Crown was prepared to ride roughshod over such minor but numerically very considerable vested interests. In accordance with the statute (Doc. 25, section XVII) the regional Auditors were required to visit each county in their charge during the period between Michaelmas (the end of the financial year) and Christmas, and there to audit the accounts of all individual bailiffs and collectors of rents. Prior to the audit notices summoning the accountants were posted in the principal towns and each 'minister' was supposed to be notified individually at least twelve days in advance. Costs of the audit were paid by the local Receiver, and he himself was present to collect the sums due from the bailiffs. Defaulters' names were reported to Westminster so that due process might be taken against them.[18] The Auditor was required to have the separate manorial or other accounts engrossed, that is copied, on parchment and to deliver them to the Chancellor by May 1st following. It is these rolls, each recording dozens of bailiffs' accounts, usually one roll for each county per year, which form the so-called Ministers' Accounts (Doc. 26). However they were submitted to the Auditor, the form in which they appear in his rolls are on the 'charge and discharge' system traditionally used on most of the great lay estates and on the more efficiently managed monastic estates. Quite simply each bailiff charged himself with (that is, listed) every item of revenue which he might be held responsible for collecting. This could begin with arrears outstanding from previous years, proceed with current rents, and end with casual revenues such as manorial court profits, profits from mills, markets and fair. He then proceeded to discharge himself of (that is, claim allowance for) such items as sums expended on repairs, outgoing rents, 'decayed' rents, and fees, including his own. The balance was then struck and was usually recorded as having been delivered in full in cash to the Receiver, apart from rents etc. carefully specified, which he had not succeeded in collecting and

[18] Richardson, *Court of Augmentations*, pp. 315–21.

which went forward to appear as arrears on his next account. But arrears were rarely a serious item at this level. Farmers who merely paid a fixed annual rent for a self-contained property such as a former monastic grange and were not responsible for collecting any other rents might not figure in such rolls and it should therefore not be taken for granted that even the earliest *Ministers'* Accounts comprehended all the former monastic property in Crown hands at the time.

It was probably at the annual audit that the Receivers and Auditors fulfilled their statutory duty (Doc. 25, section XIV) of authorizing expenditure on necessary repairs 'to the king's most profit and least charge'. Apart from this one annual ordeal the majority of bailiffs had no other contact with the court of Augmentations, whose officers will very rarely if ever have found it necessary actually to set foot on the land from which their revenue derived. Manorial courts, of course, had regularly to be held, but on the work of the stewards who presided over these as representatives of the king as lord of the manor very little has yet been written. Fees paid to one or more of them in each county figure in the Receivers' Accounts but they appear to have been responsible direct to the Chancellor,[19] as also were the county surveyors whose multifarious duties brought them into much closer contact than the financial officers with fields, pastures, sea-walls, weirs, and all manner of former monastic buildings. We know that their fees ranged from £6 to £20 a year,[20] but no one has yet worked out how their responsibilities dovetailed with those statutorily placed on the shoulders of the Auditors. As far as one can judge, the system worked, and if there were local personal rivalries and animosities there is little sign of this in the formal records.

To return to the Ministers' Accounts, these were rendered in varying detail but they normally included (Doc. 26), year after year, citations in full of the text of current leases, both conventual and Crown, the details no doubt supplied from his own or the central records by the Auditor rather than by local bailiffs. For this historians must be grateful, for the terms of leases are much more conveniently run to earth here than in the enrolment books which are neither complete nor adequately indexed. Indeed, unless a considerable number of registers has been lost, it is clear that comparatively few men took the precaution of having their conventual leases confirmed at Westminster, even those which, in accordance with the statute, might have been called in question locally. To return to the Ministers' Accounts, free and customary rents were sometimes but not always set out in detail. Regular outgoings, consisting very largely of old rents and compositions, were clearly specified. The bailiffs were not concerned with the payment of pensions to the former monks and nuns nor with the annuities etc. with which the monks had charged

[19] *ibid.*, p. 321.
[20] *ibid.*, p. 322, fn. 166.

their estates. This is important to bear in mind later when the time comes to consider the obligations incurred by purchasers of the property.

The Ministers' Accounts for Warwickshire (Doc. 26c) for the year 1546–7 are typical of their kind and call for no further comment, but those of the abbey of Cockersand in Lancashire for 1538–9 (Doc. 26a) require a little explanation. Owing to the unique combination of circumstances already referred to, the only property in Lancashire for which the court of Augmentations was responsible was that formerly appertaining to Cockersand Abbey, and the unusual step was taken of making use of the late abbey's lay Receiver, John Kechyn, as collector of its various revenues from the bailiffs and farmers. Only the rent reserved on the Crown lease of the site of the abbey and one of its rectories was paid direct to William Blithman, the Particular Receiver ultimately responsible for collecting the revenues. The account has very full details of conventual leases. John Kechyn's part was almost certainly unique. Normally there was no place in the post-Dissolution administration for the many hundreds of central monastic officials, Chief Stewards, Receivers, Auditors, etc., laymen who, provided they could substantiate claims to life-appointments by the monks, were simply paid their fees by the Particular Receivers and performed no duties in return.

Ministers' Accounts are the best known and also the least interesting of the three chief series of Augmentations accounts. Many have been printed, rarely in full and too often in the summary form used by the editors of Dugdale's *Monasticon*. Such summaries do little more than repeat the information about the location of the property available in the *Valor Ecclesiasticus*. They obscure the information which the Ministers' Accounts do provide, such as the more up-to-date details of gross and net income.[21] When the full text is used, as for the county of Lancashire by Mr R. J. Mason, the earliest Ministers' Accounts can be used to correct and amplify the *Valor*.[22] Virtually their only interest after the first year lies in their shrinking length as year by year more property left Crown possession, and their continuing evidence of the persistence under Crown ownership of so many long leases made within months of the Dissolution (Doc. 26c).

Far less known and used, especially by those engaged in purely local studies, are the Receivers' Accounts, many of them to be found in the

[21] Slightly more detailed summaries, omitting, however, all cash figures and references to leases, of the earliest surviving Ministers' Accounts relating to all the English and Welsh monasteries have been prepared by the Public Record Office and copies have recently become available for wider circulation: *Lands of the Dissolved Religious Houses* (PRO, Lists and Indexes, Suppl. series. III, i–vii), New York, 1964. For purposes of research these are no substitute for the original records.

[22] R. J. Mason, The Income, Administration and Disposal of the Monastic Lands in Lancashire, London M.A. thesis, 1962, pp. 39–61.

same PRO classification as the Ministers' Accounts and only vaguely distinguished in the printed list, or in a different place altogether, in the Land Revenue deparment of the Exchequer.[23] These are the co-ordinated annual accounts, presented, at least in the early days, separately by county, and latterly by region, but therein set out county by county. These too were drawn up on the charge and discharge system, beginning, in every year after the first, and again after the first year following the re-establishment of the court in 1547, with a sum for arrears. There then followed a detailed list of all those moneys which the Receiver should have received according to the relevant Ministers' Accounts, excluding the bailiffs' own arrears for which they alone were responsible, and including the farms paid direct to him. After these came the payments due as rent reserved on life-grants or on outright alienations of property by the Crown. As the years went by these last steadily increased in number and the former items disappeared accordingly. As already indicated, items were always arranged under headings indicating the identity of the former monastic owners and, until 1546–7, only the former religious houses actually situated within each county figure in the accounts.

The Receiver's discharges were always long and complicated. He first of all claimed allowance for the fees of himself and the other regional officers, for pensions paid to the former religious, and for fees, annuities, and cash payments in lieu of corrodies paid to laymen. The full text of many of the original conventual and Crown grants were copied out, each year, in the accounts (Doc. 29b). For all such payments the Receiver was obliged to exhibit receipts, and indeed some of these survive, fastened to the rolls. In addition to all these items relevant to his responsibilities, the Receiver also claimed allowances from time to time for sums of money furnished by him, on receipt of a royal warrant, to other officers of the Crown, to be expended, locally or elsewhere, on the king's affairs. For instance, in May 1540 Sir Thomas Arundell, Receiver for the four south-western counties, was directed by the king's general warrant to provide whatever sums should be needed to the paymaster of the coastal defence works at Weymouth and Falmouth and elsewhere along the channel coast.[24] Such warrants and the recipients' receipts were, of course, his discharge and were carefully cited to reduce his liability accordingly. Before striking his first balance the Receiver also listed all 'liveries' of cash already made to the Treasurer.

The balances still to be accounted for after all due allowances had

---

[23] The importance of Receivers' Accounts has recently been underlined by Mrs Jack's work on the dissolution of the smaller monasteries in 1536: *supra*, p. 49. They are equally, if not more, valuable for the years 1538–40 and later.

[24] PRO, Special Collections, Ministers' Accounts [sic] (SC 6), Henry VIII 7301, m. 18d. and 662, m. 10d.

been made were usually quite substantial. Great efforts were made to account for these in the list of outstanding arrears, that is, money which the Receiver claimed that he had been unable to collect. The total debit, including specified arrears, then went over to form the first item in the next year's account, and this sum was liable to build up over the years, forming a greater and greater personal liability which the Receiver carried with him, until he finally obtained discharge, sometimes many years after relinquishing office. It was open to him to institute proceedings in the court of Augmentations against those who owed him money. It was also open to the court to take proceedings against a Receiver. In practice, however, arrears were just allowed to accumulate. It has been suggested by Professor Richardson that such arrears were not always what they appeared. It seems to have been a recognized practice for all revenue officers to retain quite large sums for their own, temporary, use, and it may well have been this practice rather than genuine arrears on the part of those from whom the Receiver's cash derived which accounted for the very large sums which regularly inflated his total charge. Professor Richardson has also drawn attention to the fact that the actual amount of cash remitted to the Treasurer by a Receiver in a given year might be very small indeed. But the examples he cites are somewhat misleading. To discover how much cash was remitted it is not sufficient to point to the final 'debit' at the foot of the account, a sum which, as already indicated, merely formed part of the Receiver's total debt to the central treasury. For instance, for the financial year 1539–40 the total amount charged to George Gifford, Augmentations Receiver for the counties of Northamptonshire, Warwickshire, and Leicestershire, including arrears of over £5,000 brought forward from the previous year, was well over £12,000. His final 'debit' was £118, but in the process of arriving at such a satisfactory conclusion he had been able to obtain discharge for £1,049 3s 7d delivered to the Treasurer, Edward North, at various dates between early December and early March 1539–40. Pensions paid to the former religious had accounted for as much as £1,910 and conventual annuities to laymen for £402 odd. Agreed arrears amounted to over £8,000.[25] But single accounts, even if properly interpreted, leave many things hidden, and even an analysis of a series of such accounts, where they exist, does not reveal the whole story. Professor Richardson does well to indicate the opportunities open to regional officers, although many practices, such as the deliberate holding of funds, which today would be regarded as criminal offences, were accepted practice in Tudor England. But the possibilities inherent in the 'arrears' must not be exaggerated. Had the practice of borrowing Crown revenues at a local level been widespread it would seriously have

[25] Richardson, *Court of Augmentations*, pp. 427, 51. Gifford's account is abstracted very briefly in *LP* XVI, 92.

restricted the opportunities open to that infinitely more important officer, the Treasurer of the Augmentations himself. For the regional officers there were probably better opportunities in outright embezzlement of funds, such as the deliberate withholding of pension payments, and of fees and annuities. Such things did happen but there is no evidence to suggest that they took place on a large scale. Moreover the accounts themselves, archaic as they appear to historians, who find them difficult to interpret in terms of profit and loss accountancy, presumably made sense to contemporaries, and in the context of all the other relevant records available made it as difficult as possible for dishonesty to remain permanently undetected.

As raw material for the historian of the Dissolution the Receivers' Accounts are invaluable. Up to a point they provide for any given year a means of checking how far the property had so far been alienated, and the names of the grantees or subsequent purchasers, that is those responsible for paying the rents reserved.[26] These were not always up to date in cases where re-sales had taken place, especially if payment was in arrears. Moreover, as time went on, a number of the rents were compounded for with the Crown for capital sums (Doc. 27b, n. 5) and no rents were reserved on grants in fee made in and after 1548. Far more valuable and a good deal more reliable is the enormous amount of evidence provided about the payment of pensions, annuities, etc. These reached their upper limit in the very early 1540s when all outstanding claims had been scrutinized and before the total liability was appreciably reduced by deaths. From the Receivers' Accounts for Devon, etc. for the year 1558–9 (Doc. 27b) it is possible to calculate what proportion of the Crown's gross income was still being paid out to the former religious and to their lay friends compared with the position in 1539. On the morrow of its dissolution Buckfast Abbey's estates were charged, as already indicated, with fees and annuities totalling nearly £70 a year. The Crown added a liability for pensions to the former monks amounting to £177 odd, and altogether found itself paying out over 50 per cent of the gross abbey revenue of almost exactly £500.[27] By 1558–9 the total liability was £59 13s 4d out of a gross income in respect of what remained of the abbey property of just over £140, that is over 40 per cent. Had ex-abbot Donne not died in December 1558 the proportion would have been much greater.

In many ways the most interesting historically of the Receivers' Accounts are those relating to the financial years during which the religious houses were actually dissolved or surrendered. In 1536, as already indicated, one Receiver and one Auditor were required to be included among the commissioners detailed to visit the lesser monasteries due to be dissolved

[26] See *infra*, p. 120.
[27] Youings, *Devon Monastic Lands*, pp. 137–8.

under the act of that year. At no time after that were the local Augmentations officers as such responsible for taking the surrender of monasteries or of assigning pensions, but most of them were involved, sometimes in their own and sometimes in other regions, in a personal capacity as royal commissioners. But involved or not in the actual surrender, the Receivers include in their accounts for the relevant year a great many details concerning the actual takeover, including, in some cases, invaluable detail about the disposal of 'superfluous' conventual buildings.

An analysis of John Scudamore's accounts for 1535[sic]–36 as Particular Receiver for, among other counties, Herefordshire (Doc. 27a) shows what can be done to reconstruct the very involved accountancy necessitated by the dual operations of that year. First it is necessary to recapitulate the chronology of the dissolution process.[28] The act was passed towards the end of March and technically its provisions applied from the opening of the current parliamentary session, February 4th. In fact the act itself specified (Doc. 10, section v) a vesting day for movable goods of March 1st. As already indicated, dissolution did not proceed at once as certain things like exemption had first to be settled. But the commissioners' instructions (Doc. 11) were quite clear. They were to inform the governors of the lesser monasteries that they were now merely custodians of what already belonged to the Crown and that as such they would be required to account for all future income and expenditure. Inventories were made which were supposed to represent the situation on March 1st. The governors were instructed to collect no rents beyond what they needed for the maintenance of their communities and to expect the commissioners to return before very long. The county of Hereford was almost certainly not paid an initial visit until September and it is very likely that in its case the first and second visits of the commissioners were very close together. As Scudamore claimed allowance for 'rewards' paid to the departing religious and their servants, the actual dissolution presumably took place before Michaelmas. There is in fact some evidence that the operation was still incomplete in December, and if this is so we can only conclude that Scudamore's final reckoning was delayed and that for some reason he included the 'rewards' in his accounts for 1535–6 instead of 1536–7. He also included in his charge the proceeds of the sale of movable goods and plate, and the same argument might apply here. Unfortunately he had no occasion to insert any dates which might indicate when the sales took place. The period 'between the first survey and the dissolution', during which time the community at Clifford consumed nine young pigs, 13 quarters of rye, 40 quarters of oats, and 16 cartloads of hay, presumably commenced on March 1st, or as near as anybody could remember, rather than on the occasion of the first visit of the commissioners. The most interesting

[28] See also *supra*, pp. 47–9.

parts of the account are those in which the monastic landed income is separated into that accruing before March 1st and due to the religious communities, and all subsequent dues which were taken to belong to the king. Looking particularly at Clifford priory, the Receiver's account is almost incomprehensible at first reading owing to the excessive detail included in his charge in anticipation of his discharge. What it amounts to is that he charges himself with the whole annual revenue of the house, including the profit to be derived from the demesne in hand, with the value of all the movable goods listed in the inventory, including plate and bells, and including, of course, those later sold by the commissioners. He then proceeded to claim allowance, in respect of Clifford, for those portions of the rents from three rectories which were payable 'before the act of suppression', for the profits from the site and demesne which had been in the prior's occupation for the whole term of the account, for all the other rents due from the priory's outlying estates which had been collected by the late prior, Nicholas Hugh, and used for the maintenance of the priory, for the relevant expenses of the royal commissioners, and for cattle, grain, and other movable goods used in the monastic household before the dissolution, for beasts listed in the inventory which had since died of murrain, and for the value of a chest, also apparently listed in the inventory, which had gone to London with the priory's records. He claimed for wages due to the monks and their servants up to the time of dissolution, for rewards paid to the same, and for extra money he had had to find, with the commissioners' approval, to meet the monks' household expenses and 'things necessary for the church'. There were also debts and various administrative expenses and the plate which had been delivered to the Treasurer, Thomas Pope. From all of this it is clear that the monks of Clifford were in occupation at least until Michaelmas 1536, that although they were in receipt of the whole of their rents they were not quite able to make ends meet, and that their liabilities both current and of longstanding were met by the commissioners out of the proceeds of the sale of what remained of their movable goods. Scudamore assumed responsibility only for the revenues and goods specified in the survey and the inventory. Losses of stock he took good account of for they served to lessen his ultimate liability. But if there were any additions at littering or harvest they were not his concern, and in any case they will probably have been consumed, or quietly sold by the monks, who also had a copy of the inventory. Given the terms of the act the financial arrangements in Herefordshire appear to have worked fairly, and even mildly to the monks' advantage.

For some monasteries there have survived very detailed accounts relating to the activities of the dissolution commissioners. For St Osyth's, Essex, dissolved in July 1539, there is a survey and an account (Doc. 22) purporting to be that of the five commissioners, of whom two, Francis

Jobson and Thomas Mildmay, were Augmentations Receiver and Auditor respectively for the region of which Essex formed a part, but almost certainly completed after their departure. St Osyth's was a wealthy house, with a good deal of plate and valuable church furnishings, as well as household goods. As was the normal practice on such occasions a panel of local men had been called in to make an inventory of, and to value, the movables. Nearly 1,000 ounces of plate, gilt, parcel gilt, and silver, was valued at £185 17s 8d and all of this, apart from a few items which on the Lord Chancellor's authority were given to the late abbot, were set aside to be delivered to the Master of the King's Jewel House. The lead, still on the roofs, and the bells were valued at £1,044 and £40 respectively, but there is no indication of what was to happen to these. No doubt Lord Chancellor Audley, who was much in evidence at St Osyth's and was hoping for a grant of the abbey, exerted himself to prevent any precipitate damage to the fabric. The contents of the abbey church were listed and sold for just over £40, and household goods and stocks of corn and cattle made a similar sum. After rewards had been given to the departing monks and their servants, certain debts paid to local tradesmen and the cost of the operation met, the commissioners found themselves with a cash balance of nearly £6, of which, no doubt, Jobson took possession. No survey of the estates has survived – if indeed it was made – but pensions were assigned to the abbot and fifteen monks.

Such a document is, of course, invaluable by virtue of its detail, but a good deal of what happened could have been learned from Francis Jobson's account for 1538–9. For in order to satisfy the Auditor and to account for the £6 balance, and indeed as part of his regular duties, he had to include the accounts of the operation in his account for the year. At St Osyth's it would appear that the goods sold were paid for at once but elsewhere this was not the case. Layton's instructions for Lincolnshire were to allow no more than eighteen months for payment (Doc. 18). In other words, the commissioners' responsibilities were soon at an end, and it was left to the Augmentations Receiver – often wearing another hat – to follow up what had been done and cover the whole business in his accounts.

Finally, and more briefly because they are less concerned with the process of dissolution, something must be said about the accounts of the Treasurers of the court of Augmentations. In accordance with the statute of 1536 (Doc. 25, section xvi) these should have been complete each year by the last day of April, but this was hardly likely to be achieved. In fact the first account of Thomas Pope, the first Treasurer, covered a period of two and a half years, ending at Michaelmas 1538. Basically it was set out along the same lines as the lesser accounts, first the arrears and then a list of the actual sums of money paid over by the Receivers. Other receipts with which he was charged in his first account were the fines for exemption paid by the lesser houses (Doc. 28a), the very considerable sums already due for the purchase of parts of the monastic lands, and fines for Crown leases. The Treasurer's discharge consisted of the fees of the central officers, headquarters' expenses, a large number of other fees, pensions, and annuities, for which for various reasons, he was responsible, and enormous arrears, especially in payment for grants. As with the regional accounts these latter mounted up over the years to gigantic sums, and included not only revenue which the Treasurer had not yet succeeded in collecting but, here there is less room for doubt than in the case of the local Receivers, also cash in his hands which he had not yet handed over to the king's Chamber or some other financial department or spending agency. By Michaelmas 1538 Pope's arrears already amounted to over £23,000[29] But this was not necessarily a reflection on his efficiency. The size of his end of account debit might be due either to his lack of funds or to the fact that he had not yet been called upon to pay out. Pope relinquished his office in 1539 and during the next four years paid to his successor all but £534 2s 6d of his debt. For this he was acquitted. By Michaelmas 1543 his successor, Edward North, owed nearly £25,000, but on surrendering his office to become Chancellor in April 1544 he paid his successor over £22,000 and finally settled his debts in an exchange of land with the Crown.[30] Most of the Treasurer's deliveries of cash were, in fact, made in response to a royal warrant. As the collector of the new revenues from the monastic lands which had just about doubled the Crown's resources, the court of Augmentations replaced the king's chamber as the bank from which the king's government, and his personal extravagances, could be paid for. The cost of casual royal presents, the fees and diets of the Council of the West, the expensive replacement of departmental seals (Doc. 28c), and, of course, war expenses, all figure in the deliveries of cash made by the Treasurer. In November 1545 when £20,000 was needed within a week, £15,000 came from the royal mint, £3,000 from the Augmentations, and £1,000 each from the duchy of Lancaster and the court of Wards and Liveries.[31]

Bearing in mind the nature of the accounting system, it will be appreciated how complex is the task of recasting the accounts in order to arrive at any sort of estimate of the net profit enjoyed by the Crown as a result of the Dissolution of the Monasteries. One way of arriving at a global figure might be to extract from the Treasurers' Accounts all liveries of cash by royal warrant, adding to these the smaller sums paid out in similar fashion by the local Receivers. There would be snags, of

---

[29] Richardson, *op. cit.*, p. 329. This was the sum standing at the head of the following year's charge.

[30] *ibid.*, p. 331.

[31] *ibid.*, p. 347.

course, in such an approach but it would be a better basis of computation than many of the figures which have been offered based on attempts to add together the amount of cash collected each year by the court's officers.[32] If our present understanding of the accounts is sound that is something neither the Crown nor historians were ever intended to know for certain. The Treasurers' Accounts are far too long to print in full and for illustrative purposes a few short extracts only have been chosen.[33] To these have been added (Doc. 28b) a number of entries from one of the Treasurers' Receipt Books showing, what is never made clear in the Accounts, exactly when the purchasers of the former monastic lands actually paid the instalments of their purchase money.

Indispensable as all three series of accounts are to any investigation of the process of taking over the former monastic lands, it must be remembered that they are for the most part formal accounts, in many cases drawn up some time after the event and, without necessarily implying any really sinister intent, composed to satisfy the Auditors, and to place the accountant in the most favourable position possible. With his personal liability always in his mind the latter would naturally endeavour to keep his charge as low as possible, omitting any items for which there was no other record, and expanding his discharge in any conceivable way. But only by imposing upon its officers this personal responsibility, so that suing for arrears became a personal matter between collector and defaulter, did the Crown stand any chance of gathering in a substantial proportion of its new resources. By contemporary standards the Augmentations system was an efficient one: the Exchequer might have precluded all dishonesty, though even that is doubtful, but have achieved far less satisfactory practical results.

Local legends which persist to the effect that Henry VIII's primary objective in dissolving the monasteries was to get his hands on the vast amount of lead with which they were roofed are not without a modicum of truth. In the commissioners' instructions of 1536 (Doc. 11) lead and bells were ordered to be surveyed immediately after the religious personnel, and before dealing with the seal and other movable goods. As already indicated the disposal of the two other main categories of movables was quite straightforward: jewels, ornaments, and plate were

[32] Using only the Treasurers' Accounts Professor Richardson calculated that the net yield to the Crown via the court of Augmentations in the latter's first eight years was £899,120 odd, or about £112,390 a year: op. cit., p. 24. It appears (p. 77, n. 47) that he arrived at these figures by deducting from each year's total charge the total arrears brought forward at the beginning of the account. As long as the results are used only for averaging over the years this would appear to be realistic. But it must be remembered that these receipts were those of the Treasurer, not of the Crown.

[33] The early ones have been abstracted in LP XIII ii, 457; XIV ii, 236; XVIII ii, 231; and XIX ii,328.

sent to London or, if of little value, sold locally, and the household stuff and stock of all kinds was sold on the site. When valued, the lead and bells were normally still *in situ* on or in the conventual buildings, and their valuation often provides the only documentary evidence of the existence, size, and even lay-out of the various parts of the monastery. The relevant part of the commissioners' survey of St Osyth's priory, Essex (Doc. 22), is quite informative in this respect, and the price put on the lead, over one thousand pounds, is far in excess of that of any other of the priory's possessions, being over five times as much as that of the 986 ounces of plate. Although no doubt under considerable pressure from potential purchasers to leave the buildings weatherproof the commissioners were under instructions to pull down, or at least make uninhabitable, what were termed 'superfluous' buildings, the principal objective, no doubt, being to obliterate as quickly as possible all buildings of a peculiarly conventual character (Doc. 34c). The churches seem to have been the first target, unless they were needed for parochial use, but there is room for a careful analysis of the post-Dissolution history of monastic buildings, including wherever possible archaeological investigation of all accessible monastic sites, to discover to what extent any regular policy was followed. John Freeman, writing from Lincolnshire in 1539, warned the king that to pull down all buildings would cost a great deal of money and that as a compromise he proposed to pull down only roofs and stairs. He thought the sale of the lead would bring in £20,000 a year for four years and he seemed to be recommending that this should proceed at once before foreign princes dissolved their monasteries and no longer required our lead.[34] In some cases the lead was stripped very speedily, even if the buildings were then left to decay (or to be quarried, officially or unofficially, for building stone) and the lead immediately melted down into sows, marked with the Tudor crown. In most cases, however, the valuation required by the Crown was done while the lead was still on the roofs, as at St Osyth's (Doc. 22) and the actual stripping and storing was arranged later by the Augmentations Receiver. Such a procedure is well illustrated by the agreement made at Cirencester (Doc. 31a) between Richard Paulet, Receiver for Gloucestershire, and the representative of a local man. This was in July 1541, about eighteen months after the dissolution of the abbey. The sale of the lead throughout the country took a long time, and no positive steps to promote sales seem to have been taken until the middle of 1544.[35] Most of the lead and bell metal would appear to have been dis-

[34] *LP* xiv i, 946, quoted by Knowles, *RO* iii, 385. Mr J. C. Dickinson's statement (*British Arch. Jour.* 1968, p. 62) that the buildings of urban houses were most vulnerable is open to question: the domestic quarters were easily converted to merchant residences and workshops.

[35] Richardson, p. 236.

posed of eventually by the Crown in very large quantities to contractors who re-sold it to sub-contractors. The latter undertook its collection from various repositories. The price obtained by the Crown seems to have remained at or just over the £4 per fother estimated by John Freeman in 1539 and, as will be seen in the case of the outright sale of the land, this presumably indicates a firm determination by the Crown to sell at a pre-determined price and neither to bend to nor take advantage of market conditions. The subject has never been thoroughly investigated, although material exists in abundance.

By no means as valuable as the lead but offering more opportunities for regular annual profit were the woods which, in some areas, formed a substantial part of the former monastic estates. A Surveyor of Woods was appointed to the staff of the court of Augmentations in November 1537, at a salary of £20 a year; and in 1543 Sir Thomas Pope, late Treasurer, was appointed Master of Woods.[36] From about this time the management of woods and the organization of wood sales became an important part of Augmentations administration, and it is clear from the very detailed surveys provided by the surveyors on the occasions when woodland was being sold outright (Doc. 34b) that the business was being handled very efficiently. But there was already to hand in 1536 some fifteen years' experience of fairly high-powered woodland management and profitable wood sales by special officers appointed to the Crown lands in the charge of the General Surveyors,[37] and particular reference is made to this source of revenue in the act establishing the court of Augmentations (Doc. 25, sections VII and XIV). Supplies of timber were regularly provided for various public works by the Augmentations, another indirect profit which must be taken account of when an assessment comes to be made of the overall augmentation of royal resources which resulted from the Dissolution. At the same time administrative costs were high.

To return to the former monastic lands in general, the great estate for which the court of Augmentations had become responsible was, at the time of the Crown's assumption of ownership, very largely a *rentier* estate, the greater part of it held by traditional customary tenures which posed few problems except the regular collection of rents. That part of the estate held by leases for lives or terms of years also posed few immediate problems, because of, and indeed perhaps in spite of, the fact that so many of the current leases had been made, or renewed, shortly before the Dissolution. As already indicated, the act of 1536 dissolving the lesser monasteries had laid down (Doc. 10, section IV) that all 'crafty' leases and other grants made by the religious houses within one year preceding the passage of the act should be 'void and of none effect',

[36] *ibid.*, p. 492.
[37] *ibid.*, p. 303.

H

unless they were leases upon which the old and accustomed rents and services were reserved. This would seem to imply the cancelling of a great many of the late conventual leases of demesne not hitherto accustomed to be let and of leases made to friends of the monasteries at lower rents or for longer terms than hitherto used. The statute of 1539 (Doc. 23, sections V, etc.) repeated this and also declared invalid any leases in reversion (that is, to begin at some date in the future) made within the year previous to dissolution, or leases of growing timber. In the absence of monastic records in any quantity it is impossible for us, and it was no doubt almost as difficult for the Augmentations officers except by the use of informers, to detect which of the thousands of current conventual leases were 'new' in the statutory sense. The policy followed was certainly that of erring in favour of existing tenancies, a policy which, as already suggested, was probably officially inspired. Where doubt existed, the tenant was probably advised, and sometimes perhaps required, to exhibit his indenture to the central officers of the Augmentations at Westminster. Most of those enrolled were straightforward confirmations. In a small minority of cases the rent was raised or the term reduced. Of those conventual leases completely 'upset' by the court there is, of course, no record but it seems unlikely that many tenants were entirely deprived.

The Augmentations officers were also faced with the problem of rents payable in kind. This was solved either by commuting them very promptly into money rents (Doc. 26b), or by farming them out to third parties for a fixed sum. There is no evidence of any dissatisfaction on the part of tenants, and indeed, those who could see the way prices were going will have been very well pleased to pay a fixed money rent in place of produce whose value rose during the next few decades. Not so happy, in the long term, were those who had bought or been granted corrodies, that is food and lodging. For them the shoe was on the other foot, and their fixed money payments (Doc. 29a) will have bought them less as the years went by. Again, such arrangements were normally referred to the central officers and, as already indicated, the decision entered into one of the books of Decrees and Orders.

Far more problematical for the Augmentations officers was the placing of tenants in demesne in hand or in the actual sites recently vacated by the religious. There was no lack of prospective occupants, but there must always have been breathing down the necks of the Augmentations officers the potential purchasers who hoped to buy with vacant possession, or at least to obtain short-term tenancies themselves pending the negotiations of outright grants. A very large number of subsequent grantees, especially those in a position to exert influence, did obtain possession immediately as leaseholders. Chapuys spoke of the leasing of monastic property to noblemen as already in progress by

April 1, 1536.[38] But even the formalities of granting leases took a little time, and many vacant sites and farms were put into temporary custody pending the preparation of letters patent under the great seal of the court of Augmentations. This took months and sometimes even years. But there was little opportunity for haggling over terms. The statute establishing the court fixed the length of all new leases of the former monastic property at twenty-one years (Doc. 25, section VII) and from this the Crown never wavered. The property had to be valued to determine the rent and this was a duty placed on the shoulders of the Auditors. They resorted either to the *Valor Ecclesiasticus* of 1535 or, if available, to an 'improved' valuation made at the time of the dissolution or surrender. Even where formal leases took some time to complete it is fairly clear that the Auditors used whatever valuation was most readily to hand, and rarely bestirred themselves to make new, *ad hoc*, surveys. There were indeed those who advised delay in committing the Crown to rents which, if the matter were held over for a year, especially in the case of rectorial tithes, where the actual income could be reassessed, might reasonably be increased, but no such policy seems to have been followed. Indeed it was actually laid down in the act (clause VII) that the dissolution commissioners' certificates were to form the basis of leasehold rents. Nor did the Crown demand more than a minimal fine for its leases. For an example of the text of a Crown lease the reader is referred to that of the site of Cockersand Abbey with the grange and rectory (Doc. 26a). Thus there was laid down from the beginning, both statutorily and in practice, a policy of conservative Crown management which, in the economic conditions prevailing during the twenty-one years which the new leases had to run, almost certainly ensured a considerable advantage to the tenants.[39]

From time to time, especially in the first few years of the new court's existence, zealous local royal officers wrung their hands over official disinclination to exploit the situation in a truly commercial spirit. But whether by instinct or deliberate design, those who set the tone at Westminster knew better than to press too hard. As it was there were murmurs and complaints of harsh treatment, although these should not be taken at their face value. Even apparently unsophisticated countrymen were alive to the opportunities offered by the change of ownership to cast off old yokes and lay claim to new customs. We hear echoes of such tactics only when they were unsuccessful and when the Augmentations men proved stony-hearted. Such, one suspects, was the case at Vale Royal in Cheshire (Doc. 31b). Contemporaries were more voluble

---

[38] *LP* x, 601, p. 244.

[39] *Ag. Hist.* IV, 336–7. A statute of 1543–4, 35 Henry VIII, c. 13, provided for the granting of copyhold tenures for life or lives on the king's demesne at Walsingham: *Statutes*, III, 972. This was said to be in the interests of the town.

on the subject of the delays which, they complained, were a characteristic of the court of Augmentations at Westminster. This was perhaps inevitable in the early days and, again, one suspects that most of the complaints came from those who were hoping for favours, either for themselves or their masters, and who, in this respect, found the Augmentations officers hard nuts to crack. This was certainly the case with Thomas Warley who wrote so feelingly to his master, Lord Lisle, the king's importunate distant cousin, in February 1540.[40] The payment of fees by all who sought the services of the Augmentations was, of course, a routine matter, as in the Duchy of Lancaster Chamber on whose practice they were statutorily based (Doc. 25, section VII). For the expediting of business no doubt quite substantial extra payments were required. In this respect, and in spite of the solemn oaths provided for in the statute (section IV), practice in the court of Augmentations no doubt followed the pattern of Tudor government in general. Richard Duke, Clerk of the court from 1536 until its dissolution in 1554, received each year, in legitimate fees for enrolling indentures, writing privy seals and drafting and enrolling patents, many times his basic salary of £40.[41] What he received by way of gifts, which in contemporary eyes formed a hardly less legitimate part of his emoluments, we can only guess.

A great deal of the time of the Augmentations officers, both central and local, was taken up with the business of the alienation of the former monastic lands by the Crown to other laymen. This, which began very soon after the court was first erected, was, in a sense, leading inevitably towards its own eventual redundancy.[42] But being among the principal recipients of grants the Augmentations officers were probably little bothered at the prospect. There is no evidence that they ever deliberately hindered the process. It is to the dispersal of the monastic land that attention will now be directed.

[40] Part of his letter appears at the head of this chapter.
[41] Richardson, pp. 244, 493.
[42] No attempt will be made here to comment on the significance of the establishment of the court of Augmentations for the history of early Tudor government and administration, but readers are referred to two reviews of Professor Richardson's *History of the court of Augmentations*, by G. R. Elton in *EHR* LXXIX (1964), pp. 111–14, and by B. P. Wolffe in *Annali della Fondazioni italiana per la storia amministriva*, II (1965), pp. 660–6.

5

The Dispersal of Monastic Lands

'FOR selling of a king's livelihood is properly called delapidation of his crown, and therefore is of great infamy': from Sir John Fortescue's *The Governance of England*.[1]

Some distribution of the annexed monastic lands among the king's subjects was envisaged from the start. The act of dissolution of 1536 dissolving the smaller monasteries referred (Doc. 10, sections II and VII) to grants of the lands by letters patent 'now being thereof made' and also 'hereafter to be made', and assured to the king the right to 'give, grant, and dispose' of the property 'at his will and pleasure'. The statute creating the court of Augmentations (Doc. 25) was clearly drafted on the assumption that grants in fee would be made. Section VII, which concerned all grants made under the great seal of the court, clearly referred to lesser estates, that is grants for life, for years, or even at the king's will, but section VIII was based on the assumption that there would be grants under the Great Seal of England of 'estates of inheritance'. But, as already suggested, the very establishment of the new court implies that there was every intention at this time of retaining most of the king's new resources for his own enjoyment and that of his heirs in perpetuity.

The real dispersal can be said to have begun about two months later with a grant, dated May 25th, to none other than Richard Rich, chancellor of the court of Augmentations, of the site of Leighs Priory, Essex, with a number of its manors and other resources in the county. Rich made this his country residence. He also paid a fairly stiff price.[2] Fifteen further outright grants followed in 1536, thirty-five in 1537, seventy-five in 1538, and one hundred and twelve in 1539, in all two hundred and thirty-four before the first commission to sell monastic land was issued in December 1539. After this grants followed in spate, reaching an overall peak, both in number and in the amount of property disposed of, in 1542-4. As a result by the end of Henry VIII's reign over half of the

---

[1] Wolffe, *The Crown Lands*, p. 91.
[2] *LP* x, 1015, g. 33, and PRO, Exchequer, Augmentations Office, Particulars for Grants (E 318), 1338.

whole of the former monastic estates had been alienated. Further grants by Edward VI and rather fewer by Mary Tudor brought the total to well over three-quarters by 1558. The remainder was very largely disposed of by Elizabeth and by the early Stuarts. At county level the chronology varied a little, so that while in Leicestershire well over one-third had left Crown ownership by 1542, elsewhere, for example in Hampshire, the peak came in 1544–6, but in every county in England and Wales for which information is available, the greater part had left Crown hands by 1547 and all but a very small collection of properties by 1558. The one exception was Lancashire where so much was annexed to the duchy, with the result that well over half of all the former monastic land in that county was still in Crown ownership in 1558.[3]

At no time did the Crown put specific property on the market: the initiative in deciding what particular items were to be disposed of came from the prospective grantee. It is true that in the first flood of requests there were those who asked without specifying a particular property, but they were only the fringe and were mostly men who hoped vaguely for some token of royal favour. During the first few years many claims were made and many suits pressed. It is the letters to Cromwell which have survived and to him men revealed their unashamed acquisitiveness. At their best those on the fringes of the Court were afraid of being forgotten in the shower of royal generosity which everyone seemed to take for granted. Even then there were many, even in high places, who expressed their willingness to pay a reasonable price, and by no means all who submitted requests were gratified, at any rate not immediately (Doc. 32). Even in and after December 1539, when a series of commissions was appointed to sell Crown lands, although in each case the total amount to be sold was limited, in terms of annual value (Doc. 33), there was no attempt to sell specific properties. A certain brake was placed on the sale of lands situated near old Crown lands, and on the disposal of the larger properties, and attempts were made, by tenurial and financial concessions, to sell certain types of smaller properties.[4] But in general all the former monastic lands which at any given time were still in Crown hands were potentially on the market. Too much must not be made of efforts to pull strings and exert influence. These were important, perhaps, in the first few years, especially where there was a chance of Crown benevolence, but for the most part the market was open to all who could afford to enter it. Only by accident was more than one individual seeking to buy any particular property at one time, and there is no evidence of competitive offers. The great questions at any given time were two: would the Crown sell any more? and were there people ready to pay the Crown's price?

[3] *Ag. Hist.* IV, pp. 338–9.
[4] See *infra*, p. 120.

In choosing what to ask for, whether as a gift or purchase, people were realistic and calculating, in terms both of location and utility, with potential value or return for their money also in mind but mostly of secondary importance. The newly-vacated sites and monastic precincts, especially those with extensive adjacent demesne or home-farms still in hand, were attractive to some, more especially to those who were seeking a residence and could, like Thomas Wriothesley (Doc. 37), envisage the conversion of existing buildings. Sir Richard Grenville would have preferred a new home in his native Cornwall (Doc. 32), but finally settled for Buckland Abbey, near Plymouth (Doc. 34a), the church of which he and his successors converted most successfully into a residence. William Stumpe of Malmesbury (Doc. 34c) and Alderman Bell of Gloucester (Doc. 19) found conventual buildings convenient for conversion to industrial purposes. A very large number of sites and buildings – the latter sometimes partly defaced – were sold, sometimes several years after the Dissolution, to those who had first obtained possession from the dissolution commissioners, and then had acquired a formal Crown lease. Only in the very early years were sites available for purchase with immediate possession, and this was usually only possible for those who had already obtained a lease or were able to buy out existing leaseholders. Almost invariably, then, the sites, and also the best monastic granges, were acquired from the Crown very early on and inevitably they went to those who could either obtain them as gifts or, more important, who had at least part of the purchase price already to hand. Manorial properties were available long after most of the sites and granges had been disposed of. In the early years a few complete monastic estates, that is sites and all the property appertaining to the former community, passed *en bloc* to individual grantees, but for the most part alienation by the Crown resulted in the break-up of complexes which Augmentations administration had not divided. The manor itself, however, was rarely split up as the result of the Dissolution. Although it was not unknown for grantees subsequently to sell single tenements, especially freeholdings, the Crown rarely sold parts of manors. The Auditors of the court of Augmentations were held responsible for seeing that the Crown's administrative expenses were not further complicated by untidy grants.

Grants of sites and of manors, etc., often included also the rectorial tithes of one or more local parishes. These also had been quickly leased out if still in hand at the Dissolution, and in Edward VI's reign tenurial concessions were introduced in order to encourage the sale of 'parsonages'.[5] The passing of these rectories into Crown hands and thence into the ownership of laymen in general marked, of course, a great break with pre-Reformation practice. For centuries the regular clergy had

[5] Youings, 'Terms of Disposal', *EHR* LXIX (1954), pp. 34–5.

been expropriating their secular brethren. Laymen had collected and even farmed the tithes but not until after the Dissolution did laymen actually own the right to collect so many of these products of the land which were intended for the support of the parish clergy. Those who bought rectories were normally charged with the payment of a stipulated vicarial stipend.

The act of 1536 establishing the court of Augmentations laid down (Doc. 25, section VIII) that on all grants of 'any estate of inheritance' there should be reserved to the king and his heirs a tenure by knight service, and an annual rent of one-tenth of the current net annual value of the property concerned. The tenurial condition must be understood by reference to the Statute of Uses passed by the same session of Parliament (27 Henry VIII, c. 10) and to the energetic efforts made by the early Tudor monarchy to enlarge its 'feudal' revenues, especially those arising from its rights to wardship and marriage in respect of those who held lands of the Crown by military tenure.[6] With minor concessions introduced from 1539 in order to encourage the purchase of certain types of monastic land (Doc. 33), this provision was always adhered to, and as a result the amount of land held by knight service of the Crown, and of interest to the Office (from 1540 the court) of Wards, was considerably increased as more and more monastic land was alienated. This was another reason for not breaking up manors, which were convenient units of landholding in the feudal tenurial structure. The 'tenth', which was peculiar to Crown grants of monastic lands, was presumably partly a rather clumsy way of retaining at least some income for the Crown, and was no doubt suggested by the loss, which resulted from the Dissolution, of part of the new clerical tenth. It may also have been intended as some sort of nominal recognition of the Crown's tenurial superiority, and its collection a safeguard against concealment and evasion of feudal dues. It was always reserved on grants, whatever the other terms, until about 1544 and officially dropped in 1548, by which time it had become possible to commute such rents for a lump sum.[7] Re-sales of property even resulted in 'tenths' becoming detached from the lands on which they were originally charged, so that, as already indicated, as a register of owners the lists of reserved rents payable to local Receivers are not wholly reliable.

The first official intimation of the purchase price of the former monastic land came with the commission issued to Sir Richard Rich and Thomas Cromwell in December 1539 to sell lands to the total annual value of £6,000 for ready money at twenty years' purchase, that is a

---

[6] *Statutes* III, 539–42 and J. Hurstfield, 'The revival of Feudalism', *History* XXXVII (1952), pp. 131–45.

[7] Youings, *op. cit.*, pp. 26–7.

capital sum of twenty times their current net annual value.[8] Urban property could be sold at a lower rate. As already indicated a great many grants of monastic land had already been made since the summer of 1536 and by no means all of these had been free gifts. All had been subject to a 'tenth', sometimes quite literally this and no more, and sometimes a much larger sum which was really in the nature of a fee-farm rent equivalent to all or part of the annual value of the property. Very rarely, however, was it as much as the whole annual value. Besides this many grants had been made partly in exchange for other, carefully valued, property surrendered to the Crown. And finally there had been quite a number of sales. The payment of such cash sums as were made to the Crown for these early grants is not always recorded in the letters patent, and hence in the printed calendars, and it is essential to check the receipt books and accounts of the Treasurer of the court of Augmentations.[9] It can be shown that twenty years' purchase was already the normal formula used for sales. For instance the letters patent granting the site of Redlingfield Priory, Suffolk, in March 1537 to Sir Edmund and Lady Bedingfield mentions that the annual value is £31 4s 5d and the rent reserved is 63s 6d, that is, one-tenth exactly. No purchase price is recorded there but from Sir Thomas Pope's accounts we learn that Sir Edmund's total liability was £561 19s or almost exactly twenty years' purchase of the net annual value.[10]

The commission to Cromwell and Rich was the first of a long series, in every case providing for the sale of lands up to a specified annual value, the limit, no doubt, being set in accordance with the Crown's current financial needs. The resort to these commissions was not incompatible with a firm determination, even after Cromwell's fall, not to sell more than was necessary: in fact the limitation imposed on the commissioners argues restraint. That the Crown could never be sure of being able to sell up to the current limit may well be true but does not necessarily imply that, at least from 1540, it was a buyer's market. One's impression, from an analysis of the terms as set down in the commissions to sell Crown lands and also of those made with individual grantees, is that the king was always able to dispose of as much of the former monastic property as he needed, and, broadly speaking, on his own terms. At the same time, for those with the necessary capital there was rarely a shortage of opportunities for purchase, but little or no opportunity for haggling.

The commission of 1543 (Doc. 33) was the third of the series. After

[8] *LP* xiv ii, 780, g. 36.

[9] Virtually all Crown grants by letters patent under the Great Seal can be traced in the calendars of warrants for and enrolments of letters patent in the *Letters and Papers of Henry VIII*.

[10] *LP* xii i, 795, g. 39 and PRO, Exch., Aug. Office, Treasurers' Accounts (E 323), 1/1, m. 5. See also Doc. 28b.

Cromwell's death in 1540 Rich had acted alone, but now he was joined not only with his own joint Treasurers, Sir Edward North and Sir John Williams, and his Attorney, Walter Hendley, but also with Southwell and Moyle, General Surveyors, and their Attorney, Stanford, and with William Whorwood and Henry Bradshaw, Attorney-General and Solicitor-General respectively. Four of these were to form a *quorum* of which Rich, North or Southwell had to be one, and they were empowered to sell lands within the survey either of the court Augmentations or that of the General Surveyors up to the annual value of £10,000. It should be noted that all the purchase money was made payable to the Treasurer of the Augmentations, which introduces yet another complication to the task of calculating the profit enjoyed by the king from the sale of monastic lands. The text of the commission also made clear that the reservation of the 'tenth' should apply only to the former monastic lands and not to Crown lands in general. Moreover all grants made wholly or partially by gift or exchange or for which settlement was allowed to be made more than three months later should be dealt with by the Chancellor and officers of the court of Augmentations. There were eighteen more of these commissions during the period up to 1558, their personnel varying but usually numbering six to nine of the leading ministers, of which the Chancellor of the Augmentations was always one.

The procedure for obtaining a grant of monastic lands, as epitomized in the commissions, had already been followed very loosely in 1536-9. From 1540 onwards it was followed very precisely, whether the grant was ultimately made by sale, gift, exchange, the reservation of a fee-farm rent, or a mixture of two or more of these. The prospective grantee had first to obtain from the appropriate Auditor or Auditors of the Augmentations a detailed *valor* of the property. Like the *Valor Ecclesiasticus* or the charge in the Ministers' Accounts, this represented a statement of strictly current revenue, what ought to arise from the property barring irregular and unpredictable losses. Free and customary rents usually appeared as bare totals but, as in the accounts, the Auditors usually provided more detailed descriptions of lease-holdings, especially in the case of sites, demesne and granges which had until very recently been in monastic occupation. For these they often provided both field names and acreages, as in the *valor* of the site and demesne of Buckland Abbey, Devon, for Sir Richard Grenville (Doc. 34a). One suspects that the Auditors usually provided as much, but only as much, detailed information as they themselves had readily to hand. This would include full details of Crown leases but rather less concerning conventual grants and old fixed, or 'assessed', rents. Where appropriate the Auditor added figures representing an average year's 'casualties' by way of court profits. As with the *Valor Ecclesiasticus* no deductions were made in respect of unpredictable losses such as 'decayed' or vacant holdings or expenditure on repairs, but full allowance was made for all regular outgoings which the grantee would be obliged to make, such as 'foreign' rents, bailiffs' fees granted to them for their lives by the monks, and the stipends of vicars and various diocesan dues payable out of the 'spiritual' revenue. All of this followed very closely the basic 'charge' of the Augmentations accounts and was no doubt the result of ministerial inertia as much as of deliberate policy. But it did make sense. In any case, as clearly set down in the commissions, the compiling of the valuations was entirely the responsibility of the Auditors, and their figures could not be challenged by the commissioners (Doc. 33). Also following Augmentations accounting practice the property was not charged with the annuities and other benefits to laymen granted by the monks, nor with the pensions granted by the Crown to the religious. At the foot of their *valors* the Auditors also added notes reassuring the commissioners that the rules about the type of property which could be sold – no property worth more than a specified sum etc. – were being complied with. From 1543 the commissioners supplied the Auditors with certain *questionnaires*, the answers to which were also appended, together with any other information thought to be relevant. Always, however, the Auditors confined themselves to current values, and only very rarely did they so much as imply that any part of the property might be worth a good deal more when current leases fell in.

On separate sheets, usually of paper (the Auditors' *valors* were usually on parchment), and written in a most distinct hand, were the certificates of Woods, prepared by the appropriate surveyor. Again these were no doubt drawn as far as possible from information readily to hand, and some of the figures are suspiciously round. But most of the surveys of woods do indicate that personal visits had been made and a good deal of very meticulous surveying carried out. Due allowance was made for woods reserved for the use of tenants, and after that the residue was valued either in terms of acreage, bearing in mind the age of the timber, or, where more appropriate, according to the number of growing trees. Additions were also made in respect of the 'spring of the wood', that is the natural regenerate growth. In the case of Buckland Abbey (Doc. 34a) nothing was done about the woods, which formed an additional free bonus for Grenville, but in connection with John Leveson's grant of lands in Shropshire (Doc. 34b) the timber was valued at from 13s 4d to £1 an acre and 3d per tree. In Devon the prices ranged from as little as 6d an acre for timber of less than ten years' growth to £2 an acre for that of one hundred years.[11]

To these *valors* of the property the commissioners appended their 'rating'. Sometimes they first struck through whole items and occasion-

[11] Youings, *Devon Monastic Lands*, p. xvii.

ally reduced the allowances for bailiffs' fees, but, having seized upon the net or 'clear' annual value, their task was fairly straightforward. First they deducted the 'tenth' which was reserved on all grants made up to about 1548, then the value of any lands or revenues being surrendered in exchange, and finally any royal gift or concession of any kind. The balance was then accounted for either at a certain number of years' purchase or by the reservation of a fee-farm rent. The latter, common in the late 1530s but only rarely seen in the 1540s, was used quite often to dispose of small balances arising from the exchanges of Edward VI's reign. Finally the purchase price was completed by the addition of lump sums for woods and also for advowsons or rights of presentation which were usually valued by officers of the court of First Fruits and Tenths at one year's purchase. As might be expected from the foregoing, no charge was normally made in respect of buildings still *in situ*, even on former monastic sites. This would have added very considerably to the Auditors' responsibilities, and in any case many were already occupied by tenants and might be regarded as being accounted for in their rents. This would account for the absence of any charge for the buildings of Buckland Abbey in Grenville's rating (Doc. 34a), but the substantial sum payable by Stumpe at Malmesbury (Doc. 34c) suggests that here, as late as 1544, he was obtaining vacant possession. No doubt as an influential local man and himself an officer of the court of Augmentations (he was Receiver for North Wales), Stumpe had seen to it that the church had not been 'razed and sold' as intended. The same argument presumably applied to the terms of the grant to the Mercers' Company of London who in 1542 paid a round sum of £100 for the fabric, including the lead, of the church of St Thomas of Acon.[12] In some cases, however, the grantees had themselves already purchased part or all of the fabric, including the lead if the buildings were to stand, from the dissolution commissioners, so the absence of any charge for fabric in the particulars for grants is not to be regarded as conclusive evidence that the Crown had waived all chance of profit from the conventual buildings. To return to the rating, various details were added about tenure, and, for the benefit of the Treasurer, requirements about settlement, that is the time allowed for payment. Finally the commissioners concerned appended their signatures. To the file of documents already accumulated the grantee usually added a formal request to purchase on the terms already settled, signed and sealed by himself. These files containing *valors*, ratings, and requests form the class of records known as Particulars for Grants and they are remarkably complete for the period from 1540 onwards. The dating of their constituent parts makes it possible to obtain an impression of the speed with which applications for grants

[12] PRO, Exch., Aug. Office, Particulars for Grants (E 318), 758 and *LP* XVII, 283, g. 55.

were dealt with. The Auditors took their time and the extraction of the essential valuations from these bureaucrats was undoubtedly the most difficult, and expensive, part of the process of obtaining a grant. In so far as influence could be brought to bear on the progress of a suit, this is where it was most necessary, and where those inside had the edge over those on the fringes of the government machine. The commissioners' rating followed fairly quickly. Then followed a delay of a month or so, and sometimes much longer, before the necessary royal warrant, either by privy seal or signed bill, could be obtained. The date of the arrival of this warrant in the office of the Lord Chancellor was the one used for the actual date of the grant which appeared in the letters patent.

As already indicated there is no evidence in the records of any bargaining between the Crown or its officers and would-be grantees. Nor, where straightforward sales were concerned, was it necessary for prospective purchasers to obtain royal favour, or in any way to pull strings, except, perhaps, to expedite completion. It might be argued that arguments over terms carried on verbally would hardly be likely to be recorded and that all that survives are the terms finally agreed. But there remain the terms as stipulated in the commissions, terms which can be shown to have been almost invariably adhered to. There is also the fact that the 'twenty years' purchase' formula was so consistently the norm that deviations from it, especially in the period up to 1547, are thrown into high relief. Moreover those deviations can be shown to have had a rational basis. Where the rate was less than twenty times the clear annual value the reason can usually be found in the nature of the property and in the commissioners' instructions. It is on those cases where the rate was higher than twenty years' purchase that interest has recently been focused, chiefly by Professor H. J. Habakkuk, whose very convincing analysis, largely of the 'ratings' for Devon, has shown the way towards a real understanding of the government's reaction to market conditions.[13] It was, in fact, the new body of commissioners to sell Crown lands appointed in May 1543 who, in accordance with their instructions (Doc. 33), used their discretion to step up the rate. Almost immediately merchants of Totnes in Devon were paying twenty-one years' purchase, and in one case as much as twenty-five times the certified annual value.[14] In Professor Habakkuk's view this increase is not to be interpreted as a result of competition among men able to afford to outbid their neighbours, and certainly not to any hard bargaining by the Crown with grantees, but merely reflects an attempt by the Crown's agents to realize something nearer the real value of the property. Fixed,

[13] H. J. Habakkuk, 'The Market for Monastic Property, 1539–1603', *EcHR*, Ser. 2, x (1958), pp. 362–80.
[14] Youings, *Devon Monastic Lands*, pp. 27, 30.

or already 'improved', rents of course offered no scope but in each of the Devon examples the Auditor hinted that the property was let at a less than economic rent. Only after 1550, however, by which time most of the former monastic land had left Crown lands, was the practice of increasing the number of years' purchase in full swing, and then it became almost the rule except for fixed rents. By the late 1550s the rate was often as high as thirty years' purchase, and by the 1590s it had crept up, in some cases, to forty. According to Professor Habakkuk the rise in the ratings never quite caught up with land values. Whether this was due to administrative inertia or deliberate policy, it probably helped to sustain interest after the first wave of demand had been satisfied. Supply and demand were probably always fairly evenly balanced. Most purchasers were prepared to pay a fair price: they could neither afford inflated prices nor did they really hope for bargains unless they were leading politicians or civil servants.

Those who write about the dispersal of monastic lands sieze very readily on the word 'speculator' to describe all those who bought, and, at some later date, re-sold their new property, in whole or in part. It was, of course, Professor R. H. Tawney who called historians' attention to the very large number of these re-sales. He spoke of a 'furore' and certainly gave the impression that most of them implied a considerable profit on the part of the sellers. Recently Professor Habakkuk has invited historians to be more precise in their terminology. A man who buys up a substantial block of property and then, over a period gradually sells it in portions, at a profit, may justifiably be called a speculator if, when he made his purchases, he had only a hope and not a certainty of sale. But many of those who bought, especially indeed those who bought certain carefully selected properties located in many widely-separated parts of the kingdom, and who obtained licences to alienate almost at once, even within days of purchase, were much more likely to have been acting as agents for other would-be purchasers.[15] Not all men knew the ropes or had the courage to apply direct to the court of Augmentations. Besides, the process of obtaining grants was an expensive one and there was almost certainly an economy to be achieved in one man making a number of direct purchases and then distributing the property to those who had probably already paid him an agreed sum, including some profit for his trouble. In 1558 one Thomas Savage of Marylebone pursued his purchase of thirty-two acres of woodland at East Barnet, late of St Albans Abbey, to the point of paying the cash to the Crown officers. He then arranged for the conveyance to be included in a much larger grant to one John Marsh of Chipping Barnet and his partner William Rolfe. Marsh's executors subsequently conveyed the property to Savage,

[15] Habakkuk, 'The Market for Monastic Property', *passim* and especially pp. 377–80.

taking 30s for their commission, a much less expensive operation for Savage, apparently, considering the size of the grant, than the obtaining of separate letters patent from the Crown.[16] Those purchasers who really were bent on speculating in monastic lands were much more likely to buy properties in certain limited localities, for there was no method of advertising nationally, and anyone wishing to sell to local men, especially to tenants in occupation, would need to go themselves to the areas concerned. If the re-sales are looked at carefully on these lines the proportion of them which will be dubbed 'speculative' will certainly be greatly reduced.

Evidence of re-sales is not hard to find. In the first place all who held their grants by military tenure of the Crown were required to obtain a licence to alienate the land, and their licences, by letter patent, were normally enrolled on the patent rolls. A great deal of information is also available from the survival of original conveyancing documents and from their enrolments in one of the courts of record. Unfortunately it was no part of the licence to specify the purchase price, and this information is not always available from the original indentures of bargain and sale or their enrolments. The licence granted to William Riggs and Leonard Brown in 1544 (Doc. 35) allowing them to alienate a small part of a very large grant came barely a month after the initial purchase was complete. Robert Martyn was a local man, probably a relative of the Martyns named as tenants of the Tolpuddle property and possibly himself the present occupant. How much Riggs and Brown made from the deal we have no means of discovering but they were almost certainly acting as agents, commissioned in advance to make the purchase, not buying it on the off-chance of selling.[17] But, agents or speculators, it was on the activities of such men that the Crown depended to get rid of most of the small properties up and down the country which formed part of no manorial complex and whose administration was hardly worth the cost involved. Incidentally the licence had cost Riggs and Brown at least £3 8s 8d which would have to be added to the purchase price of £186 for the Dorset property.

On the other hand there has recently come a warning that by relying on the formal records we may be *under*-estimating the activities of speculators. According to the patent roll the site of Selby Abbey, Yorkshire, was purchased not long after the Dissolution by Sir Ralph Sadler and subsequently re-sold by him to Leonard Beckwith, the local Receiver. From this one might assume that this was arranged between

[16] *Cal. Patent Rolls, Philip and Mary* IV (1557–8), pp. 410–11, and Hertfordshire Record Office, 43591, to which Dr John Kew kindly drew my attention, and supplied me with a transcription.

[17] The selling of such property to friends and associates has recently been equated with the exercise of patronage: A. J. Slavin, *Politics and Profit, a study of Sir Ralph Sadler,* Cambridge, 1966, p. 201.

them because of Beckwith's official position. But the story which emerged several years later (Doc. 36), the accuracy of which we have no reason to doubt, is that Sadler in fact disposed of his interest at considerable profit to a third party, Henry Whitereson, his one-time attorney and also an officer of the court.[18] Whitereson, on going north to realize from his deal some of the cash which was still owed to the Crown (Doc. 28b), found difficulty in selling any part of the property or even leases for the same. He was eventually helped out of his difficulty by accepting an offer from Beckwith which left him with a respectable profit of nearly £200. Unless and until a few more details of this kind emerge it would be foolish to adopt too cynical an approach to the general run of recorded evidence upon which it will always be necessary to rely, but the case serves to alert us to the probability that where many of the grants are concerned, the official records tell only part of the story.[19]

The case just cited is also interesting from the point of view of settlement of the purchase money. The Augmentations Treasurer's receipt books (Doc. 28b) show that final payment to the Crown for Selby was not made until after March 1541, that is after Beckwith had settled with Whitereson. The commissioners' ratings usually included instructions about settlement, depending on current official policy, and grantees were usually required to enter into bonds promising payment, bonds upon which the Crown could take proceedings in case of default. At first approximately half was required to be paid in hand, that is before the grant could be completed, and the rest within six months. But the commission of 1543 (Doc. 33) stipulated that half be paid at once and the rest within three months except by special arrangement with the Chancellor and officers of the court of Augmentations. In the last years of Henry VIII's reign the position was eased, but in Mary's reign all was required to be paid in hand or at most within a matter of days.[20] The Treasurer's accounts and receipt books enable us to discover how promptly payment was actually made (Doc. 28b). Ten years after his grant of Buckland Abbey (Doc. 34a) Grenville's heir still owed the Crown 15s 9d. The system ensured that even such relatively small debts were not forgotten, but there can be little doubt that many purchasers were allowed considerable latitude, despite their bonds. It was money due for purchases of monastic land that helped to swell the arrears which mounted up year by year in the Treasurers' Accounts. That each of the early Treasurers was able to obtain his acquittal eventually does

---

[18] Slavin, p. 198, and Richardson, *Court of Augmentations*, p. 52, n. 53.

[19] For another story of a deal in a local setting see J. A. Youings, 'The city of Exeter and the property of the dissolved monasteries', *Transactions of the Devonshire Association* LXXXIV (1952), pp. 135–40.

[20] Youings, *Devon Monastic Lands*, p. xviii.

suggest that most defaulters paid up in the end, but the subject needs to be more fully investigated.[21]

It is not very difficult to trace the post-Dissolution ownership of the great majority of monastic manors, granges and rectories. When the Chancery and Augmentations records fail or, as in the case of the later Receivers' Accounts, are unreliable, there will often be the evidence of estate papers, title deeds and inquisitions *post mortem* to fall back upon. Where so many local historians and those who have set out to deal with the disposal of monastic land on a county or regional basis have so often fallen short is in their failure to pursue ownership beyond the initial Crown grant, and this in spite of the preoccupation of many writers with 'speculators'. The most difficult items to trace are the smaller rents and odd tenements, for the re-sale of which no Crown licence was required, but though important in indicating the number of persons among whom the land was ultimately dispersed, they comprehend only a small proportion of the whole monastic landed estate.

Considerable progress has indeed been made in assessing the effect of the disposal of monastic lands by the Crown on the pattern of local landownership. In a county like Essex, so near to London, the effect was to introduce into local society the new royal servants who could begin at once to establish residences and indeed, in the case of Richard Rich, even conduct the king's business from his Essex home at the former Leighs Priory. Far away in south-west Wales the monastic lands were sold very largely to strangers such as Roger Barlow, a wealthy merchant of Bristol. But the process was a slow one and the effect on local society was far from revolutionary. Over in Lincolnshire the property was widely dispersed among peers like the earl of Rutland, Crown officers, and local gentry. Several local families like the Heneages, some of whose members were in the king's service, were thereby enabled to put themselves firmly on the map. Excluding syndicates of London merchants the initial Crown grants, of which there were 109 between 1538 and 1547, went to 85 persons.[22] No quantitative analysis of the effect of this on landownership in the county has been made, but one gets the impression that in Lincolnshire, as elsewhere, the dispersal of monastic lands only facilitated changes in landownership, and the emergence of new local wealth with its concomitant social and political power, which was happening anyway. The availability of monastic lands enabled the market to expand and simply quickened things up.

[21] For a somewhat inconclusive discussion of the achievements of the late-Edwardian commission for the collection of debts see Richardson, *Court of Augmentations*, pp. 183–7.
[22] H. A. Lloyd, *The Gentry of South-West Wales*, Cardiff, 1968, pp. 30–40, and G. A. J. Hodgett, 'The Dissolution of the religious houses in Lincolnshire', *Lincs. Archit. and Archaeolog. Society*, Ser. 4. i (1951), pp. 86–9.

I

This was certainly the case in Devon, where, even if the Russells be included with the strangers, well over fifty per cent of the monastic property disposed of by 1558 was in the possession of local families, more particularly, of course, those whose more enterprising and energetic members had acquired the essential capital in the service of the Crown. The position in Lancashire was very similar, although in this county much less had been alienated, so that by 1558 only just over one-quarter of the total monastic estate had passed into the hands of local laymen.[23] It is now almost a truism to add that in Lancashire, as in every county for which information is available, conservatism in matters of religion was no bar to the acquisition and retaining of monastic lands.

Judging by the county studies so far completed and published very few new or appreciably enlarged estates were built up, by 1558, entirely or even principally out of monastic lands. It was not a matter of men being uneasy about concentrating their purchases in monastic lands but that few found it convenient to do so. There were, of course, the notable exceptions such as the estates of the Russells, of the Wriothesleys, and of Sir Ralph Sadler, and every county produces a small number, even among the lesser fry. In Devon about nine can be identified and in Leicestershire some fourteen; but in each case these were only a small percentage either of the grantees of monastic lands or of the new landowners of the middle decades of the sixteenth century. But this is what one might expect if one moves away from the study of the dispersal of monastic lands *in vacuo* and sees it in proper perspective as part of the mid-Tudor land market. This surely is the direction in which we should now be moving. Is it not time to forget, for the moment, the admittedly substantial gifts of monastic land, gifts which are really part of the political history of the period, and also to leave the shifting sands of social classes, aristocracy, gentry, etc., and think about the land market pure and simple. There are firmer footings to be found here, in spite of the difficulties of distinguishing between genuine conveyances and mortgages and trusts. The survival, for the county of Devon, of a remarkably complete series of enrolments, both locally and at the courts at Westminster, of deeds of bargain and sale, has enabled Dr John Kew to study, not only the pattern of land sales in the county but something

---

[23] R. J. Mason, 'The income, etc., of the monastic lands in Lancashire', London University M.A. thesis, 1962, pp. 227–8. See also T. H. Swales, 'The redistribution of the monastic lands in Norfolk at the Dissolution', *Norfolk Archaeology*, XXXIII (1966), p. 43. In Norfolk nearly 270 monastic and other ecclesiastical manors had been disposed of by the Crown between 1536 and 1566. Of these over 200 had gone to gentlemen, presumably very largely of local birth, and only 15 to peers. While the gains of the former had gone steadily up since 1545, those of the latter had risen steeply by 1545, thereafter to fall. An analysis based on annual value rather than on the counting of manors would slightly modify these figures but would probably not alter the trend substantially.

at least of the financial ramifications thereof and thus, among other things, to throw a good deal of light on the ways in which minor local landowners in particular managed, by judiciously-timed sales, to raise the money necessary to buy carefully chosen portions of the monastic lands. They did, on occasion, borrow money and even speculate in land which had not yet been paid for. But for the most part, unlike the really large landowners, they planned ahead and put off their purchases until they could afford them.[24] It was to an extent which at the moment we can only guess at that such men kept the demand for monastic land buoyant if not brisk when the first flush of the Dissolution was past. Dr Finch's pioneer study of five Northamptonshire landowning families is an indication of what can be done where substantial family and estate records survive. In her case-studies monastic lands formed only a minor part, probably less than would have been the case had her selection, even of Northamptonshire estates, been a more random sample.[25] It would perhaps be more realistic if future work were to be carried out on a regional basis, or at least on a group of counties (possibly Augmentations-wise) rather than within the narrow confines of single counties.[26]

[24] J. Kew, 'The Disposal of Crown Lands and the Devon land market, 1536–58', *Agricultural History Review*, XVIII ii, (1970), p. 101.

[25] M. Finch, *The Wealth of Five Northamptonshire Families, 1540–1640*, Northants. Record Society XIX (1956).

[26] The important subject of the identity of the new owners of the monastic lands and the effect of the dispersal on the pattern of landownership has been dealt with very briefly, partly for reasons of space but also because the relevant documentary sources do not lend themselves so readily to publication in a book of this kind. A very valuable contribution to the later history of the Crown's dispersal of monastic lands has recently appeared in R. B. Outhwaite's 'Who bought Crown lands? The pattern of purchases, 1589–1603', *BIHR*, XLIV (1971).

DOCUMENTS

1. A Petition of some Knights of Parliament, 1410

FROM *The St Albans Chronicle* (Bodleian Library MS 462), edited by V. H. Galbraith, 1937, pp. 52–5. This represents an attempt, though not the first, to disendow the Church in order to augment the Crown's resources. Tainted with Lollardy, it probably had only limited support, was stoutly opposed, and was rejected. [Translation from Latin.]

To our most excellent lord the king and to all the lords in this present parliament assembled, show meekly all the faithful commons, saying truly that our lord king may have of the temporal goods occupied and greatly wasted by bishops, abbots and priors in the kingdom fifteen earls, fifteen hundred knights, six thousand two hundred esquires and a hundred more almshouses than there are now, well and properly supported from lands and tenements. And besides this he could have a clear twenty thousand pounds over as may be computed and proved . . . As to how this can be done know that the temporalities of bishops, abbots, and priors amount to 332,000 marks a year, that is to say the temporalities of the archbishop of Canterbury with two abbeys there, with Shrewsbury, Coggeshall and St Osyth's are worth 20,000 marks; those of the bishop of Durham and the abbey 20,000 marks; those of the archbishop of York and two abbeys there 20,000 marks; those of the bishop of Winchester and two abbeys there 20,000 marks; those of Clerkenwell and its parts, 20,000 marks. And so the first sum amounts to 100,000 marks. . . . And so the second sum amounts to 100,000 marks; . . . third sum 100,000 marks; . . . fourth sum 32,000 marks . . . And we have not yet dealt with colleges, chantries, white canons, cathedral churches and churches appropriated to them, Carthusian monks, French monks, nor with glebe, with leper houses [etc.]. And therefore the faithful commons desire, for the honour of God and the good of the kingdom, that these worldly clerks, bishops, abbots and priors who are such worldly lords should live on their spiritual revenues . . .

2. Bath Cathedral Priory lease, 1528

The text of an indenture of a reversionary lease by the cathedral priory of Bath, Somerset, dated 11 November 1528, of its manorial demesne and stock at Combe: BM, Harl. MS. 3970, fo. 20, printed in W. A. J. Archbold, *Somerset Religious Houses*, 1892, pp. 355–63. This is from a register of the leases of Prior William Holway (1525–39), mostly dating from 1537–8. For what happened after the dissolution of the priory in 1539 see Doc. 26b.

To all true Christian [people] to whom this present writing indented shall come, William Holway by the sufferance of God prior of the monastery and cathedral church of St Saviour and of the holy apostles Peter and Paul of Bath in the county of Somerset and [the] convent or chapter of the same place send greeting in our lord God everlasting . . . Know ye that we the aforesaid prior and convent or chapter with one assent have let . . . to William Pole of Combe in the county aforesaid, husbandman, to Edith his wife, and to Thomas their son all that our farm, barn, and shippen set and being within our manor of Combe aforesaid, with all lands, meadows, leasows [*pastures*], pastures, woods and underwoods, with all and sundry their appertenances to the farm of old time by right appertaining and belonging, except . . . the rents, reliefs, and all other services of all other tenants there . . . [and except] the mansion or place of our manor of Combe aforesaid with all the court and dovehouse, garden, and orchard there and also the way that goes from the kitchen wall until the highway by the shippen . . . [and except] our lordship or royalty there, with waifs and strays and all rights and profits of our courts . . . [and tithes, etc.]. And moreover know ye that we . . . have granted . . . to the said William Pole, Edith his wife, and Thomas their son all that our wether flock of Combe aforesaid, containing in number 360 wethers, with all and all manner of issues, profits, and revenues yearly coming and growing of the said wether flock, together with pastures, 'sleytes' [? *sheep-folds*], closes, meadows, hills or downs and all other manner of lands or fields belonging or appertaining to the sustentation or feeding of the said wether flock of old time within the lordship of Combe aforesaid and elsewhere, with the customary works of our tenants there, that is to say of washing and shearing of the wether flock at the season or times meet and accustomed. To have and to hold all the aforesaid . . . to the aforesaid William Pole, Edith his wife, and Thomas their son from the last day of April in the 23rd year of the reign of our sovereign lord king Henry the eight [1531] for term of their lives and of every of them [the] longer liver successively, quietly,

well, and in peace. Yielding and paying therefore yearly ... for the
aforesaid farm of our manor and other the premises in grain or corn as
follows: that is to say they shall pay or cause to be paid, carry or cause
to be carried, at their own proper costs and expenses yearly during the
term aforesaid into the garner of the said prior and convent and their
successors within the said monastery of pure and clean and of the best
wheat, and not of the 'orffes' [? *offal*, i.e. waste] of any wheat, well and
purely threshed and winnowed, 16 quarters of good and lawful and
reasonable measure, to be paid and delivered always between the feasts
of St Michael the Archangel and Whitsuntide weekly as shall be demanded and required of them by the said prior and his successors or
their servants or officers; and in pure and of the best barley, well and
purely threshed and winnowed, 22 quarters of good, lawful and reasonable measure, to be paid, brought in, and delivered as is aforesaid,
yearly, always between the feasts of All Saints and St David the Con-
fessor the first day of March, weekly likewise, as shall be demanded ... ;
and moreover they shall cut down, clean, and make before the month
of May, and carry or cause to be carried at their own proper costs and
expenses yearly during the term aforesaid, four wain loads of wood or
fuel, out of our wood of Prysten or elsewhere as there shall be assigned,
into the 'Bruerne Orte' within our monastery or to our manor of Combe
if they be so commanded, and there to pile the same where they shall
be assigned, at their own costs and charges. And also they shall feed and
fatten in stall ... from the feast of St Martin the bishop in winter
[*11 November*] until the Invention of the Holy Cross [*3 May*] one ox ...
and for the said wether flock with their pastures and other their appertenances £6 of good and lawful money of England, to be paid yearly in
the feast of the Nativity of St John the Baptist [*24 June*] in the chapel
of All Saints within our monastery aforesaid ... And furthermore they
and every of them shall yearly during the said term gather, pay, and
levy all the rents of the said prior and convent and his successors of their
tenants there and bring it home to their monastery and there pay it to
the said prior and his successors, or their deputies in that behalf,
quarterly, and thereof at their audit make a true account, without any
fee therefore demanding ... And furthermore ... they ... shall stand
obliged and bound by their writing obligatory under the pain of £100
to us the said prior and convent and to our successors that they or one
of them whom it shall chance to be last, or his executors or assigns in
that behalf, in the end of the aforesaid term [will] well and truly yield
[and] deliver to us ... the aforesaid wether flock containing in number
360 whole, sound, and strong, not rotten, bandy nor otherwise diseased,
or at the least for every poll [*head*] or piece 18d, to be esteemed, valued,
or judged by the whole homage there, so that always notwithstanding it
shall be at the liberty and choice of us the said prior and convent and

our successors whether we will then take the aforesaid sheep or the price aforesaid . . . In witness whereof to the one part of this writing indented remaining with the aforesaid William, Edith, and Thomas we the aforesaid prior and convent have put to our common or convent seal and to the other part of the same writing indented remaining with us . . . the aforesaid William, Edith, and Thomas have put their seals. Given in our chapter house, with our whole assent, consent, and will, the 11th day of November in the 20th year of the reign of our sovereign lord King Henry the eight . . . [1528].

3. A Petition from the Parish of Wembury, Devon

A petition from some of the parishioners of Wembury, Devon: PRO, State Papers Domestic (SP 1), 100/106–9, calendared in *LP*, IX. 1147. Although undated, this 'Memorandum' is among Thomas Cromwell's papers and was probably presented in about 1535–6, some three years before the dissolution of Plympton Priory, an Augustinian house which owned the rectory, and advowson of the vicarage, of Wembury. Written in a large, bold hand, and clearly compiled with little or no professional assistance, it shows no sign of having been intended for the bishop, nor is there any trace of the complaint among the archives of the diocese of Exeter. The rectory of Wembury was part of a large grant made by the Crown in 1547 to the Dean and Canons of St George's Chapel, Windsor: Youings, *Devon Monastic Lands*, pp. 98–9.

Memorandum, that the prior of Plympton and his proctors [*officers*] doth make and hath made a year [out] of the parish of Wembury to the sum of £50 sterling[1] and the said parish hath not with them no priest uprising neither downlying [i.e. *resident*], not within the space of four miles to the said parish, but if they have need of a priest they must go to Plympton after him, the which is eight miles going and coming to the said parish, wherefore, for lack of a priest the said parish shall well and truly [? perish]. And bear witness at all times that there hath been many [a] one dead and hath died without shrift and housel [the eucharist] or any other sacrament ministered unto them [such] as christening, burying, 'nayling' [? *annealing*] and such other.

Also the said parish hath no priest no day in the week for to say to them neither mass, matins, evensong neither none other service no day except the Sunday. Then the priest or a canon cometh from Plympton and sayeth mass, matins, and evensong before noon, and so he goeth home again to the priory to dinner and cometh no more at the said parish till the next Sunday following.

Also the said parish hath been without a priest many Sundays and holy days in the year in times past so that they have had neither mass, matins nor evensong said to them, ...

Also the said prior nor his convent will not come nor send no priest to the said parish to bury a corpse, poor nor rich, old nor young, but they

---

[1] In 1535 the tithes and oblations belonging to the 'chapel' of Wembury were said to be let by the priory for a term of years at a rent of £43 13s 4d: *VE* II, 376.

will have for their labour 7d. Also the said prior and his convent hath yearly of the said parish of Wembury for to have the sacrament ministered unto them, 13s 4d, the which he calleth his fee farm, and this he hath besides all other oblations, and yet he is never content nor satisfied. . . .

These be the names of them that have died within the said parish without shrift or housel or any sacrament ministered unto them: Master Thomas Wessell, John Weryn, John a Lowe, William Fox, Joan Peperell, Cecily Mechell, Master Wessell's servant that was. Moreover one John Weryn in the said parish did send his servant in the morning early for to have a priest to christen his child and the said child was very sick and almost dead, and they answered and promised to send a priest in all haste that might be possible, and so his servant was home again by 7 o'clock in the morning to his master's house. And at 8 o'clock the child was a church, and there the godfathers and godmothers did tarry there till 4 o'clock at afternoon and there came no priest. Then they went home with the child and before they came home the child was dead, unchristened except that [which] the midwife did to it. And when it was night the priest was come and sent for the child and then the godfathers and godmothers then went to church and buried the child.

. . . .

Also the one half of the said parish belongith to the said prior and are his tenants and the Thursday before the nativity of Our Lady last past his steward and his bailiff came to the said parish for to keep the said prior's courts and the steward and his bailiff said, 'Sires, you are all my lord of Plympton's tenants and my lord is informed that you labour and go about for to have the hire of his parish or to find a priest, uprising and downlying. Wherefore and if you make any such labour therefore', the said steward and his bailiff said that the said tenants should be forfeit their holdings if they so did. And for that we, the other half of the parish, have made them no thing or counsel of this matter. . . .

Also, we of the said parish, considering how many times we have lacked a priest, and could never have one at our need, have hired a priest at our own proper costs and charges, and the prior not therewith satisfied nor content did send his steward and his bailiff to the said parish of Wembury and they commanded his tenants that and if any of them did give anything to the priest's wages that they should forfeit their holdings. The which priest hath served with us for the space of ten years . . .[2]

Also it is not only the said parish of Wembury that is thus served but it is three parishes more, that is to say Plymstock, Brixton, and Shaugh, and the least parish of them all is worth yearly to the said prior of

[2] It would be interesting to know whether the bishop was privy to this arrangement. Was this priest perhaps the instigator and writer of the petition?

Plympton £30 or better, and no parish of them all hath no priest uprising or downlying without it be to the poor parish's costs and charges.

Whereupon we all of the said parish will desire you of your great goodness and for the love of God that you will [provide for] all such articles as is before written and rehearsed to be corrected and amended. And to satisfy you that it is of a very truth, I, William Pernyng, being the church warden, and also Nicholas Rede, John Weryn, William Hogge, William Spicer, John Stephen, John Cavytt, with many other more of the said parish shall testify and bear witness at all times if need require that it is evidently so as is here written.

4. Monastic Resources

(a) The royal commissioners' valuation of the resources of Walsingham Priory in 1535: from *The Valor Ecclesiasticus*, III, pp. 385–8. Both Henry VII and Henry VIII paid many visits to Walsingham and the continuing popularity of the shrine right down to the eve of the Dissolution is shown by the amount of money offered by visitors in the year preceding the commissioners' survey, no less than two-thirds of the priory's net income from other sources. Even without the Crown's removal of the statue of Our Lady and the Holy Child in 1538 such revenue was of course beyond the reach of the king when the priory was dissolved in 1539. [Translation from Latin]

Priory or Monastery of Walsingham
Richard Vowell prior there

It is valued in

SPIRITUALITIES IN THE COUNTY OF NORFOLK

Rectory of All Souls in Great Walsingham and the rectory of St Peter's there, as well as the rectory of All Souls in Little Walsingham, with the prior's tithes (60s) there, £59 10s 5d

Tithes of garb [*wheat sheaves*] appertaining to the church of Walton, 40s

.   .   .   .   [Total]   £61 10s 5d

TEMPORALITIES IN THE COUNTY OF NORFOLK

Manor of Great Ryburgh, valued in rents and farms p.a., £32 14s 7⅞d

Farm of the grain mill there, 113s 4d

Sale of wood in an average year, 76s

Profits of the court there in an average year, 8s 8d

In all   £42 12s 7⅞d

Manor of Little Ryburgh Woodhall, valued in rents and farms p.a., £4 19s 4¾d

Sale of wood in an average year, 14s 9d

In all   £5 14s 1¼d

[Twelve more manors and a considerable number of odd rents follow]

[Total] £446 14s 5⅝d, from which there is to be

DEDUCTED OR ALLOWED ACCORDING TO THE STATUTE

Sinodals paid: .   .   .   .   .   [In all]   6s 8d

Procurations paid: .   .   .   .   .   [In all]   30s 6d

Annual Pensions paid: .   .   .   .   [In all]   54s 3d

Alms paid:

Distributed of old at Houghton St Giles for the soul of William Lexham esquire by the founder's provision, 13s 4d

Given of old to certain poor men out of the manor of Peterston by the provision of the founder, King Henry VI, 17s 4d

Distributed to 25 poor men at Bedingham at the feasts of St Mary and on Perasceves Day for the souls of Edward I, Edward II and John Uvedale, knight, by the founder's provision, 12s 6d

[In all]   43s 2d

[Stipends, etc. £13 13s 4d]

Rents paid ... [a long list of small sums]   [Total]   £23 19s 11½d

Fees:

to Roger Townshend, knight, Chief Steward of Little Walsingham and other lordships of the monastery, 40s

to William Salmon, Auditor there, 26s 8d

to William Cocks, bailiff of Great and Little Riburgh, 46s 8d

to Robert Hanke, bailiff of Swanton Novers and Kerdiston, 8s 4d

to John Tye, bailiff of Houghton St Giles, 7s

to Thomas Seaman, bailiff of Peterston, 2s

to William Tichefield, bailiff of Foulsham with Bintree and Norton, 13s 4d

to the aforesaid Thomas Seaman, bailiff of the following lordships, Burnham Overy, 2s; Sall with Reepham, 5s; Sperham, 2s, and Wyneton and others, 2s   In all   11s

to Roger Hopkyns and Nicholas Marshall, bailiffs of Little and Great Walsingham, 60s

[Total]   £10 15s

[Total]   £55 2s 10½d

And there remains clear per annum £391 11s 7¾d
The tenth of this is £39 3s 2d

Also [belonging to] the prior of Walsingham there is valued in

OFFERINGS

In the chapel of the Blessed Virgin Mary last year £250 0s 12d

To the Holy Milk of the Blessed Virgin Mary there the same year, 42s 3d

In the chapel of St Laurence the same year, £8 9s 1½d

[In all]   £260 12s 4d
of which the tenth is £26 0s 15d

(b) A grant to Thomas Cromwell by the abbot of Pipewell, North-amptonshire, 4 June 1531, of 26s 8d a year for his life: PRO, Ex-chequer, Augmentations Office, Miscellaneous Books (E 315), 96, fo. 122. This conventual grant, the earliest of the batch in date, was one of thirty submitted by Cromwell and confirmed by the officers of the Court of Augmentations on 31 October 1539. Note that the conventual seal has been used on the authority of the abbot alone. [Translated from the Latin]

To all Christian people to whom this present writing shall come, We, Thomas, by divine permission abbot of the monastery of the Blessed Virgin Mary of Pipewell in the county of Northampton, send greeting in the Lord Everlasting. Know that we, the aforesaid abbot, have given, granted, and by this our present writing confirm, to Thomas Cromwell esquire, for his good and gratuitous counsel and aid, and for his good-will already shown to us and to be shown, an annual rent or annuity of twenty six shillings and eightpence sterling charged on our manor of Elkington in the county of Northampton aforesaid,[1] the abovementioned Thomas Cromwell or his assigns to have, hold, and receive the aforesaid annual rent . . . during his lifetime, to be paid twice a year, namely at the feast of Michaelmas and the Annunciation of the Blessed Virgin Mary, in equal portions, by the receiver, bailiffs, occupiers, or farmers, or other tenants for the time being . . . [Clause of distress for non-payment] And we, Thomas, abbot, have placed the aforesaid Thomas in full possession and seisin of the aforesaid annuity by the payment of four pence sterling. In witness whereof, to this our present writing, I have placed our seal. Given 4 June in the twenty-third year of the reign of Henry VIII, by the grace of God of England and France king, defender of the faith, and lord of Ireland.

[1] In the *Valor* of 1535 it appears as a charge on the general revenues of the abbey: *VE* IV, 296.

5. A Plan for Root and Branch Disendowment of the Church

An anonymous paper concerning clerical income: BM, Cotton MS. Cleop. E IV, fos. 174-5, printed by L. Stone, *Bulletin of Institute of Historical Research*, XXIV (1951-2), pp. 9-11. This document which, on internal evidence, can be dated quite confidently to the early autumn of 1534, quite clearly indicates a scheme in the mind of the author for the wholesale resumption by the Crown of all ecclesiastical endowments above parish level, to be followed by the provision of fixed incomes according to need. It comprises both the secular hierarchy of the Church and the communities of regular clergy.

Preparation for the Suppression[1]
THINGS TO BE MOVED FOR THE KING'S HIGHNESS FOR AN INCREASE AND AUGMENTATION TO BE HAD FOR MAINTENANCE OF HIS MOST ROYAL ESTATE, AND FOR THE DEFENCE OF THE REALM, AND NECESSARY TO BE PROVIDED FOR TAKING AWAY THE EXCESS WHICH IS THE GREAT CAUSE OF THE ABUSE IN THE CHURCH.

1. First that it may be provided by authority of parliament by an act in due form to be made that the archbishop of Canterbury for maintenance of his estate shall have 2000 marks yearly, and not above, and that all the residue of the possessions appertaining to the said archbishop may be made sure to the king's highness and his heirs for the defence of his realm and maintenance of his royal estate.
2. Item that it may be likewise provided that the archbishop of York may have £1000 yearly, and not above, for maintenance of his estate and the residue to be to the king and to his heirs in form abovesaid.
3. Item that it be likewise provided that every bishop that may dispend above 1000 marks yearly to have assigned to him 1000 marks, and not above, for maintenance of his degree, and the residue to be to the king in form abovesaid.
4. Item that his highness may have for the maintenance of the estate of the supreme head *to him and to his* [heirs] of the church of England the first fruits of every *bishopric*, benefice, dignity, or promotion spiritual for one year next after every vacation thereof, of whose gift so ever it be, and that the first fruits to the bishop of Norwich may cease and no longer be paid, *but to the king*.
5. Item that the king's highness may have to him and to his heirs for

[1] Words in italics were added in another hand.

K

the maintenance of his royal estate and *theirs* [to use and disburse for the defence of the realm][2] all the lands and possessions of monasteries, abbeys, priories, and houses of religion or conventual whereof the number in any one house is *or of late hath been* less than a convent, that is to say, under 13 persons.

6. Item that in such abbeys and monasteries of monks and other religious men where the number is above a convent be it provided that for every monk being a priest there may be assigned of the possessions of the house 10 marks. And for every novice not being priest, £5.[3] And to the abbot or governor of the house as much of the possessions of the house in yearly value as the whole convent shall have assigned amongst them all, to the intent that every such abbot or governor shall keep hospitality and the reparations [repairs] of the house. And the residue of the possessions of the house to be to the king and to his heirs.

7. Item in abbeys and monasteries of religious women where the number be above a convent be it provided that every nun of the house may have assigned to them for their finding yearly [£5][2] *10 marks*. And the abbess or prioress to have yearly as much as all the nuns for hospitality and the reparations of the house, and the residue to be to the king and to his heirs.

[fo. 175] 8. Item that the king's highness may have the moiety and halfendeal of the dividend in every cathedral or collegiate church, and the other moiety to go to the residencers as has been accustomed.

9. Item that the king's highness and his heirs may have the third part of the revenues of every archdeaconry within the realm.

10. Item that the lord of St John's [the head of the English order of St John of Jerusalem] during his life may have 1000 marks, and not above, and the residue of his possessions to the king and to his heirs. And immediately after the decease of the said lord of St John's the king's highness to have all the whole lands and possessions now appertaining to the said lord of St John's, and likewise all the lands and possessions of every commandery after the decease of the knights now living and being in possession thereof, to the intent that his highness after these possessions shall fall and come to his hands may with the profits thereof devise and practice for the [defence and annoyance of the Turk][2] [invasion][2] *the maintenance of his estate and his children and for invasion* [and][2] *defence and enterprise of against the Irishmen* [which in manner of living][2]

11. Item to the intent that justice may be truly and indifferently ministered by the king's only [only the king's] officers and ministers to all the king's subjects that all franchises and liberties [belonging] to any

---

[2] Erased.

[3] These were exactly the stipends which were suggested by the abbot of Pershore in 1536 as adequate for his monks: *LP* XI, 1145.

archbishopric, bishopric, cathedral church, church collegiate, monastery, priory or other house conventual *or cathedral* may be resumed and annexed to the [? Crown] for ever, court barons and leets only excepted. And over this that his highness may have aswell towards the charges of the wars now present and begun for defence of Ireland as [well as] for the making of the haven of Dover and divers piles, fortresses, block-houses and other munitions against Scotland and other confines of the realm necessary for the surety and defence thereof the rates following: First, of every spiritual person that may expend £20 or above, 4s of the pound, to be paid in two years, that is to say every year 2s of the pound. Item, of every spiritual person that may dispend under £20, 2s of the pound, that is to say 12d one year and 12d another.
Item, of every temporal person that may dispend in lands £20 or above, or be worth in movable substance £100 or above, 2s of every pound in two years, that is to say, 12d every year.
Item, of every temporal person that may spend 40s or above and under £20, or be worth in movable substance £5 or above and under £100, 12d in the pound in two years, that is to say, in every year 6d.
Item, that all strangers inhabited and resident in the realm to pay double the rates of the king's temporal subjects.

6. Departing Canons of Bodmin: the Prior's Letter, 1535

FROM a letter from the prior of Bodmin, Cornwall, 25 May 1535, to a Mr Lock, mercer, of Cheapside: BM Cotton MS, Cleop. E IV, fo. 116, printed in Wright, *Letters*, pp. 130–1. Thomas Mundy had been appointed prior against the wishes of the Arundell family of Lanherne. Canon John Bandon had obtained from the archbishop of Canterbury, on 7 May and on payment of £4, a dispensation to leave his order and hold a secular benefice, conditional on his obtaining the prior's consent. On 7 June following he obtained another 'capacity', which cost him 26s 8d, this time without any obligation to obtain the prior's approval. Within a matter of months he was vicar of Broadwoodwidger in Devon, with a stipend of £8 a year from the prior of Frithelstock, who owned the rectory (Chambers, *Faculty Office Registers*, pp. 26–7, 40 and *VE* II, 335).

... Sir, I am sore disquieted with a set of unthrifty canons, my convent, and their bearers [*supporters*], which of long continuance have lived unthriftily and against the order of religion ... for the reformation thereof the bishop at his last visitation gave certain and divers injunctions, ... wherewith they [the canons] be sore grieved and intend the most part of them to depart with capacities without my consent and will. And one of them hath purchased a capacity in the last term without my licence, which is against the words of his capacity, whereof I have restrained his departing, for no great loss that I should have of him but for the ill example to others. For if I should suffer this man to depart in this manner I shall have never a canon to bide with me. I am sore threatened with [by] one Master Roger Arundell, a great bearer and maintainer of my brethren against me, and the procurer of their capacities, to be brought before the king's grace's honourable Council, for that I have not suffered this lewd canon to depart with his capacity according to their intent ...

[The prior goes on to ask Lock to persuade Cromwell to refer the matter to some of the local gentlemen.]

7. The Visitors' Injunctions, 1535

The King's Injunctions for Monasteries and other religious houses: BM, Cotton MS., Cleop. E IV, fos. 21–5, printed, with some errors, in Wilkins' *Concilia* (1727), III. 789–91, following Burnet, *History of the Reformation*, 1715, I. ii. 129–32. These were the injunctions which led to the shower of protests from frustrated heads of religious houses such as that from the Abbot of St Augustine's, Bristol (Doc. 8).

GENERAL INJUNCTIONS TO BE GIVEN ON THE KING'S HIGHNESS'S BEHALF IN ALL MONASTERIES. . . .
First, that the abbot, prior or president and all other brethren of the place that is visited shall faithfully, truly and heartily keep and observe, and cause, teach and procure to be kept and observed of others, as much as in them may lie, all and singular [the] contents as well in the oath of the King's highness's succession, given heretofore by them, as in a certain profession lately sealed with the common seal and signed with their own hands.

[2] Also that they shall observe and fulfil by all the means that they best may the statutes of this realm made or to be made for the extirpation and taking away of the usurped and pretended jurisdiction of the bishop of Rome within this realm. . . .

[3] Also that the abbot, prior or president and brethren may be declared by the king's supreme power and authority ecclesiastical to be absolved and loosed from all manner [of] obedience, oath and profession by them heretofore perchance promised or made to the said bishop of Rome or to any other in his stead or occupying his authority or to any other foreign power or person; . . .

[4] Also that no monk or brother of this monastery by any means go forth of the precincts of the same.

[5] Also that women, of what state or degree soever they be, be utterly excluded from entering into the limits or circuit of this monastery or place unless they first obtain licence of the King's highness or his visitor.

[6] Also that there be no entering into this monastery but one and that by the great fore-gate of the same. . . .

[7] Also that all and singular brethren and monks of this monastery take their refections all together in a place called the 'misericorde' such days as they eat flesh, and all other days in their refectory; and that at every mess there sit four of them, not of duty demanding to them any certain usual or accustomed duty or portion of meat, as they were wont to do, but that they be content with such victual as is set before them, and there take their refections soberly without excess, giving due thanks

to God; and that at every such refection some chapter of the New Testament or Old by some of the said brethren be read and recited to the others, [they] keeping silence and giving audience to the same.

[8] Also that the abbot and president do daily prepare one table for himself and his guests thither resorting, and that not oversumptuous and full of delicate and strange dishes but honestly furnished with common meats, at which table the said abbot or some senior in his stead shall sit to receive and gently entertain the strangers [and] the guests.

[9] Also that none of the brethren send any part of his meat or the leavings thereof to any person but that there be assigned an almoner which shall gather the leavings both of the convent and strangers' tables, after that the servants of the house have had their convenient refections, and distribute the same to poor people, amongst whom special consideration be had of such, before other, as be kinsfolk to any of the said brethren, if they be of like power and debility as other be; and also of those which endeavour themselves with all their will and labour to get their living with their hands and yet cannot fully help themselves for their chargeable household and multitude of children (yet let not them be so cherished that they shall leave labour and fall to idleness); with consideration also specially to be had of them which by weakness of their limbs and body be so impotent that they cannot labour; and by no means let such alms be given to such valiant, mighty and idle beggars and vagabonds as commonly use to resort about such places, which rather as drove beasts and michers should be driven away and compelled to labour than in their idleness and lewdness, against the form of the King's grace's statute in this behalf made,[1] [be] cherished and maintained, to the great hindrance and damage of the commonweal.

[10] Also that all other alms or distributions due or accustomed to be made by reason of the foundation statutes or custom of this place be made and given as largely and as liberally as ever they were at any time heretofore.

[11] Also that the abbot, prior or president shall find wood and fuel sufficient to make fire in the refectory from Allhallows Eve to Good Friday.

[12] Also that all the brethren of this house, except the abbot and such as be sick or evil at ease, and those that have fulfilled their Jubilee, lie together in the dormitory, every one by himself in several beds.

[13] Also that no brother or monk of this house have any child or boy lying or privily accompanying with him, or otherwise haunting unto him, other than to help him to mass.

[14] Also that the brethren of this house, when they be sick or evil at

---

[1] This must be the Act Concerning the punishment of Beggars and Vagabonds, 22 Henry VIII, c. 12 (1531): *Statutes* III, 328.

ease, be seen unto and be kept in the infirmary duly, as well for their sustenance of meat and drink as for their good keeping.

[15]   Also that the abbot or president keep and find in some university one or two of his brethren, according to the ability and possessions of this house, which brethren after they be learned in good and holy letters when they return home may instruct and teach their brethren and diligently preach the word of God.

[16]   Also that every day by the space of one hour a lesson of Holy Scripture be kept in this convent. . . .

[17]   Also that the brethren of this house, after divine service done, read or hear somewhat of Holy Scripture, or occupy themselves in some such like honest and laudable exercise.

[18]   Also that all and every brethren of this house shall observe the rule, statutes, and laudable customs of this religion as far as they do agree with Holy Scriptures and the word of God; and that the abbot, prior or president of this monastery . . . [shall teach them] that their ceremonies and other observances of religion be none other things than as the first letters or principles and certain introductions to true Christianity, or to observe an order in the church, and that true religion is not contained in apparel, manner of going, shaven heads, and such other marks, nor in silence, fasting, uprising in the night, singing and such other kind of ceremonies, but in cleanness of mind, pureness of living, Christ's faith not feigned and brotherly charity. . . .

[19]   Also that the abbot and president of this place shall make a true and full reckoning and account of his administration every year to his brethren, as well of his receipts as [of his] expenses, and that the said account be written in a great book remaining with the convent.

[20]   Also that the abbot and president of this house shall make no waste of the woods pertaining to this house, nor shall set out unadvisedly any farms or reversions, without the consent of the more part of the convent.

[21]   Also that there be assigned a book and a register that [there] may [be] cop[ied] out into that book all such writings, word by word, as shall pass under the convent seal of this house.

[22]   Also that no man be suffered to profess or to wear the habit of religion in this house or [before] he be 24 years of age complete and that they entice nor allure no man with persuasions and blandishments to take religion upon him.

[23]   Also that they shall not show any relics or feigned miracles for increase of lucre but that they exhort pilgrims and strangers to give that to the poor that they thought to offer to their images or relics.[2]

[2] An interesting anticipation of Cromwell's First Injunctions to the Clergy of 1536: Williams, *English Historical Documents*, v, 806.

[24]   Also that they should suffer no fairs or markets to be kept or used within the limits of this house.

[25]   Also that every brother of this house that is a priest shall every day in his mass pray for the most happy and most prosperous estate of our sovereign lord the King and his most noble and lawful wife Queen Ann.

[26]   Also that if either the master or any brother of this house do infringe any of the said injunctions any of them shall denounce the same or procure to be denounced as soon as may be to the King's Majesty or to his visitor-general or his deputy; and the abbot or master shall minister spending money and other necessaries for the way to him that shall so denounce.

[27]   Other spiritual injunctions may be added by the visitor as the place and nature of the comperts [findings] shall require, after his discretion, reserving power to give more injunctions and to examine and discuss the comperts, to punish and reform them that be convict of any notable crime, to search and try the foundations, charters, donations, appropriations and muniments of the said places and to dispose all such papistical escripts as shall be there found to the right honourable Mr Thomas Cromwell, general visitor to the King's said highness, as shall seem most expedient to his high wisdom and discretion.

8. Representations from the Monks of St Augustine's, Bristol

A letter from the abbot of St Augustine's, Bristol, to Thomas Cromwell in the early Autumn of 1535: PRO, SP 1, 96, pp. 32–3.

Right honourable Mr Secretary, Principal Visitor under the King's most royal majesty, supreme head of the church of England next under God in earth. So it is that the reverend and discreet man Master Doctor Layton by his great authority lately visited us at the King's monastery of St Austins where he left at his gentle departing with me and my brethren certain injunctions somewhat hard and strait to be observed and kept. Wherefore I most heartily desire your good mastership to grant to me and to my officer chamberlain licence and liberty to go and to ride to see good order, custom, and manner to be kept within the lordships of the said monastery at times convenient for the profits of of the same. Secondly I heartily pray you to give to me licence and liberty to walk to my manor places nigh to Bristol for the comfortable health of my body and for the saving of expenses. Thirdly I beseech you that I may walk within the circuit of the monastery, that is to say within the Green and Canons Marsh next adjacent to the precincts of the said monastery. Furthermore both I and my brethren instantly prayeth, desireth, and beseecheth your good mastership to grant to me power to give them licence some times to walk, three or four together, the juniors with the seniors (refraining the town) about the hills and fields to recreate their minds and to lax their veins, whereby they may be more apt to continue both night and day in the service of God. Yet we most heartily desire you to suffer us to have some poor honest woman to keep us if any pestifer[ous] plague or distress of sickness do fall amongst us, as it hath been there of long consuetude. . . .

9. The Uses of Founders: Bridlington Priory, 1535

A letter from William Wood, prior of Bridlington, Yorkshire, to Thomas Cromwell, 23 October 1535: BM, Cotton MS, Cleop. E IV, fo. 53, printed in Wright's *Letters*, pp. 80–1. Cromwell's letter to the prior has not survived but the tenor of the vicar-general's requirements is very clear from the prior's reply. No further pressure appears to have been exerted but in fact the priory and its estates came to the Crown in 1537 following the attainder of prior Wood for being implicated in the Pilgrimage of Grace.

Right Worshipful, my duty in my most humble manner remembered, I recommend me to your good mastership, and for so much as your said mastership by your last letters to me directed advised me, and in like manner counselled me to recognise the King's Highness to be our patron and founder, forasmuch as no article, word, sentence or clause in our original grant to us made by Sir Gilbert de Gaunt . . . appeared to the contrary why of equity his Highness ought not so to be, or else to appear before your mastership and other of his Grace's Council the last day of October as I would avoid his Grace's high displeasure. In this matter, even so humble as I can, I shall beseech your good mastership to be good master to me and your poor and daily orators my brethren, for, notwithstanding the King's Grace's noble progenitors' titles and claims heretofore made to our said patronage and foundership (though all we are and ever will be at his most gracious commandment and pleasure) yet we have ever been dismissed clear without any interruption in this behalf nigh this two hundred years . . . And whereas I am detained with divers infirmities in my body . . . I shall humbly beseech your goodness to have me excused and . . . to accept this bearer my brother as my lawful deputy . . . of whom also you shall receive a poor token from me. . . .

10. Parliamentary Half-measures: The Act of 1536

An act (27 Henry VIII, c. 28) whereby all Religious Houses of Monks, Canons, and Nuns which may not dispend Manors, Lands, Tenements and Hereditaments above the clear yearly value of £200 are given to the King's Highness, his heirs and successors for ever: *Statutes* III. 575–8.

I   Forasmuch as manifest sin, vicious, carnal, and abominable living is daily used and committed among the little and small abbeys, priories, and other religious houses of monks, canons, and nuns, where the congregation of such religious persons is under the number of twelve persons, whereby the governors of such religious houses and their convent spoil, destroy, consume, and utterly waste, as well their churches, monasteries, priories, principal houses, farms, granges, lands, tenements, and hereditaments, as [also] the ornaments of their churches and their goods and chattells, to the high displeasure of Almighty God, slander of good religion, and to the great infamy of the king's highness and the realm if redress should not be had thereof, and albeit that many continual visitations hath been heretofore had, by the space of two hundred years and more, for an honest and charitable reformation of such unthrifty, carnal, and abominable living, yet nevertheless little or none amendment is hitherto had, but their vicious living shamelessly increases and augments . . . so that without [*unless*] such small houses be utterly suppressed and the religious persons therein committed to great and honourable monasteries of religion in this realm, where they may be compelled to live religiously, for reformation of their lives, there can else be no reformation in this behalf:

In consideration whereof the king's most royal majesty, being supreme head on earth under God of the Church of England, daily finding and devising the increase, advancement, and exaltation of true doctrine and virtue in the said Church, to the only glory and honour of God and the total extirping and destruction of vice and sin, having knowledge that the premises be true, as well by the accounts of his late visitations as by sundry credible information, considering also that divers and great solemn monasteries of this realm wherein (thanks be to God) religion is right well kept and observed, be destitute of such full numbers of religious persons as they ought and may keep, has thought good that a plain declaration should be made of the premises, as well to the Lords spiritual and temporal as to other his loving subjects the Commons in this present Parliament assembled.

Whereupon the said Lords and Commons, by a great deliberation, finally be resolved that it is and shall be much more to the pleasure of Almighty God and for the honour of this his realm that the possessions of such small [printed text has 'spiritual'] religious houses, now being spent, spoiled, and wasted for increase and maintenance of sin, should be used and converted to better uses and the unthrifty religious persons so spending the same to be compelled to reform their lives: and thereupon [they] most humbly desire the king's highness that it may be enacted by authority of this present Parliament that his majesty shall have and enjoy to him and to his heirs for ever all and singular such monasteries, [etc.] . . . which have not in lands, tenements, rents, tithes, portions, and other hereditaments, above the clear yearly value of two hundred pounds. And in like manner [his majesty] shall have and enjoy all the sites and circuits of every such religious houses and all and singular the manors, granges, meases [*demesnes*], lands, tenements, rents, reversions, services, tithes, pensions, portions, churches, chapels, advowsons, patronages, annuities, rights, entries, conditions, and other hereditaments appertaining or belonging to every such monastery, priory, or other religious house . . . in as large and ample manner as the abbots [etc.] now have, or ought to have, the same in the right of their houses. And also his highness shall have to him and to his heirs all and singular such monasteries, [etc.], which at any time within one year next before the making of this Act have been given and granted to his majesty by any abbot, [etc.], under their convent seals, or that otherwise have been suppressed or dissolved, and all and singular the manors, [etc.], to the same monasteries, [etc.], appertaining or belonging; to have and to hold all and singular the premises, with all their rights, profits, jurisdictions, and commodities, unto the King's majesty and to his heirs and assigns for ever, to do and use therewith his and their own wills, to the pleasure of Almighty God and to the honour and profit of this realm.

II And it is ordained and enacted by authority aforesaid that all and every person and persons and bodies politic which now have, or hereafter shall have, any letters patent of the king's highness, of any of the sites, circuits, manors, [etc.], which appertained to any monasteries, [etc.] heretofore given or granted to the king's highness or otherwise suppressed or dissolved, or which appertain to any of the monasteries, [etc.] that shall be suppressed or dissolved by authority of this Act, shall have and enjoy the said sites, [etc.] contained and specified in their letters patent now being thereof made, and to be contained and expressed in any letters patent hereafter to be made, according to the tenors, purports, and effects of any such letters patent, and shall also have all such actions, suits, entries, and remedies . . . in like manner, form, and condition as the abbots, [etc.] which had the same might, or ought to have had, if they had not been suppressed or dissolved.

III Saving to every person and persons and bodies politic, their heirs and successors (other than the abbots, [etc.] and the convents of the same and their successors, and such as pretend to be founders, patrons, or donors of such religious houses or of any lands, [etc.] belonging to the same and their heirs and successors) all such right, title, interest, possession, leases for years, rents, services, annuities, commons, fees, offices, liveries and livings, pensions, portions, corrodies, synodies, proxies, and all other profits, as they or any of them ought or might have had in or to any of the said monasteries, [etc.] or in or to any manors, [etc.] appertaining or belonging, or that appertained to any of the said monasteries, [etc.] as if the same monasteries, [etc.] had not been suppressed by this Act but had continued in their essential bodies and states that they now be or were in.

IV Provided always, and be it enacted, that forasmuch as divers of the chief governors of such religious houses, determining the utter spoil and destruction of their houses, and dreading the suppressing thereof, for the maintenance of their detestable lives, have lately fraudulently and craftily made feoffments, estates, gifts, grants, and leases, under their convent seals, or suffered recoveries, of their manors, [etc.] in fee simple, fee tail, for term of life or lives, or for years, or charged the same with rents or corrodies, to the great decay and diminution of their houses, all such crafty and fraudulent recoveries, [etc.] made by any of the said chief governors of such religious houses under their convent seals within one year next before the making of this Act, shall be utterly void and of none effect; provided always that such persons as have leases for term of life or years whereupon is reserved the old rents and services accustomed, and such as have any office, fees, and corrodies that have been accustomed or used in such religious houses, or have bought any livery or living in any such houses, shall have and enjoy their said leases, [etc.] as if this Act had never been made.

V And it is also enacted by authority aforesaid that the king's highness shall have and enjoy to his own proper use all the ornaments, jewels, goods, chattels, and debts which appertained to any of the chief governors of the said monasteries, [etc.] in the right of their said monasteries, [etc.] at the first day of March in the year of our Lord God 1535 [*1 March 1536*], or any time since, wheresoever and to whose possession soever they shall come or be found, except only such beasts, grain and woods, and such other like chattels and revenues as have been sold in the said first day of March or since for the necessary or reasonable expenses or charges of any of the said monasteries or houses.

VI [Discharge of payment of first fruits.]

VII   [Clear yearly value to be as recently certified to the Exchequer, without need of further inquisition.]

VIII   In consideration of which premises to be had to his highness and to his heirs as is aforesaid, his majesty is pleased and contented, of his most excellent charity, to provide to every chief head and governor of every such religious house, during their lives, such yearly pensions and benefices as for their degrees and qualities shall be reasonable and convenient; wherein his highness will have most tender respect to such of the said chief governors as well and truly conserve and keep the goods and ornaments of their houses to the use of his majesty, without spoil, waste, or embezzling the same; and also his majesty will ordain and provide that the convents of every such religious house shall have their capacities, if they will, to live honestly and virtuously abroad [outside], and some convenient charity disposed to them towards their living, or else shall be committed to such honourable great monasteries of this realm wherein good religion is observed, as shall be limited [determined] by his highness, there to live religiously during their lives.

IX   And it is ordained by authority aforesaid that the chief governors and convents of such honourable great monasteries shall take and accept into their houses, from time to time, such number of the persons of the said convents as shall be assigned and appointed by the king's highness, and keep them religiously during their lives within their said monasteries in like manner and form as the convents of such great monasteries be ordered and kept.

X   [Discharge of all archbishops, bishops, and other persons chargeable with the collection of the tenths, of sums still owing from the monasteries to be suppressed by this Act.]

XI   [Discharge of arrears of the hundred thousand pounds granted to the king by the clergy of the province of Canterbury, in so far as this concerns religious houses suppressed by this act.]

XII   And also the king's majesty is pleased and contented that it be enacted by authority aforesaid that his highness shall satisfy, content, and pay all and singular such just and true debts which are owing to any persons by the chief governors of any of the said religious houses, in as large and ample manner as the said chief governors should or ought to have done if this Act had never been made.

XIII   Provided always that the king's highness at any time after the making of this Act may at his pleasure ordain and declare by his letters patent under his great seal that such of the said religious houses which his highness shall not be disposed to have suppressed nor dissolved by authority of this Act shall still continue, remain, and be in the same body corporate and in the [same] essential estate, quality, and condition, as well in possession or otherwise, as they were before the making of this Act, without any suppression or dissolution thereof. . . .

XIV [Discharge of arrears owing by the clergy of the province of York similar to that for Canterbury.]

XV [The Act not to apply to cells of the greater monasteries.]

XVI Saving always and reserving unto every person and persons being founders, patrons, or donors of any abbeys, [etc.] that shall be suppressed by this Act, their heirs and successors, all such right, title, interest, possession, rents, annuities, fees, offices, leases, commons, and all other profits whatsoever which any of them have or should have had, without fraud or covin, by any manner of means otherwise than by reason or occasion of the dissolution of the said abbeys, [etc.]. . . .

XVII And further be it enacted . . . that all and singular persons, bodies politic and corporate, to whom the king's majesty, his heirs, or successors, hereafter shall give, grant, let, or demise any site, or precinct with the houses thereupon builded, together with the demesnes of any monasteries, [etc.] and the heirs, successors, executors, and assigns of every such person, [etc.] shall be bounded by authority of this act, under the penalties hereafter ensuing, to keep or cause to be kept an honest, continual house and household in the same site or precinct, and to occupy yearly as much of the same demesnes in ploughing and tillage of husbandry . . . which hath been commonly used to be kept in tillage by the governors, abbots, or priors of the same houses, monasteries, or priories, or by their farmer or farmers occupying the same, within the time of 20 years next before this act. And if any person . . . then he or they so offending shall forfeit to the king's highness for every month so offending £6 13s 4d, to be recovered to his use in any of his courts of record.

XVIII [Justices of the Peace to inquire into and deal with offences against this act.][1]

[1] In the original engrossment of the act (House of Lords Record Office) sections XVII and XVIII are on a separate sheet, headed by the King's sign manual. For a suggestion that this indicates additions by the Commons see Lehmberg, *Reformation Parliament*, p. 228, but see also Doc. 14, p. 169 and *supra*, p. 46.

11. The Commissioners' Instructions, 1536

Instructions for the Commissioners appointed in 1536 to survey the smaller, i.e. the less wealthy, monasteries in the bishopric of Llandaff: PRO, Suppression Papers (SP 5), 4/fos. 186–9. In Wales the ecclesiastical administrative unit was used in place of the English county. Similar sets of instructions, with minor verbal variations, for a number of bodies of commissioners have survived: cf. *LP* x, 721.

INSTRUCTIONS for the King's Commissioners for a new Survey and an Inventory to be made of all the Demesnes, Lands, Goods, and Chattels appertaining to any house of religious monks, canons and nuns within their Commission, according to the Articles hereafter following, the number of the which houses in every county limited in their commission being annexed to the said commission.[1]

HENRY R[2]

First, after the division made, one Auditor, one particular Receiver, one Clerk of the Register of the last visitation,[3] with three other discreet persons to be named by the King in every county where any such houses be, after their repair to such house shall declare to the Governor and [the] Religious Persons of the same the Statute of Dissolution, their Commission and the cause and purpose of their repair for that time.

Item, that after the declaration made the said Commissioners shall swear the Governors of the Houses or such other of the officers of the same houses or others, as they shall think can best declare the state and plight [*condition*] of the same, to make declaration and answer to the articles hereunder written.

Item, of what Order, Rule or Religion the same house is and whether it be a cell or not. And if it be a cell then the commissioners to deliver to the governor of the house a Privy Seal and also injoin him in the King's name under a great pain [*penalty*] to appear without delay before the Chancellor of the Augmentations of the Revenues of the King's Crown and the Council of the same, and in the meantime not to meddle with the same cell till the King's pleasure be further known.

Item, what number of persons in religion be in the same and the conversation of their lives [*their conduct*], and how many of them be priests,

---

[1] For the text of the Yorkshire commission see Williams, *Eng. Hist. Docs.* v, p. 770.

[2] The King's sign manual.

[3] One of the clerks attached to the *Valor* commission of 1535.

and how many of them will go to other houses of that religion, or how many will take capacities, and how many servants or hinds the same house keepeth commonly, and what other persons have their living in the same house.

Item, to survey the quantity or value of the Lead and Bells of the same house, as near as they can, with the ruin, decay, state and plight of the same.

Item, incontinently [*without delay*] to call for the Convent Seal with all Writings, Charters, Evidences and Muniments concerning any of the possessions to be delivered to them and put them in sure keeping, and to make a just Inventory betwixt them and the Governor or other head officer, by indenture, of the Ornaments, Plate, Jewels, Chattels, ready money, stuff of household, Corn, as well severed as not severed, stock and store in the farmers' hands and the value thereof, as near as they can, which were appertaining to the same houses the first day of March last, and what debts the house doth owe and to what person, and what debts be owing to them and by whom.

Item, after to cause the convent or common Seal, the Plate, Jewels and ready Money to be put in safe keeping and the residue of the particulars specified in the Inventory to be left in the keeping of the governor or some other head officer without wasting or consumption of the same unless it be for necessary expenses of the house.

Item, that they command the Governor or other receiver of the same house to receive no rents of their farmers until they know further of the King's pleasure, except such rents as must needs be had for their necessary finding or sustenance or for payment of their servants' wages.

Item, to survey discreetly the Demesnes of the same house, that is to say such as be not commonly used to be letten out, and to certify the clear yearly value thereof.

Item, to examine the true clear yearly value of all the farms of the same house, deducting thereof rents resolute [*paid*], pensions and portions paid out of the same, synodals and proxies, bailiffs', receivers', stewards' and auditors' fees and the names of them to whom they be due and to none other.

Item, what Leases have been made to any farmer, of the farms pertaining to the same house, and what rent is reserved, and to whom and for how many years, and a copy of the indenture if they can get it, or else the counterpane.

Item, to search and enquire what Woods, Parks, Forests, Commons or other profit belonging to any of the possessions of the same house, the number of acres, the age and value, as near as they can.

Item, what Grants, Bargains, Sales, Gifts, Alienations, Leases of any lands, tenements, woods or offices hath been made by any of the said governors of any of the said houses within one year next before the 4th day of February last past.[4] and of what things or to what value and to whom and for what estate.

Item, if there be any house of any of the religious aforesaid dissolved or omitted and not certified in the Exchequer then the said commissioners to survey the same and to make certificates accordingly.

Item, that they straitly command every governor of every such house limited [included] in their commission to sow and till their ground as they have done before till the King's pleasure be further known.

Item, every of the said commissioners . . . immediately after they have perused one shire, parcel of their charge, in form aforesaid, shall send to the Chancellor of the Court of the Augmentation of the Revenues of the King's Crown a brief certificate of their comperts [findings] according to the instructions aforesaid, what they have done in the premises, and in every county so surveyed, then to proceed further to another county, and as they pass the said counties to make the like certificate, and so forth till their limits be surveyed, and there to remain till they know further of the King's pleasure. . . .

Item,[5] if there be any house given by the King to any person in any of the said several limits of the said commission, the names whereof shall be declared to the said commissioners, then the said commissioners immediately shall take the convent seal from the governor and take an inventory indented of the lead, bells, debts, chattels, plate, jewels, ornaments, stock and store, to the King's use, and to make sale of the goods, chattels, and other implements, plate and jewels only excepted.

Item, the said commissioners in every such house to send such of the Religious Persons that will remain in the same religion to some other great house of that religion by their discretion, with a letter to a governor for the receipt of them, and the residue of them that will go for their Capacities, with the letter of the same commissioners.

Item, the said commissioners to give the said persons that will have capacities some reasonable rewards, according to the distance of the place, by their discretions to be appointed.

Item, the said commissioners to command the Governor to resort to the Chancellor of the Augmentations for his yearly stipend and pension.

Item, if there be any house dissolved or given up to the King by their Deed then the commissioners shall order themselves in every point and purpose as of the houses given by the King to any other person, in form aforesaid.

---

[4] The first day of the last session of the late Parliament.

[5] This item, and all those which follow, except the last, relates to houses which are to be dissolved forthwith.

Item, if it appear to the said commissioners that any of the said houses within the survey be of the order of Gilbertines that then they shall no further proceed but enjoin the governors of the same houses that they with all celerity do appear before the Chancellor and Council of the court of Augmentations at Westminster where they shall know further of the king's pleasure.

12. Popular Reactions at Exeter

Very little is on record about the reception accorded to the commissioners by laymen, but the following account of what happened at Exeter was set down from memory some years later by John Hooker, the Elizabethan City Chamberlain: Exeter Record Office, Book 51 (Hooker's *Annals*), fo. 343, printed in G. Oliver, *Monasticon Dioecesis Exoniensis* (1861), p. 116.

. . . who [the commissioners] came to this city in the summertime to execute their commission, and beginning first with the priory of St Nicholas, after that they [had] viewed the same they went thence to dinner and commanded [a man] in the time of their absence to pull down the rood loft in the church. In the meanwhile, and before they did return, certain women and wives in the city, namely Joan Reeve, Elizabeth Glandfield, Agnes Collaton, Alice Miller, Joan Reed and others, minding to stop the suppressing of that house, came in all haste to the said church, some with spikes, some with shovels, some with pikes, and some with such tools as they could get and, the church door being fast, they broke it open. And finding there the man pulling down the rood loft they all sought, [by] all the means they could, to take him and hurled stones unto him, in so much that for his safety he was driven to take to the tower for his refuge. And yet they pursued him so eagerly that he was enforced to leap out at a window and so to save himself, and very hardly he escaped the breaking of his neck, but yet he brake one of his ribs. John Blakealler, one of the aldermen of the city, being advertised thereof, he with all speed got him to the said monastery, he thinking what with fair words and what with foul words to have stayed and pacified the women. But how so ever he talked with them they were plain with him and the aforesaid Elizabeth Glandfield gave him a blow and set him packing. The Mayor [William Hurst], having understanding hereof and being very loathe the visitors should be advertised of any such disorders and troubles,[1] he came down with his officers, before whose coming they [the women] had made fast the church doors and had bestowed themselves in places meet as they thought to stand to their defences. Notwithstanding, the Mayor broke in upon them and with much ado he apprehended and took them all and sent them to ward. The visitors being then made acquainted herewith, they gave thanks to the Mayor for his care and diligence . . . and so they proceeded to the

---

[1] The city was on the point of obtaining a new royal charter conferring upon it the status of a separate county.

suppressing of the house, and before their departure they intreated the Mayor for releasing of the women.[2]

[2] When inquiries were made into the incident on the King's behalf a few months later it was reported that the troublemakers were in fact women and not men in disguise and that they claimed that 'their only intent was to let [hinder] two Breton carvers [?carpenters] which made their avaunt [boasted] that they would pull down the crucifix of the said church of St Nicholas, with all the saints there, naming them to be idols': PRO, State Papers Domestic (SP 1), 102, fo. 33.

13. Brief Certificate for the County of Sussex, 1536

The returns of the king's commissioners for the county of Sussex, 1536: PRO, Suppression Papers (SP 5), 3/128, calendared in *LP*, XI p. 591. This tabulated summary of the commissioners' findings relates to the smaller houses surveyed in 1536 following the act of that year (Doc. 10).

COUNTY OF SUSSEX: The brief certificate of the Commissioners appointed for the survey of the monasteries and priories within the county of Sussex as hereafter shall appear:-

The priory of Tortington: Black Canons of the order of St Augustine [a]¹ The clear yearly value at the first survey, £75 12s 3½d [b] The clear yearly value of the same house at this new survey, £82 9s 4½d with [c] £6 17s of increase, viz the demesnes [d] 40s
[e] Religious persons, 6; whereof [f] priests, 5, [g] novices, 1, [h] Incontinent, 1, [j] desiring capacities, 4, and the others desire to go to other houses.
[k] Servants, 12; whereof [m] waiting servants, 2; [n] hinds, 8; [p] women servants, 2; and a prior quondam having a pension by resignation of £10
[q] Bells, lead (nil) and other buildings to be sold, by estimation £20 The house wholly in ruin.
[r] The entire value of the movable goods, £39 5s 2d; [s] in store with farmers, nil; [t] debts owing to the said house £13 3s 6½d
[u] Woods there, 60 ac., all above 20 years' age, at 13s 4d the acre, £40
[v] Common, 80 acres. [w] Parks, none.
[y] Debts owing . . . [by the monastery], £12 16s 8d

The priory of Boxgrove: Black monks of the order of St Benedict
[a] £145 10s 2½d; [b] £148 14s, with [c] 63s 9½d and [d] 8s 2d
[e] 9; [f] 8; [g] 1; [h] none; [j] 8
[k] 28; [m] 10; [n] 8; [p] 2 and children, 8
[q] £13 6s 8d [No lead] The house in good estate
[r] £83 15s; [s] nil; [t] nil
[u] 60 acres, all above 20 years' age, at 10s the acre, £30; [v] 60 acres [w] none
[y] Debts owing by the same house as appeareth particularly by a book thereof made remaining with the commissioners, £42 10s 6¼d

¹ Each letter in square brackets indicates a column in the original return.

The new priory of Hastings: Black monks of the order of St Augustine
[a] £51 9s 5½d; [b] £47 2s 1½d And so decayed for certain lands in Peasmarsh now surrounded by the sea, £4 7s 4d. The demesnes increased 4s 8d
[e] 4; [f] 3; [g] 1; [h] 4; [j] 4
[k] 6; [m] 4; [p] 2
[q] £20 [No lead] The house wholly in ruin
[r] £16 14s 7d; [s] nil; [t] nil
[u] 100 acres, all above 20 years' age, at 3s 4d the acre, £16 13s 4d; [v] nil; [w] nil;
[y] £12 13s 4d

The priory of Michelham: Black canons of the order of St Augustine
[a] £160 12s 6d; [b] £163 14s 6d with [c] 62s and [d] nil
[e] 9; [f] 8; [g] 1; [h] none; [j] all
[k] 29; [m] 18; [n] 11;
[q] £30 The house in good estate
[r] £55 14s 4d; [s] nil; [t] £9 15s 2d
[u] 80 acres, all above 20 years' age, at 13s 4d the acre, £53 6s 8d; [v] for 40 beasts [w] none
[y] £26 9s 1d

The priory of Shulbred: Black canons
[a] £72 14s 10½d; [b] £75 17s 6½d with [c] 62s 8d and [d] 46s 8d
[e] 5; [f] all; [g] nil; [h] none; [j] 4
[k] 13; [m] 5; [n] 6; [p] 2 and prior quondam having a pension by resignation of £12
[q] 53s 4d [No lead] The house in good estate
[r] 30s; [s] nil; [t] nil
[u] 100 acres [w] nil
[y document decayed]

The abbey of Durford: Canons of the order of Prémontré
[a] £98 4s 5d; [b] £98 17s 9d with [c] 13s 4d and [d] nil
[e] 9; [f] 8; [g] 1; [h] nil; [j] all
[k] 24; [m] 8; [n] 12; [p] 4
[q] £20 The house in competent estate
[r] £63 16s [s] nil [t] nil

[The rest of the document lists houses with which, for various reasons, the commissioners were not concerned.]

14. Thomas Starkey and the Redisposition of Monastic Wealth

From Thomas Starkey's letter to Henry VIII, *c.* June 1536, printed in *Starkey's Life and Letters*, ed. S. J. Herrtage, Early English Text Society, extra series, XXXII (1878), pp. liii–lviii. After expressing his hope that the passage of the recent act will enrich the king's subjects Starkey presents arguments defending a limited diversion of monastic resources, even if this appears to run counter to the founders' wishes. He concludes with a plea that the sites and buildings of the dissolved monasteries will not be depopulated and turned into sheep-runs.

. . . Wherefore, considering that this worldly treasure is no such thing wherein any noble heart can take his delight and pleasure, sure hope I have that your grace, whom I know so deeply can weigh the nature of things, will most liberally dispense this treasure and dispose these riches to the aid, succour, and comfort of your most loving and obedient poor subjects . . . I trust to see now many a noble gentleman relieved by these acts and, exercising themselves in all feats of arms, made apt and meet to the defence of their country. I trust now to see many a noble wit encouraged to learning by your grace's liberality and made apt to celebrate your fame and glory, commending your princely virtues to eternal memory. I trust now to see many notable preachers spring forth to light and declare to your people the truth of Christ's doctrine sincerely. And finally I trust now to see all such superfluous riches, which among them that bare the name of spiritual nourished nothing but idleness and vice, to be converted and turned by your gracious goodness to the increase of all virtue and honesty. . . .

. . . many there be which are moved to judge this act of suppression of certain abbeys both to be against the order of charity, and injurious to them which be dead because the founders thereof and the souls departed seem thereby to be defrauded of the benefit of prayer and alms deed there appointed to be done for their relief by their last will and testament . . . [but in the writer's view] the will and deed of every private man for a common weal may be altered by the supreme authority in every country . . . it is always by reason thought that if he were present he would give his consent to all such things as be judged by common authority to be expedient to the public weal, to the which no private weal may be lawfully repugnant. . . .

And yet many men further, as it appeareth to them not without reason, have required in this matter much rather a just reformation than this utter ruinous suppression. How be it those men, as I think, have not in diligent consideration such things as in this act are principally to be pondered and weighed. For though it be so that prayer and alms deed be much to the comfort of them which be departed, and though God delights much in our charitable minds thereby declared, yet to convert over much possessions to that end and purpose, and to appoint over many persons to such office and exercise, cannot be without great detriment and hurt to the Christian common weal, good order, and true policy . . . and though it be a good thing and much religious to pray for them which be departed out of this misery, yet we may not give all our possessions to nourish idle men in continual prayer for them, leaving others destitute of help which be in life, for to the one we are bounden by express commandment, whereas the other cometh but of mere devotion. . . .

But here is a thing which many wise men fear and greatly distrust, and what it is I shall to your highness briefly declare. It is openly judged and commonly thought that the farm and occupation of these abbeys and monasteries shall be leased and set unto great lords and gentlemen of much possessions, and to them which have thereof no great need at all, the which doubtless, if it be so, shall much deface and greatly diminish the profit of your act and public utility, for then shall the great commodity thereof run but to few and . . . your people thereby shall be little then increased. Whereas if the farms thereof were leased, by copyhold and of a mean rent, to younger brethren living in service unprofitably and to them which be of lower state and degree, they should greatly help to set forward Christian civility and much increase the number of your people, especially if the farm of the whole monasteries and demesnes of the same were divided into sundry portions and divers holdings and not leased to one [man] to turn it into a grange. And this thing should not be utterly without reason and good consideration, for pity it were that so much fair housing and goodly building, which might with commodity be maintained to the comfort of man, should be let fall to ruin and decay, whereby our country might appear so to be defaced as [if] it had been lately overrun with enemies in time of war, the which must needs ensue if the whole monastery be leased but to one to whom it shall not be necessary to maintain so much housing, but a sheep-cote peradventure shall be to him sufficient. . . .

15. The King's Instructions Regarding the Monks of Whalley, 1537

The draft of a letter from the King to the earls of Sussex and Derby, and others, 17 March 1537: printed in *State Papers of Henry VIII*, ii (1830), pp. 540–1. This was no doubt in reply to letters received from Sussex, who was acting as the King's lieutenant in Lancashire, and others, on 11 March (*LP* XII, i, 630).

. . . And whereas upon the execution of the abbot of Whalley [*on 10 March*] you have taken order for the direction of the house and the safe keeping of the goods, without embezzlement, till further knowledge of our pleasure, approving much your good foresight thereof we have thought convenient to signify unto you that for as much as it appears that the house of Whalley has been sore corrupt, among others, that it should seem there remain very few therein that were meet to remain and continue in such an incorporation, we think it shall be meet that some order be taken for the removal of the monks now being in the same and that we should take the whole house into our hands, as by our laws we be justly, by the attainder of the said abbot, entitled unto it, and so devise for such a new establishment thereof as shall be thought meet for the honour of God, our surety, and the benefit of the country. Wherefore our pleasure is that you shall, with good dexterity, lay unto the charges of all the monks there their grievous offences towards us and our commonwealth, and therewith assay their minds, whether they will conform themselves gladly for the redubbing [*amending*] of their former trespasses to go to other houses of their coat, where they shall be well treated, or else whether they will rather take capacities and so receive secular habit. Albeit we require you so to move them to enter into other houses that they may choose the same, for we think it cannot be wholesome for our commonwealth to permit them to wander abroad, and therefore we require you to frame them to that point that they may enter into other places as is aforesaid, wherein you shall do unto us good service. . . .

16. The Priors' Fee'd Men

(a) The text of the grant of an annuity to William Blake, yeoman, made by the prior of Newstead, Nottinghamshire, in May 1537: PRO, Exchequer, Augmentation Office, Misc. Brooks (E 315), 93/fo. 54v. Newstead was an Augustinian priory with an annual net income, according to the 1535 survey, of £167. It was dissolved in July 1539, but it was not until over two years later, on 23 November 1541, that Blake himself appeared before the officers of the court of Augmentations and had his grant formally approved and enrolled.

Be it known unto all men by these presents that we, John, the prior of the monastery of Newstead in Sherwood, and the convent of the same place, for the good and faithful service that William Blake of Eastwick within the county of Nottingham, yeoman, hath heretofore done unto us, have given to the said William Blake one annuity or yearly fee of forty shillings by year, yearly to be paid to the said William Blake or his assigns forth of our lordship of Rowthorn within the county of Derby . . . during the life natural of the said William Blake . . . of the which said annuity or yearly fee of 40s the said prior and convent have put the said William Blake in full and peaceable possession by paying to him at this present day 4d of lawful money of England in the name of possession . . . [clause of distress]. In witness whereof we the said prior and convent to this our present writing have set to our common seal, dated in our chapter house at Newstead aforesaid the 10th day of May . . . [1537]

(b) An indenture of March 1538 whereby Ulverscroft Priory, Leicestershire, another and even less well endowed house of Augustinian canons, granted to one Richard Standish, gentleman, the office of bailiff and surveyor of its lands: PRO, E 315, 94/fo. 95. No such office was mentioned in the *Valor* of 1535: *VE* IV. 175. This house too was dissolved in 1539 and in November 1541 Richard Standish's claim to his fee was approved by the court of Augmentations, to be paid, with arrears, by its local finance officers.

Be it known to all Christian people by these presents that we, Edward Dalby, prior of the priory of Our Lady of Ulverscroft in the county of Leicester, and the convent of the same place, of one whole assent and consent hath named . . . Richard Standish, gentleman, our chief bailiff and surveyor of and upon all manner [of] lands, [etc.] during the time of his natural life, to gather, receive, and levy all manner farms, rents, [etc.] within any of our manors, [etc.] that is to say, in Syston, Swithland, Dusty Markfield, Stanton, Shenton, Bunny, and Stanford, and in all parcels in any other place wheresoever they be belonging to the said house of Ulverscroft, at such days as it is and hath been accustomed heretofore, and more plainly doth appear in the rent rolls of the said prior and convent, and duly and truly to pay and deliver yearly at two times in the year, that is to say at the feast of Easter and St Michael the Archangel, unto the hands of the said prior and convent and their successors or lawful deputies within the limits above expressed in that behalf all such farms, rents, [etc.] as he shall gather, receive, and levy, and thereof to make a just and faithful account once in the year and yearly to the said prior and convent and their successors or their auditor in that behalf, and moreover the said Richard shall oversee and survey all the said tenements and lands to the best and most profit of the said prior and convent and their successors. In consideration of all and singular the premises well and truly to be performed, done, and kept by the said Richard or his able and lawful deputy during the term aforesaid, the abovesaid priory and convent hath given and granted and by these presents giveth and granteth to the said Richard Standish a yearly rent or annuity of three pounds sterling, to be paid to the said Richard yearly at the feasts of Easter and St Michael the Archangel . . . [clause of distress]. In witness whereof we the said prior and convent to these patents hath set to our common seal, given in our chapter house the tenth day of March . . . [1538].

17. Pressures and Responses, 1538-9

(a) A letter from Richard Whittington, cellarer of Bordesley Abbey in Worcestershire, to Mr Thomas Evans, 8 May 1538: PRO, State Papers Domestic (SP 1), 132, p. 67, calendared in *LP* XIII i, 957. In fact Abbot John Day remained in office to surrender the house himself, together with nineteen monks, on 17 July 1538 (*LP*, XIII i, 1401).

Right worshipful my singular good master . . . thanking you of your good advertisement and counsel when I did speak with you last, and this my writing is to advertise you that our father and master is purposed to resign or, as we hear say, hath resigned his office of abbé, for that he is aged, impotent, sick, and also not of perfect remembrance, as you know right well. In consideration whereof I pray you and also desire you to stand good master unto me in the preferment to the same, and that you please to write your favourable letters in my favour unto the right honourable and my singular good lord the Lord Cromwell, lord privy seal. And I promise unto you by these presents that I will accomplish, fulfil, and obey such order as you did advise me unto at our last conversation, that is to say to surrender and yield up the same monastery of Bordesley with appertenances unto the king's hands at such days and time as my said honourable Lord Cromwell the lord privy seal shall require and command me, after that I am once in possession and able to do the same, and trusting only in my said lord's goodness for a reasonable means of living, according as you promised me in his good lordship's behalf. This fare you heartily well, from Bordesley this present 8th day of May anno domini 1538.

By your own to his little power Richard Whittington, cellarer there.

(b) A letter to Cromwell from John Massey, abbot of Combermere in Cheshire, 10 May 1538: PRO, SP 1, 132, p. 86, calendared in *LP* XIII i, 969. The formal deed of surrender of this Cistercian house, signed by the abbot, the prior, and eleven monks, was dated 27 July 1538 (*LP* XIII i, 1476). Massey appears to have made the journey to London, setting off towards the end of May with a letter of commendation from Rowland Lee, bishop of Coventry and Lichfield, who as President of the Council in the Marches of Wales, had enjoyed the abbot's hospitality (*ibid.*, 1087).

Right honourable and my singular good lord, I meekly have me commended unto your good lordship. And where of late it pleased your lordship to send to me your honourable letters willing me by the same to come up to you for the intent I should surrender the monastery to the king's grace, I beseech you for God's sake to be my good lord. I had my office and the house by the king's grace and your lordship, and when it shall please his grace and your lordship to take it again I am and shall be ready at his grace's commandment as his faithful and true subject, trusting [that] his noble grace and your good lordship's pleasure may be that I and my poor brethren may continue in the monastery as his grace's true bedesmen and daily orators. And [we] shall continually, according to our most bounden duties, pray to God for the prosperous estate of his most noble reign and the long continuance of your lordship's good health. At Combermere the 10th day of May. By your daily bedesman and orator, John, abbot there.

(c) Letter to Thomas Cromwell from John Stonywell, last abbot of Pershore, Worcestershire, 23 February 1539: PRO, SP 1, 143/pp. 146–7, calendared in *LP* xiv i, 349. At Pershore Stonywell had been at odds both with his community – over stipends – and with his tenants (*LP* xi, 1145 and xiv i, 1162). Less than a year before this letter was written he is reputed to have made the dangerous remark, 'I trust and I pray God that I may die one of the children of Rome' (*LP* xiii i, 822), but Cromwell knew that Stonywell was no martyr and he was left in possession until he finally surrendered his house on 21 January 1540. He was given a pension of £160 *per annum*, and also part of the abbey buildings (*LP* xv, 92).

With humble reverence it may please your lordship to be advertised that afore the last Christmas I desired Master Doctor Layton to give you knowledge that I would resign my monastery to the King's Grace and you if it be your pleasure I shall do, which I will gladly follow immediately after I have the resignation made in due form. And then I pray your lordship give me licence to intreat of my pension and you to determine it at your own pleasure after your hearing of these my petitions. Because I have born all charges of my monastery from Michaelmas to the feast of [the] Annunciation [25 *March*] next following I pray your lordship cause me to receive this half year's rent[1] and then I will leave the monastery out of all debt, which I found indebted £1,000 and much more, as my acquittances thereof maketh mention. Item, I have let to farm for term of years eight lordships by reason of the King's most honourable letters and yours. And I have increased the annual rents of the said lordships above the true valor of the King's Books yearly forty pounds and more, as it appeareth by the indentures of the said lordships,

---

[1] The abbot was quite clearly expecting very shortly to be called upon to surrender.

and no rent of any tenants there augmented by one farthing. And therefore I pray your lordship to consider that profit in your assigning of my pension, and that I may have an honest house to dwell in and my monks to have pensions according to the virtues of their livings. Item, I will leave the monastery well stored with lead, wood, corn, and with all manner [of] other household stuff, and therefore I pray your lordship to give me my books and other convenient stuff to serve me at your pleasure. Item, I will leave £100 and more leviable debts mentioned in my auditor's book. And therefore I pray your lordship that all such fees which I have used to pay yearly, both that hath been granted by convent seal afore my days and within my days, may be affirmed. And because I have not sufficient ability to prefer this my trusty servant, bearer hereof, according to his desire, I pray your good lordship to show your goodness unto him. And with my daily prayers Almighty God preserve your honourable lordship in honourable prosperity long to endure. Written at Pershore the xxiii day of February.

Your honourable bond orator, John Politensis,[2] abbot of Pershore
To the right honourable lord Cromwell, Lord Privy Seal, this to be delivered [endorsed] Anno xxx The abbot of Pershore

[2] Since 1524 he had been titular bishop of Pulate in Epirus: Knowles, *RO* III, 340–1.

18. Royal Authority to Dissolve, 1539

A commission under privy seal issued to Dr Richard Layton and four others in February 1539, to dissolve ten monasteries in Lincolnshire: PRO, Exchequer, King's Remembrancer, Ecclesiastical Documents (E 135), 3/13. The four houses asterisked surrendered, along with Fosse in the same county, in July 1539 to Dr London (*LP* XIV i, 1222, 1235, 1242, 1251, 1280, 1321) but of the rest Torksey had probably already been dissolved, Thornton became a secular college, and the others surrendered in the autumn (*ibid.*, ii, 173, 235, 631, 652). The survival of this commission is probably due to its never having been despatched from Westminster. For a draft commission in almost identical terms see BM, Cotton, Cleop. E IV, fo. 193. Freeman and Wiseman were Receiver and Auditor, respectively, of the court of Augmentations, for Lincolnshire.

Henry the eighth, by the grace of God king of England . . . [etc.] to our trusty and wellbeloved Richard Layton and John London, doctors, Robert Cotton, John Freeman, and John Wiseman, greeting. Forasmuch as we understand that the monasteries and nunneries of Thornton, Spalding, *Heynings, Crowland, Torksey, *Kyme, Grimsby, *Orford, *Nun Cotham and Stixwould[1] in our county of Lincoln remain at this present in such state as they be neither used to the honour of God nor to the benefit of our common weal, we let you therefore wit [*know*] that, being minded to take them into our own hands for a better purpose, like as we doubt not but the heads and convents of the same will be content to make their surrender accordingly, we for the special trust and confidence we have in your fidelities, wisdom, and discretions, have, and by these presents do authorise, name, assign and appoint you, three and two of you, that immediately resorting to the said houses you shall receive of the said heads and convent[s] such a writing under their convent seals as to your discretions shall seem requisite, meet, and convenient for the due surrender to our use of the same. And thereupon taking possession of all the goods, chattells, plate, jewels, implements and stuff being or appertaining unto the same and further causing all the goods and implements, the lead and bells excepted, to be indifferently sold, either for ready money or else at days upon sufficient sureties, so that the same days pass [*exceed*] not one year and a half, you shall deliver to the heads and brethren such part of the money and goods for their dispatch and assign unto them such pension to be levied out of the goods, lands or revenues of the same houses as by your dis-

---

[1] The names of the houses do not quite fill the space left for them.

cretions and wisdom shall be thought meet and convenient, which done, further seeing the rightful and due debts paid and satisfied as to reason and good conscience appertaineth, and your own charges reasonable allowed, you shall proceed to the dissolution of the said houses and further in our name taking possession of the same and of all the goods and lands thereunto belonging or appertaining, you shall deliver the custody of the said houses, lands, bells, and lead to some substantial and convenient persons, safely and surely to be kept to our use and profit, bringing and conveying to our Tower of London all the rest of the money, plate, jewels, and ornaments that in any wise shall come to your hands by means of the premises or of any part thereof. Wherefore we straitly charge and command all mayors, sheriffs, bailiffs, constables and all others aiding, helping and assisting as they will answer unto us for the contrary at their peril. Given under our privy seal at our palace of Westminster the 21st day of February the 30th year of our reign.

19. Eyewitnesses at Gloucester, 1538

(a) Memorandum by the mayor and three aldermen of Gloucester describing the suppression of the three houses of friars in their city, 28 July 1538: BM, Cotton MS., Cleop. E IV, fo. 252, printed in Wright, *Letters*, pp. 202–3. Richard Ingworth had already visited Gloucester on 23 May and taken possession of the friars' seals, whereby he was confident of their ultimate surrender, 'for they have no living' (Wright, *Letters*, pp. 193–4).

Memorandum, this 28th day of July in the 30th year of our most dread sovereign lord king Henry the eighth, Richard, bishop of Dover and visitor under the lord privy seal for the king's grace, was in Gloucester, and there before the mayor and aldermen in the houses of friars there at two times in two days put the said friars at their liberties [*gave them the choice*], whether they would continue in their houses and keep their religion, and injunctions according to the same, or else give their houses into the king's hands. The injunctions he there declared among them, the which were thought by the said mayor and aldermen to be good and reasonable, and also the said friars said that they were according to their rules, yet as the world is now they were not able to keep them and live in their houses, wherefore voluntarily they gave their houses into the visitor's hands to the king's use. The visitor said to them, 'Think not, nor hereafter report not, that you be suppressed, for I have no such authority to suppress you but only to reform you, wherefore if you will be reformed according to good order you may continue for all me.' They said they were not able to continue. Wherefore the visitor took their houses and charitably delivered them and gave them letters to visit their friends and so to go to other houses, with the which they were very well content and so departed. This we the said mayor and aldermen testify by our hands subscribed.

Master William Hasard, mayor Master William Mathew, alderman
Mr Thomas Bell the elder, alderman Thomas Payne, alderman

(b) From a letter from Ingworth to Thomas Cromwell written shortly after the occasion described above: BM, Cotton MS., Cleop. E IV, fo. 251, printed in Wright, *Letters*, pp. 198–201.

. . . In Gloucester I have discharged three houses, as by the mayor and aldermen's hands you may perceive. The Black Friars is a proper little house, little lead but one aisle, no rents but their gardens, the which Master Bell the alderman hath in lease under their convent seal for

many years, and I heartily desire you be good lord to him that he also
may have [i.e. *occupy*] that house. He doth much good in that town
among the poor people, setting many on work, above 300 daily, and I
am much bound to him for his great comfort in all my business there at
both times, and for the more part I have been at board with him. I
beseech you be good lord to him.[1] The Grey Friars is a goodly house,
much of it new builded, especially the church, quire and dorter, the
rest small lodgings, divers leases out for years of lodgings and gardens,
no lead but a small conduit and small gutters. The White Friars but a
small house and in decay. . . . Young Thomas Bell hath part of the gardens of it for years. I would he might have that house if it pleased the
King's grace and your lordship. . . .

. . . I would do all things with so much quiet and without any clamour
so near as I know. If that I knew your pleasure there shall no part be left
undone so near as I may. My commission givith me no authority to put
any out without they give up their houses, but if that I knew your
pleasure I may find causes sufficient to put them out of many places for
their misliving and for disobeying the instructions and the King's acts.

. . . I beseech your lordship to have discharge for these friars to change
their apparel [*to become secular priests*]:

The Black Friars of Gloucester: Friar John Reynolds, bachelor in
divinity, late prior, Friar John Howper, Friar Richard Bylond, Friar
William Swan, Friar William Walton, Friar Ralph Howell, Friar
Thomas Meykyns

The White [Friars] of Gloucester: Friar Thomas Knight, Friar
William Plesans, Friar Henry Byschewood

The Grey Friars of Gloucester: Friar William Lightfoot, Friar John
Barclay, Friar Henry Jaket, Friar George Cooper, Friar John Rebull

.   .   .   .

[1] Thomas Bell senior purchased the Black Friars about twelve months later
and converted it into a workshop for the manufacture of cloth: *LP* XIV, 1354,
g. 48 and Williams, *Eng. Hist. Docs.* V, 211.

(a–d) Letters from the Commissioners to Thomas Cromwell, 26 January, 20 February, 10 and 30 March, 1539: PRO, State Papers Domestic (SP 1), 142. 155–6; 143. 115–6; 144. 81–2, 191–2; printed in W. A. J. Archbold, *Somerset Religious Houses*, pp. 70–6, and calendared in *LP* XIV i, 145, 324, 491, 629. The two more important commissioners were John Tregonwell and William Petre, both doctors of civil law. No record of their first commission has survived, but their 'circuit' seems to have commenced at Poulton, Wiltshire, on 16 January and to have been completed at Bruton, Somerset, on 1 April 1539. On 17 January Petre wrote to Cromwell with a query arising out of the 'book of names' of houses to be visited: *LP* XIV i, 78.

(a) [26 January 1539]
Our most bounden duties remembered, it may please your good mastership to be advertised that from dissolving of the late monastery of Keynsham [*on 23 January*], because Hinton lay best in our way and at the request of the lord Hungerford [*of Heytesbury, Wilts.*] to whom your lordship wrote the King's highness's pleasure to be that we should leave the demesnes of the same, we came thither yesternight. And immediately after our coming [we] entered communication with the prior there of the cause of our coming and [? used such] means and persuasions unto him for this purpose as we thought most meet and might best take place in him. Whose answer in effect was that if the King's majesty would take his house [as if] it proceeded not of his voluntary surrender he was contented to obey, but otherwise he said his conscience would not suffer him willingly to give over the same. In the end after long communication he desired delay to make us answer unto this morning, at which time we eftsoons using like diligence in persuading him as we did before, he declared himself to be of the same mind he was yesternight, or rather more stiff in the same. In communication with the convent we perceived them to be of the same mind the prior was and had much like answer of them as we had of the prior (three excepted which were conformable). And amongst the rest one Nicholas Baland, monk there, being incidentally examined of the King's title of supremacy, expressly denied the same, affirming the bishop of Rome to be the vicar of Christ, and that he is and ought to be taken for the supreme head of the church. The prior and others showed us that this Baland hath been in times past, and yet many times is, lunatic. We have not yet done anything touching this man but (not putting him in any fear) have let him remain un[til] your lordship's further pleasure be known herein. In the premises it may

please your lordship to declare your pleasure unto us, which [being] known we shall, according to our most bounden duties, conform ourselves accordingly. And in the meantime, because we thought that the other Charterhouse [*Witham*], taking example by this will not conform themselves, we have determined (your lordship's pleasure saved) to defer the same unto our return. Thus Almighty God have your good lordship in his most blessed keeping. From Hinton the 26th of January [1539]

    Your lordship's most bounden, John Tregonwell
    Your lordship's most bounden bedesman and servant, William Petre

(b) On 27 January the commissioners took the surrender of Bath Cathedral Priory (*LP* xiv i, 148) and then proceeded through Somerset and so into Devon, taking just under three weeks to reach Exeter and en route taking eight further surrenders as detailed in their letter of 20 February.[1]

[20 February 1539]
Our most bounden duties remembered, it may please your good lordship to be advertised that since our last letters we have, with as good expedition as we might, taken surrender of the houses of St Johns in Wells [on 3 February], St John's in Bridgewater [7 February], Athelney [8 Feb.], Minchin Buckland [10 Feb.], Taunton [12 Feb.], Dunkeswell [14 Feb.], Canonsleigh [16 Feb.] and Polsloe [19 Feb.], and in all these houses have found as much conformities as might be desired, saving that in many of them we have found great waste and many leases of late passed, which nevertheless we have stayed and called in again as near as we might. And because we would, as much as in us is, take away the occasion of attempting the like in other houses, we have thought good, having now received from your lordship the commission in which Mr Pollard is joined with us, to divide ourselves, so that two of us being at one house the other two may in the same time despatch another, by which means we think we shall not only stay many such wastes and spoils as being passed before our coming could never be recovered again, but also, we trust, make an end of all the others committed unto us by your lordship before the Annunciation of Our Lady, whereby shall remain to the King's majesty the half year's rent of those houses, and yet pass all other things as much to the king's highness's profit as [if] we were all together. We think there will be a great sum of money that shall be saved to the King's highness thereby. Our purpose herein we think our most bounden duties to signify unto your lordship to know your pleasure in the same. In the meantime we shall, as we ever hitherto

---

[1] The dates in square brackets are those of the deeds of surrender as calendared in *LP* xiv i, *passim*.

have done, endeavour ourselves according to our most bounden duties and your good lordship's advertisement (for the which we most humbly thank the same) to do all things as far as our poor wits will serve as circumspectly for the profit of the king's majesty as we may, most humbly beseeching your lordship to take our proceedings herein in good part and to signify unto us your further pleasure touching Bruton[2] and Hinton, to the despatch whereof we think we shall be ready (your lordship's pleasure so standing) by the return of this messenger. And thus we pray God to have your lordship in his blessed keeping. From Exeter the 20th day of February [1539]

> Your lordship's most bounden, John Tregonwell
> Your lordship's most bounden bedesman and servant, William Petre
> Yours evermore to command, John Smyth

(c) On the same day as the above letter was written the commissioners took the surrender of St John's Hospital at Exeter (*LP* xiv i, 323) and then, dividing as planned into two parties, completed their mission to the eight remaining houses in Devon and Cornwall in less than two weeks. Both parties were back on the Devon-Dorset border by 8 March, on which day both Forde and Newenham abbeys surrendered (*LP* xiv i, 468–9).

[10 March 1539]

Our most bounden duties remembered, it may please your lordship to be advertised that this day (the surrender of the late monastery of Forde being before by us taken) we resorted to the priory of Montacute for the execution of the King's highness's commission there. Where, after long communication with the prior, and as many persuasions for the setting forth of the King's grace's pleasure in this behalf as we could devise, we found the prior in like obstinacy as we had before found the abbot of Bruton, and by so much as by his answer we might conjecture there had been some privy conference between them in this matter.[3] Before our coming he had leased almost all his demesnes to divers persons. The premises we have thought our bounden duties to signify unto your lordship, being at all times ready to do further herein as your lordship shall command us. Thus we pray God have your good lordship in his most blessed keeping. From Montacute the 10th of March [1539]

> Your lordship to command, Hugh Pollard
> Your lordship's most bounden bedesman and servant, William Petre

(d) Still dividing forces, but without Pollard, the commissioners pro-

---

[2] An Augustinian priory lying about 20 miles south of Hinton. It was presumably visited by the commissioners en route for Wells.

[3] Montacute was a Cluniac house.

ceeded to obtain the submission of ten further houses, mostly in Dorset and Wiltshire, but including Witham, Somerset, on 15 March and Montacute on 20 March (*LP* xiv i, 524, 575). All three were at Amesbury on 30 March.

[30 March 1539]
Pleaseth it your good lordship to be advertised, yesterday (the surrenders of the monasteries of Shaftesbury and Wilton being before [by] us taken) we came to Amesbury and there communed with the abbess [*Florence Bonnew*] for the accomplishment of the King's highness's commission in like sort. And albeit we have used as many ways with her as our poor wits could attain, yet in the end we could not by any persuasions bring her to any conformity but at all times she rested and so remaineth in these terms, 'If the King's highness command me to go from this house I will gladly go, though I beg my bread. And as for pension I care for none.' In these terms she was in all her conversation, praying us many times to trouble her no further herein for she had declared her full mind, in the which we might plainly gather of her words she was fully fixed before our coming. This we have thought good according to our most bounden duties to signify unto your lordship, ready with all our powers to accomplish that [which] your lordship shall further command us herein. We have sent to Bruton again and yesterday had answer from thence that the abbot as yet is at London. We trust to finish the rest of our business by your lordship committed unto us before Easter and so with as much speed as we may to wait upon you and declare the full of all our proceedings herein. Thus praying Almighty God to have your lordship in his most blessed keeping, from Amesbury the 30th of March.

Your lordship's most bounden, John Tregonwell
Your lordship's most bounden bedesman and servant, William Petre
Your lordship's most bounden, John Smyth

Abbess Bonnew resigned her office on 10 August and the house was finally surrendered by her successor, Joan Darrell, to new commissioners on 7 December 1539 (*LP* xiv ii, 27, 646). The prioress and thirty-three nuns were granted pensions. The abbot of Bruton, John Ely, with his prior and thirteen monks surrendered to Petre on 1 April 1539. He was granted a pension of £80 (*LP* xiv i, 664). Meanwhile, on 31 March, Dr Tregonwell had at last met with success at Hinton Priory (*ibid.*, 637).

(e) A letter from Edmund Horde, prior of Hinton in Somerset, to his brother Alan, 10 February 1539: BM, Cotton MS., Cleop. E IV, fo. 270, printed in Archbold, *op. cit.*, pp. 83–4 and in Ellis, *Letters*, Ser.

II, ii, p. 130. The royal commissioners, as already indicated, had been at Hinton on 26 January and found the prior difficult (above, p. 180). He finally surrendered on 31 March, and on 24 April was granted a pension of £44 (*LP* XIV, i, 637, and XV, p. 543).[1]

Jesus

In Our Lord Jesus shall be your salutation. And where you marvel that I and my brethren do not freely and voluntarily give and surrender up our house at the motion of the King's commissioners but stand stiffly and (as you think) obstinately in our opinion, truly brother I marvel greatly that you think so, but rather that you would have thought us light and hasty in giving up that thing which is not ours to give but dedicate[d] to Almighty God for service to be done to his honour continually, with many other good deeds of charity which daily be done in this house to our Christian neighbours, and considering that there is no cause given by us why the house should be put down but that the service of God, religious conversation of the brethren, hospitality, alms deeds, with all other our duties be as well observed in this poor house as in any religious house in this realm or in France, which we have trusted that the King's grace would consider. But because that you write of the King's high displeasure and my lord privy seal's, who ever hath been my especial good lord, and I trust yet will be, I will endeavour myself, as much as I may, to persuade my brethren to a conformity in this matter, so that the King's highness nor my said good lord shall have any cause to be displeased with us, trusting that my poor brethren (which know not where to have their living) shall be charitabl[y] look[ed] upon. Thus Our Lord Jesu preserve you in grace.

Hinton, 10 day of February   E[dmund] Horde
To his brother Alan Horde in Middle Temple deliver

[1] Thomas Arundell, Augmentations Receiver for the south-western counties, arrived shortly afterwards, and, presumably in ignorance of Cromwell's promise to Lord Hungerford, who later claimed that he had paid cash to the commissioners, proceeded to pull down and carry away much of the priory fabric: *LP.* XIV, i, 1154.

21. Deed of Surrender of Ford Abbey, 1539

A deed of gift, with warranty, dated 8 March 1539, whereby the abbot and convent of Forde in the county of Devon (now in Dorset) surrendered themselves, the monastery, and all its possessions to the king, to be at his absolute disposal: PRO, Exchequer, Augmentations Office, Deeds of Surrender (E 322), 88. The text, including the dating clause, is in one hand throughout and is subscribed with what appear to be the signatures of the abbot, the prior, and twelve monks, all of which suggests that, although drawn up in accordance with common form, the document was in fact written on the spot, and at the time of surrender, probably by a clerk accompanying the royal commissioners. [Translated from Latin]

To all the faithful in Christ to whom the present writing shall come, Thomas Charde, abbot of the monastery or abbey and church of the Blessed Virgin Mary of Forde in the county of Devon, of the Cistercian order, and the convent of the same place, Greeting in the Lord everlasting:

Know that we, the aforenamed abbot and convent, by our unanimous assent and consent, our minds resolved, from our certain knowledge and mere motion, for certain right and reasonable causes specially moving our minds and consciences, voluntarily and freely have given, granted and by [these] presents give, grant, render, and confirm to our most illustrious prince and lord, Henry VIII, by the grace of God of England and France king, defender of the faith, lord of Ireland, and supreme head on earth of the English Church, all our said monastery or abbey of Forde aforesaid, together with all and singular manors, lordships, messuages, gardens, curtilages, tofts, lands, and tenements, fields, meadows, pastures, woods, underwoods, rents, reversions, services, mills, ferries, knights' fees, wards, marriages, serfs, bondmen with their issue, commons, liberties, franchises, jurisdictions, offices, courts leet, hundreds, view of frankpledge, fairs, markets, parks, warrens, fishponds, waters, fisheries, highways, tolls, vacant grounds, advowsons, nominations, presentations and donations of churches, vicarages, chapels, chantries, hospitals, and of other churches and benefices whatsoever, rectories, vicarages, chantries, pensions, portions, annuities, tithes, oblations, and all and singular our emoluments, profits, possessions, hereditaments, and rights whatsoever, both in the county of Devon and in the counties of Dorset, Somerset, and elsewhere in the kingdom of England, Wales, and the marches thereof, to the same monastery or abbey of Forde aforesaid in any way appertaining, adjoining, attaching, or incumbering, and all our charters, evidences, writings, and muniments, to the same monastery or abbey, manors, lands, tenements and other premises or parcel thereof attaching or concerning whatsoever. To have, hold, and enjoy the said abbey or monastery, the site, ground, circuit, and precinct of Forde aforesaid, together with all and singular manors [etc.] to the aforesaid most illustrious prince and our lord the king, his heirs and assigns, for ever . . . [and] we ourselves and the said monastery or abbey of Forde aforesaid and all our rights in whatsoever manner acquired as is due we surrender and submit. And having given and granted in accordance with [these] presents, we give and grant to the same king's majesty, his heirs and assigns, all and all manner of full and free permission, authority, and power to dispose of us and the said monastery or abbey of Forde aforesaid, together with all and singular manors, [etc.] and all the premises with their rights and appurtenances whatsoever, and, at the free will of the king, to whatever use his majesty shall please, to alienate, give, convert, and transfer, and all such alienations, [etc.] we promise by these presents to ratify. . . .

[There follow clauses renouncing to the king any rights or property which may become due to the monastery as the result of any settlements or legal actions, and promising to warrant and defend the king's rights in the property against all men for ever.] In witness whereof we, the aforesaid abbot and convent, have set to these presents our common seal. Given in our chapter house of Forde aforesaid the eighth day of May in the thirtieth year of the reign of the abovesaid king Henry.

Acknowledged before me William Petre, one of the clerks, etc., the day and year abovewritten, by me William Petre

[*Alongside are the following names*]: per me Thomas, abbot; [?] Rede, prior; Richard Were, John Cosyn, Robert Ilminster, John Newman, John Bridgeman, Thomas Stafford, John Fawell, W[illiam] Wynsor, Ellis Oliscombe, William Keynston, William Dynyngton and Richard Kingsbury.[1]

---

[1] The pension list, signed by John Tregonwell and William Petre, runs as follows (*LP* xiv i, 468): Thomas Charde alias Tybbes, abbot, £80 and 40 wainloads of firewood; William Sherneborne alias Rede, £8; Richard Exmester alias Were, £8; John Brydgewater alias Stone, £8; John Newman, £6; John Cosyns, £6 13s 4d; Robert Ylmester alias Roose, £7; Ellys Olescum alias Potter, £7; John Fawell, £3 6s 8d; Thomas Stafforde alias Bate, £3 6s 8d; William Grene (*sic*), £5 6s 8d; William Wynsor alias Hyde, £5; William Denyngton alias Wylshire, £5 and Richard Kingesbury alias Sherman, £5.

22. Dissolution Accounts of St Osyth's Abbey, Essex, 1539

The survey of movables and the account rendered by the commissioners engaged in the dissolution of St Osyth's Abbey, Essex, July 1539: PRO, Exchequer, King's Remembrancer, Church Goods (E 117), 10/26, with extracts from a more detailed account of cash received for sales of movable goods and of disbursements in cash by the commissioners: PRO, State Papers Domestic, Suppression Accounts (SP 5), 2/264–82.[1] St Osyth's surrendered on 28 July 1539.

THE LATE MONASTERY OF ST OSYTH'S IN THE COUNTY OF ESSEX
Hereafter ensueth the state, value, and condition as well of all and singular the jewels, plate, ornaments of the church, goods, chattells, lead, and bells appertaining and belonging to the late monastery . . . as also the costs, charges, and expenses had and sustained for and about the dissolution of the same, together with sundry sums of money paid to divers creditors . . . surveyed, seen and examined by Sir John Sinclair and Sir William Pirton, knights, John Pekyns, clerk, Thomas Mildmay, and Francis Jobson, the King's commissioners. . . .
JEWELS: First 2 old mitres whereof the ground is all small pearl set upon plate of silver gilt garnished with counterfeit stones and glasses; Item a pair of gloves called Pontificals garnished with silver gilt set with glass having in either of them a brooch of silver gilt set with counterfeit stones and glasses; Item 5 rings of gold set with glass, pearl, and crystal; Item 4 rings of silver gilt set with counterfeit stone; Item the skull of St Osyth [en]closed in silver, parcel gilt; Item a crown of silver gilt too [*also*] set upon the said skull, garnished, and with counterfeit stones; Item 12 plates of silver whereon [have] been relics enclosed
These parcels . . . remain undefaced until the King's Highness pleasure in the same be known.
The value of the Plate:—
Gilt . . . 483 oz, which after the rate of 4s the oz amounteth to £96 12s
Parcel Gilt . . . 327½ oz, which after the rate of 3s 8d the oz amounteth to £59 19s
White Plate . . . 176 oz which after the rate of 3s 4d the oz amounteth to £29 6s 8d

[Total] 986½ oz . . . £185 17s 8d

---

[1] The first of these, which comprehends the whole operation, is here printed in full. The second has been drawn upon only very selectively, for footnotes, a rather less confusing arrangement than that adopted in M. E. C. Walcott, 'The Inventory of St Osyth's Abbey', *Essex Archaeolog. Trans.*, Old Series, v, 53–69.

Ornaments of the Church:— Divers and sundry copes, vestments, albs, tunicles, towels and other vestry and church stuff, praised by Adam Sampson and others and sold by the forenamed commissioners . . . amounting to the sum of £40 2s 10d[2]

Corn, cattle and other movable goods:— Item corn, cattle, bedding, napery, vessels, kitchen stuff, buttery, pantry and other implements and utensils of household, praised by the said Adam Sampson and sold by the said commissioners to divers persons,[3] over and besides certain tables, forms, standards, brewing vessels, and other necessaries fixed in the ground, remaining as implements of the house until the King's pleasure therein may be known . . . £40 16s 9d

Edifications and Buildings: None removed nor sold by the commandment of my Lord Chancellor till the King's pleasure be known

Iron, glass and stone: all yet remaining untouched for like cause

Debts due to the late monastery: by John Pomell of Ely, freemason, as appeareth by his bill, 60s

Lead remaining:[4] Upon the Presbytery over the High Alter by estimation in fothers, 20; the Chapel of the South side by estimation in fothers, 6; the Cross Aisle on the South side, 10; the Steeple, 6; the South Aisle against the body of the church, 10; the Body of the church, 35; the Chapel and the Vestry on the North side adjoining together 10; the Cross Aisle on the North side 6; the Chapter House on the North side 6; the Dorter roof 18; the rear Dorter 8; the Aisle of the North end of the Great Dorter 6; the Great Chamber over the Hall 8; the Parlour joining to the Great Chamber 2; the Chapel adjoining to the Great Chamber 3; the Gallery next the Hall 3; the little roof joining to the Dorter on the West part 3; the Frater 16; the four panes [sides] of the Cloister 15; the Chapel joining to the West end of the church on the north side 4; the old Hall and the chamber joining to it 15; the Pastry roof joining to the kitchen 4; the Entry roof between the Moon Chamber and the New Hall 3; the New Hall 11; the roof joining to the west end of the New Hall on the north side 2; the

[2] The sales made by Sampson and three other 'appraisers indifferent' employed by the commissioners, included that of a blue cope made of taffeta to one William Newman, for 5s, and a similar vestment to Sir Cornelius Willinson, the sub-prior. The table at the high altar was sold to Sir William Pyrton for 40s, and a pair of organs in the Lady Chapel to a Thomas Clarke for 20s: fos. 274–5.

[3] Sir Francis Jobson, one of the commissioners, bought six cart horses, with carts and gear, for £5; the abbot three great latten candlesticks for 3s; and Sir John Sinclair all the furniture in the infirmary for 2s. All the contents of the Great Chamber, the Hall, the Kitchen and other domestic offices, as well as everything in the Bishop's Lodgings, the Moon, the Star, and the Sun Chambers, were marked as sold to Audley: fos. 276–82.

[4] A fother of lead = 19½ cwt, or 1950 lbs.

Gallery of the Garret 15; the Bakehouse 10; the Bishop's Lodgings 2; the Gatehouse 4:

[Total] 261 [fothers], which after the rate of £4 for every fother amounteth to £1,048

Bells: 5, weighing by estimation 40 hundredweight, which after the rate of 25s the hundredweight amounteth to £40

Sum total of the plate, ornaments, goods and chattells, lead and bells before written, over and besides the jewels above mentioned here not valued, and over and besides £59 10d for the price of certain plate delivered to the creditors towards the payment of their debts, £1,353 17s 3d

Whereof divers sundry sums of money advanced and paid by the said commissioners:—

Wages and rewards: Paid as well to the religious persons[5] there as to waiting servants, hinds and others[6] by the discretion of the same commissioners as by a book of parcels thereof made more plainly it doth appear, £33 9s 10d

Debts paid to divers creditors for sundry sums of money by them due for sundry necessaries by them provided to the use of the late monastery, over and besides £59 10d paid in plate to divers creditors and over and besides [blank] yet due [and] not demanded nor asked, £27 4s

Plate delivered and given to the late abbot there by the commandment of my lord Chancellor, with and by the assent of the forenamed commissioners, parcel of the plate above mentioned, amounting in the whole to the sum of £12[7]

Costs and expenses of the Commissioners: And for the costs of the King's commissioners and their servants sustained in the execution of the premises, with also the costs of measuring the lead and bells, weighing of the plate and defacing of the shrine[8] . . . £12 6s 8d

Total: £85 0s 6d

And so remaineth: in Lead by estimation as aforesaid   £1,044

     Bells   £40

     Debts due to the late monastery   60s

     Plate to be delivered to the Master of the Jewel House

---

[5] Fifteen monks received together the sum of £15 13s 4d.

[6] These included one Edward Short, schoolmaster (20s), five kitchen servants, eight cooks, six waggoners, five boys, and three laundresses, of whom 'Mother Paten' and 'Hans' wife' received 5s each, and Joan Cooper, 3s 4d: fos. 265–6.

[7] This included a gilt cup with cover, 15½ oz @ 4s, 62s; a nut garnished with silver, parcel gilt, with a cover, 66s 8d; and 33 spoons, white plate, 37 oz @ 3s 4d, £6 3s 6d: fos. 271–2.

[8] To the goldsmith and his servant for the weighing of the plate, and for defacing the shrine, the commissioners paid 6s 8d; to a plumber for melting the lead, 5s; to the Augmentations Auditor and Receiver, and their servants, who rode over from Chelmsford and back over a period of seven days, £7 10s: fo. 266.

to the King's use according to the rates of prices above
mentioned   £175 18s 6d

Ready money received by the said commissioners yet in
their hands to the King's use   £5 18s 3d

[Total] £1,268 16s 9d

Pensions assigned by the King's Commissioners to the late abbot and
religious persons of the monastery aforesaid, from the feast of the Annunciation of Our Lady the Virgin in the 30th year of the reign of King
Henry VIII [1539], during their lives, to be paid by the hands of the
Particular Receiver of the Augmentations within the county of Essex by
even portions according to the effect of their commission: That is to
say, to:

The late abbot there by the year, £100; The Prior by the year, £10;
The sub-Prior by the year, £8; The Cellarer by the year, £8; The
Bailiff by the year, £8; The Sexton by the year, £8; The Cantor by
the year, £8; 9 other religious persons, priest every [one] of them, at
10 marks by the year, £60

[Total] £210

23. Statutory Confirmation of the King's Title, 1539

'An Act for the Dissolution of Abbeys', 31 Henry VIII, c. 13: *Statutes* III, 733-9. First introduced into the Lords, this was passed by the Commons in May 1539, at a time when the last stage, the 'induced' surrenders, was well under way but by no means completed. Considerable portions of the monastic property had by now been disposed of by the Crown.

Where divers and sundry abbots [etc.] of their own free and voluntary minds, good wills and assents, without constraint, coaction [*coercion*] or compulsion of any manner of person or persons, since [4 February 1536] by the due order and course of the common laws of this his realm of England and by their sufficient writings of record under their convent and common seals, have severally given, granted, and by the same their writings severally confirmed all their said monasteries [etc.] and all their sites, circuits and precincts of the same, and all and singular their manors, lordships, granges [etc.], to have and to hold all the said monasteries [etc.] to our said sovereign lord [the king], his heirs and successors, for ever, and the same . . . voluntarily, as is aforesaid, have renounced, left and forsaken . . . Be it therefore enacted by the King our sovereign lord and the lords spiritual and temporal and the Commons in this present parliament assembled, and by authority of the same, that the King . . . shall have, hold, possess, and enjoy to him, his heirs and successors for ever all and singular such late monasteries [etc.] which since the said [4 February 1536] have been dissolved, suppressed, renounced, relinquished, forfeited, given up or by any other means come to his highness . . . and . . . shall have, hold, possess and enjoy all the sites, circuits . . . manors . . . in as large and ample manner and form as the late abbots [etc.] . . . at the time of the said dissolution [etc.].

II. And it is further enacted . . . that not only all the said late monasteries [etc.], forthwith, immediately, and presently, but also all other monasteries [etc.] which hereafter shall happen to be dissolved, suppressed, renounced, relinquished, forfeited, given up or by any other mean come unto the King's highness . . . as soon as they shall be dissolved [etc.] shall be vested, deemed, and adjudged by authority of this present parliament in the very actual and real seisin and possession of the King our sovereign lord, his heirs and successors for ever, in the state and condition as they now be, and as though all the said late monasteries [etc.] so dissolved [etc.] were in this present act specially and particularly rehearsed, named and expressed by express words, names, titles [etc.].

III. [All the said monasteries and their possessions, except those coming to the King by attainder, to be under the survey of the court of Augmentations as in 27 Henry VIII, cc. 27, 28.]

IV. Saving to all and every person and persons and bodies politic and their heirs and successors . . . other than the said late abbots [etc.] and such as pretend [claim] to be founders, patrons, or donors of such monasteries [etc.], all such right, title, claim, interest, possession, rent charges, annuities, leases, farms, offices, fees, liveries and livings, portions, pensions, corrodies, commons, synodals, procurations and other profits which they . . . have, claim, ought, may, or might have had, in or to the premises or to any part or parcel thereof, in such like manner, form and condition, to all intents, respects, constructions and purposes as if this act had never been had nor made, rents services, rents sec and all other services and suits only excepted.

V. [Cancellation of all leases and grants for life or years made within a year before dissolution of lands not formerly usually let to farm, or in reversion, or not reserving the rent reserved during the twenty years prior to the first day of this parliament (28 April 1539), and of any sale of woods still growing made within a year before dissolution.]

VI. [Cancellation of all feoffments, fines and recoveries made by the abbots, etc. without royal licence within a year before dissolution of land given by the King or his predecessors, or belonging to monasteries of the King's foundation.]

VII–VIII [As clauses V–VI but referring to houses still to be dissolved.]

IX. [Leases in reversion made within one year of the dissolution or of the first day of this parliament to tenants in occupation may be confirmed for terms of 21 years or less from the date of the reversionary leases, provided the old rent is reserved.]

X. [Leases for life made within one year before dissolution to tenants already in occupation as tenants for life or years, the term not having expired, may be confirmed, provided the old rent is reserved.]

XI. [Leases by copy of court roll for lives protected if in accordance with local custom and the old rent reserved.]

XII. [Leases made by the court of Augmentations and leases, sales of wood, etc., confirmed by that court, to be confirmed.]

XIII. [Those who have paid for wood sales nullified by this act to be compensated for their outlay.]

XIV. [Protection for those who have purchased lands, etc., from abbots, etc., since 4 February 1536 with the king's licence.]

XV. [Confirmation of all purchases and exchanges made by the King since 4 February 1536.]

XVI. And where it hath pleased the king's highness of his abundant grace and goodness, as well upon divers and sundry considerations his

majesty specially moving, as also otherwise, to have bargained, sold,
[ex]changed, or given and granted by his grace's several letters patent,
indentures or other writings, as well under his highness's great seal as
under the seal of his highness's duchy of Lancaster and the seal of the
office [*sic*] of the Augmentations of his Crown, unto divers and sundry
of his loving and obedient subjects divers and sundry honours, castles,
manors, monasteries ... lands, rents [etc.] in fee simple, fee tail, for term
of life or for term of years, for avoiding of [*making void*] which said
letters patent, and of the contents of the same, divers and many ambiguities, doubts and questions might hereafter arise, be moved and
stirred, as well for misrecital or nonrecital as for divers other matters,
things or causes to be alleged, objected or invented against the said letters
patent, as also for lack of finding of offices or inquisitions, whereby the
title of his highness therein ought to have been found before the making
of the same letters patent, or for misrecital of leases as well of record as
not of record or for lack of the certainty of the values or by reason of
misnaming of the honours, castles, manors, monasteries [etc.], albeit
the words in effect contained in the said letters patent be according to
the true intent and meaning of his most royal majesty. Be it therefore
enacted by the authority of this present parliament that as well all and
every the said letters patent, indentures or other writings and every of
them made under the seal or seals abovesaid, or of any of them made or
granted by the king's highness since the said ... [4 February 1536] as
[well as] all and singular other his grace's letters patent, indentures or
other writings to be had, made or granted to any person or persons
within three years next after the making of this present act of any honour
[etc.] ... shall stand and be good, effectual, and available in the law of
this realm to all respects, purposes, constructions and intents against
his majesty, his heirs and successors, without any other licence, dispensation, or tolerance of the kings' highness, his heirs and successors,
or of any other person or persons whatsoever they be, for any thing or
things contained or hereafter to be contained in any such letters patent,
indentures or other writings, any causes, considerations or thing material
to the contrary in any wise notwithstanding. [General saving of rights in
the properties so granted to all but the king, his heirs and successors, the
governors and governesses of monasteries, etc., donors, founders and
patrons.]

XVII. And where divers and sundry abbots [etc.] ... have had, possessed and enjoyed divers and sundry parsonages appropriated, tithes,
pensions and portions and also were acquitted and discharged of and
for the payment of tithes to be paid out or for their said monasteries
[etc.], be it therefore enacted by the authority abovesaid that as well the
king ... as [well as] all and every such person and persons, their heirs
and assigns, which have or hereafter shall have any monastery [etc.] or

N

any manors [etc.] which belonged or appertained or which now belong or appertain unto the said monasteries [etc.] shall have, hold, retain, keep and enjoy, as well the said parsonages appropriate, tithes, pensions and portions . . . as [also] the said monasteries [etc.] discharged and acquitted of payment of tithes, as freely and in as large and ample manner as the said late abbots [etc.] at the days of their dissolution [etc.], saving to the king's highness, his heirs and successors all and all manner of rents, services and other duties . . . as if this act had never been had nor made.

XVIII. [Exempt monasteries and churches and chapels belonging to them to be in future within the visitation of the ordinary (*the bishop*) of the diocese within which each lies.]

XIX. [Confirmation of verbal royal licences to Thomas duke of Norfolk to purchase the monastery of Sibton in Suffolk from the abbot, and to Lord Cobham to purchase the college or chantry of Cobham in Kent.]

24. A Moment in Time: Evesham, 1540

From notes inserted in an English Bible formerly belonging to Evesham Abbey: M. D. Knowles, *EHR*, LXXIX (1964) pp. 775-7. The bible is a copy of the first edition of the Matthew Bible of 1537, no doubt acquired by the abbey in response to an injunction of Bishop Latimer of Worcester in the autumn of 1537 to all monasteries within his jurisdiction. The writer was John Alcester, lately sacristan of the abbey.

. . . And the year of Our Lord [1540] the monastery of Evesham was suppressed by King Henry the VIII, the xxxi year of his reign, the 30 day of January at evensong time, the convent being in their choir at this verse: *Deposuit potentes* . . . And [they] would not suffer them to make an end. Philip Hawford being abbot at that time and 30 were at that day alive in the said monastery. The steeple and the tower were 11 score [feet] in length, the tower 4 score and ten and the spire 7 score.

The above lines occur on the last leaf of the Old Testament. Elsewhere John Alcester tells us that there were 36 monks alive at the time of the suppression, including the abbot, but as he also includes the name of a former abbot who had been 'retired' in March 1538, the statement above may be more accurate, and may even include some lay servants. A pension list of 27 January contains only 21 names but another, also from an official source, of 16 February lists 34 former monks (Knowles, *op. cit.*, p. 776). The abbey church was destroyed shortly after the departure of John Alcester and his brothers.

25. The Act establishing the Court of Augmentations, 1536

27 Henry VIII, c. 27, *Statutes* III, 569–74. This act, which must be read in conjunction with the previous one dissolving the lesser monasteries (Document 10) was passed on or about 1 April 1536, shortly before the dissolution of the Reformation Parliament.

Forasmuch[1] as in this present parliament begun at London on the third day of November . . . [1529] it is enacted . . . that his majesty should have and enjoy to him, his heirs, and successors for ever all and singular such monasteries, priories and other religious houses of monks, canons and nuns . . . which have not in lands, tenements, rents [etc.] above the clear yearly value of two hundred pounds . . . and . . . all and singular such monasteries, abbeys, and priories which at any time within one year next before the making of the said act have been given and granted to his majesty by any abbot [etc.], or otherwise have been suppressed or dissolved, and all and singular the manors, lands [etc.] to the same . . . appertaining and belonging, to do and use therewith his and their own wills to the pleasure of Almighty God and to the honour and profit of this realm, and further. . . . For the more surety and establishment whereof and to the intent that the king's majesty, his heirs and successors shall be yearly as well truly and justly answered, contented, and paid of the rents, farms, issues, revenues and profits rising, coming, and growing of the said manors, lands, tenements, and other hereditaments before specified as [he shall] of the goods, chattells, plate, stuff of household, debts, money, stock, store, and other whatsoever profits and commodities given, granted, or appointed to the king's majesty by the same, in such court, place, form, manner, and conditions as hereafter shall be limited, declared and appointed, BE IT ENACTED, ordained, and established by the assent of the king's majesty, his Lords spiritual and temporal, and the Commons in this present parliament assembled, and by authority of the same, in manner and form as hereafter followeth in articles, that is to say: First the king our sovereign lord, by authority aforesaid, maketh, establisheth, and erecteth a certain court commonly to be called the Court of the Augmentations of the Revenues of the King's Crown, which court by authority aforesaid continually shall be a court of record, and shall have one great seal and one privy seal, to be engraved and made after such form, fashion, and manner as shall be

---

[1] The original engrossment of the act (House of Lords Record Office) is headed by the King's sign manual.

appointed by the king's highness and shall remain and be ordered as hereafter shall be declared.

II   Also be it enacted by authority aforesaid that there shall be one certain person to be named and assigned by the king's highness which shall be Chancellor of the said court and shall be chief and principal officer of the same court . . . and shall have the keeping of the great seal and the privy seal to be assigned for the said court. Also that there shall be one person to be named by the king's highness which shall be called the king's Treasurer of the Court of the Augmentations of the Revenues of the King's Crown and [he] shall be the second officer of the same court.

III   Also it is ordained by authority aforesaid that there shall be one person learned in the laws of the land to be named by the king's highness which shall be called the king's Attorney of the said court and [he] shall be the third officer of the same court. Also there shall be one person to be named by the king's highness which shall be called the king's Solicitor of the said court and [he] shall be the fourth officer of the court. Also that there shall be ten particular Auditors to be named by the king's highness which shall be called Auditors of the Revenues of the said Augmentations [sic]. Also there shall be 17 particular Receivers to be named by the king's highness which shall be called Receivers of the said Revenues. Also that there shall be one person to be named by the king's highness which shall be called Clerk of the said court, and one other person which shall be Usher of the same court, and one other person which shall be called Messenger of the same court, which Usher and Messenger shall be named by the king's highness, and every [one] of them shall have such yearly fees, rewards and profits as the Usher and Messenger of the Duchy Chamber of [Lancaster at] Westminster have and perceive.

IV   Also the said Chancellor which shall be appointed by the king's highness shall take a corporal oath before the Lord Chancellor of England for the time being after the tenor ensuing: You shall swear that you well and truly shall serve the king in the office of Chancellorship of the Augmentations of the Revenues of the King's Crown and shall minister equal justice to rich and poor to the best of your cunning, wit, and power, and that you shall diligently procure all things which may honestly and justly be to the king's advantage and profit and to the augmentation of the rights and prerogatives of his crown, and truly use the king's seal appointed to your office, and also endeavour yourself to the uttermost of your power to see the king truly answered of all such rents, revenues, issues, and profits which shall or may arise or grow in your office, and from time to time deliver with speed such as shall have to do before you, and that you shall not take nor receive of any person any gift or reward in any cause or matter depending before you, or wherein the king's highness shall be party, whereby any prejudice, hindrance, loss, or [disinheritance] shall grow or be to the king's highness, so help you God and all Saints. Also that the said Treasurer shall take a corporal oath before the said Chancellor of the said court according to the tenor ensuing: You shall swear that you shall well and truly serve the king our sovereign lord and his people in the office of Treasurer of his court, and you shall reasonably and honestly procure the king's profit and do right to all manner of people, poor and rich, in those things which touch your office, and the king's treasure you shall truly keep and dispend and true declaration and account shall make from time to time without any concealment, according to this act made for the establishment of this court, and further [you] shall do everything that of right appertain to your office, so help you God and all Saints. Also either [*each*] of the said Attorney and Solicitor shall take a corporal oath before the said Chancellor according to the tenor ensuing: You shall swear that you well and truly shall serve the king as his Attorney in all courts for and concerning any matter or cause that shall concern or touch the possession and hereditaments limited to the survey and governance of this court, and procure the king's profit thereof, and that you shall truly counsel the king and the Chancellor of this court in all things concerning the same to the best of your cunning, wit, and power, and with all speed and diligence from time to time at the calling of the said Chancellor you shall endeavour yourself for the hearing and determination indifferently of such matters and causes as shall depend before the said Chancellor, and that you shall not take any gift or reward in any matter or cause depending in the same court or elsewhere wherein the king shall be party whereby the king's majesty shall be hurted, hindered, or disinherited, and further do all and every thing that shall appertain to your office, so help you God and all Saints. Also that every of the said Auditors shall take a corporal oath before the said Chancellor after the tenor ensuing: You shall swear that you shall well and truly serve the king in your office and true allowance make to every person which shall be account[able] before you, you shall not take or receive of poor or rich any gift or reward in any matter or cause depending to be discussed in the same court but such as shall be your ordinary fees, and you shall do all and every other thing which shall appertain to your office, so help you God and all Saints. Also that every of the said particular Receivers shall take a corporal oath before the said Chancellor after the tenor ensuing: You shall swear that you truly shall serve the king in your office and nothing conceal, but true account make of all such revenues, rents, sums of money, and other profits wherewith you shall be lawfully charged by reason of your office, you shall make no petition nor ask allowance but such as shall be good, just, and true and reasonable, and you shall do all and every thing and things which you ought to do by reason of your office according to the form and effect of this act, so help you God and all Saints. Also that the said Clerk of the Council [*sic*] shall take a corporal oath before the said Chancellor after the tenor ensuing: You shall swear that you shall well and truly serve the king in your office of Clerk of the Council of this court and truly do and execute all and every thing and things which you ought to do by reason of your office according to the form and effect of this act, so help you God and all Saints.

V   Also be it enacted by authority aforesaid that all the said monasteries, priories and other religious houses which be dissolved and [be] come or shall come to the king's highness by the act aforesaid, and all the manors, [messuages], lands, tenements, rents, services, tithes, pensions, portions, advowsons, patronages, and all hereditaments appertaining or belonging to any [of] the said monasteries, priories, or other religious houses shall be in the order, survey and governance of the said court, and of the officers and ministers thereof, and all the farms, issues, revenues and profits coming and growing of the premises or any part thereof shall be taken and received to the king's use by the ministers and officers of the same court, in manner and form as hereafter shall be declared, except always and reserved such and as many of the same monasteries . . . which the king's majesty by his letters patent under his great seal shall declare and limit to continue . . . as they were before the working of the said act.

VI   Also be it enacted by authority aforesaid that all those manors, lands, tenements, and hereditaments which the king's highness hath purchased and now remain in his Grace's hands, or in the hands or possession of any person or persons to his use, and [all those] which hereafter his highness shall purchase, shall be and remain in the order, survey, and governance of the said court in form as is above rehearsed.

VII   Also be it enacted by authority aforesaid that all gifts, grants, releases, confirmations, leases, letters patent, and other writings which shall be in the name of the king's highness, his heirs or successors, of any estate of freehold only,[2] or for any term of years, or at will, or at pleasure, of any manors, lands, tenements, or other hereditaments whatsoever they be which be before assigned to the order, survey and governance of the said court, or of any rent charges, annuities, next avoidance of advowsons, offices, or wards to be given, [leased], or granted out of the same or any part thereof or by any means concerning the said court or any of the premises committed to the survey of the said court, to any person or persons or bodies politic, or of any office appertaining or belonging to the said court of Augmentations, shall be made by the Clerk of the said court or his deputy or deputies and [be] subscribed with his own proper hand and name, and sealed with the great seal assigned to and for the said court. And that all and every such

[2] i.e. life grants only: for grants in fee see section VIII.

gifts . . . shall be good and effectual in the law, without livery and seisin or attornment, against the king's highness, his heirs, and successors, according to the tenor, purport and effect of such gifts, grants [etc.]. And that the said Chancellor upon every warrant to be directed to him under the king's sign manual shall have power and authority to cause to be made, by the said Clerk of the said court or his deputy or deputies in due order and form, all such gifts, grants [etc.] according to the tenor and effect of every such warrant which to him shall be directed, and to seal all such patents and writings with the great seal remaining in his custody. The said Chancellor and other officers to take for his and their fees for the ensealing and writing of every patent such fee or fees as is taken by the Chancellor or other officer or officers of the king's Duchy of Lancaster in like case. . . . Also the said Chancellor by the consent of the Treasurer, Attorney, and Solicitor, or two of them, without any warrant from the king's highness, shall have power and authority to make any woodsales in or upon any [of] the manors . . . , and shall also have like power and authority in the king's name to make leases for terms of 21 years and not above by letters patent to be written by the same Clerk of the same court and his deputy or deputies, and the name of the said Clerk to be subscribed as is aforesaid, and to be sealed with the said great seal, of any of the manors [etc.] . . . the said Chancellor and other officer or officers taking for his or their fees thereof as is aforesaid. . . . Provided always that upon every such lease to be made by the said Chancellor there shall be reserved to the king's highness and to his heirs so much yearly rent and profit as the lands, tenements, or hereditaments comprised in such leases have been [let] heretofore, or more, or after such yearly value as they shall be certified by the king's commissioners[3] into the said court. Provided also that no leases for term of years shall be made of any reversion without the king's special warrant for the same. Also the said Clerk of the said court shall enroll and register in a great book in parchment all and every [of] those gifts, grants, releases, confirmations, leases, letters patent, and all other writings which shall be made and granted under the great seal and also the day, time and year of the surrender of any of them when any such surrender shall happen, which register of enrolments shall remain and be safely kept in the said court as a record to the king's use by the appointment of the said Chancellor. And that also the said Clerk shall enter in a book the appearances of every person that shall be called to appear before the said Chancellor, and all acts, decrees, and orders that shall be made by the said Chancellor and Council, taking such fees for the same and for writing and enrolling of any gifts, grants [etc.] as the clerk of the Duchy of Lancaster hath been accustomed to take and have.

VIII   Also it is enacted by authority aforesaid that upon all and singular

[3] Those appointed to dissolve, i.e. to take the surrenders of, monasteries.

letters patent to be made under the great seal of England of any manors, lands, tenements, and hereditaments belonging or appertaining to any of the said houses comprised in the said act and committed to the survey of the said court, to any person or persons or body politic, for any estate of inheritance, there shall be always reserved to the king's highness, his heirs and successors a tenure by knight service [in chief] and a yearly rent of the tenth part of the yearly value of the lands to be comprised in every such letter patent, according to such rate as the same manors, lands, and tenements given shall be expressed to be of yearly value in the same letter patent, any thing or clause contained in any warrant to the contrary thereof notwithstanding, and that the said rent so reserved upon any such estate shall be contented and paid to the officers of the said court [of Augmentations] to the king's use according as other revenues there shall be paid, and that none avowal shall be made or admitted by or for the king or any other person that the same manors, lands, and tenements be of more yearly value than in the same letters patent shall be declared.

IX   Also the said Chancellor shall have power and authority to take recognisances of every particular Receiver which shall be assigned for the said court, and of his sureties, for the sure payment of his receipts, and . . . of every farmer, bailiff, reeve, or other accountants for the true payment of receipts, and of every person and persons which shall be indebted to the king's highness for any arrearages of his receipt, farm, or charge, or for any other cause for and concerning any of the premises. And that all such recognisances, of what sum soever they be, shall be good and effectual in the law to all intents and purposes as recognisances taken in the king's Chancery or elsewhere before any Judge of Record.

X   Also it is ordained by authority aforesaid that the Chancellor of the same court for the time being shall have full power and authority to award writs of *Scire facias*[4] under the great seal of his office upon every such recognisance in the said court to be taken, if case so require, and to hold pleas upon the same and to award execution, to all intent and purposes as is used and accustomed to be done in the king's high court of Chancery. Provided always that if any issue of trial, triable by the verdict of twelve men, fortune to arise in the pleading of the same, that then in every such case the said Chancellor shall and may deliver the record thereof to the Justices of the King's Bench for the time being, and thereupon the said court of the King's Bench to do everything for the trial of the same issue as they ought to do in case the said issue or trial had been sent or delivered to them out of the king's court of Chancery. And after the trial thereof in due form had, and the judgement thereupon given, the Justices of the King's Bench to have power

----

[4] Writs summoning persons to appear before the court to show cause why action should not be taken against them.

to award execution accordingly, and the money thereof coming to be delivered by the same Justices, or clerk of the papers of the same court, to the Treasurer of the said court of Augmentations to the king's use.

XI   Also that the said Chancellor for the time being shall have full power and authority to award, under the privy seal appointed to the said court, in the king's name, such process and precepts with reasonable pains to be therein limited as be now commonly used in the court of the king's Duchy Chamber of Lancaster being at Westminster, against every person or persons, whatsoever they be, for and concerning the interest, right and title of the king's majesty, his heirs, and successors, of, in, or to any of the premises limited to the survey and governance of the said court, or of or for any rent, account, receipt, or services in any wise touching or concerning the same premises or any part of them, for and on behalf of our said sovereign lord the king, or of or for any debt rising or growing by occasion of the same.

XII   Also it is ordained by the authority aforesaid that the said Attorney and Solicitor shall diligently from time to time attend upon the Chancellor in the said court for the hearing and ordering of matters and causes in the said court, and procure with all diligence that all rents, farms, [etc.] . . . shall be truly and justly paid and answered to the Treasurer of the said court for the use of the king's highness, without concealing any part thereof, and shall also cause and procure process to be made against such as shall be indebted to the king's highness and their sureties of and for any part thereof from time to time as the time and case shall require.

XIII   Also it is enacted by authority aforesaid that if any of the said officers appointed for the same court do conceal or withdraw willingly any rents, revenues, casualties, or other goods given to the king by the said act, that then the officer so offending shall lose the double value of the thing so concealed or withdrawn.

XIV   And it is ordained and enacted by authority aforesaid that every of the said particular Auditors and Receivers shall be attendant upon the said Chancellor from time to time as causes shall require, and that every of the said particular Receivers shall well and diligently and effectually gather and levy to the king's use all such farms, issues, and profits as shall be limited to his charge and distrain for the same if need so require. And that every of the said particular Receivers and Auditors so joined together by the appointment of the said Chancellor shall well and truly survey all manner of [repairs] needful to be done in or upon any of the said manors, lands, tenements, or hereditaments limited to his charge and appoint the said [repairs] to be done to the king's most profit and least charge, and also to survey the woods limited to their charge, and what wood sales shall be convenient to be made, and make certificate of the premises from time to time to the said Chancellor.

XV   Also it is ordained by authority aforesaid that all the rents, [etc.] ... as they shall grow due and be payable, shall be paid and delivered to the hands of the said Treasurer by every of the said particular Receivers, to be safely kept to the king's use. And that every acquittance which shall be subscribed with the name and hand of the said Treasurer made to any of the said particular Receivers, or to any person or persons whereby [it] shall appear that the said Treasurer shall have received of any of the said particular Receivers or other person or persons any of the farms, rents, issues, and profits in the charge of the said particular Receivers, or for any debt that shall be done to the king's highness by occasion of the premises or any part thereof, or for any sums of money which the said Treasurer shall have power to receive to the king's use by reason of his office, and all other acquittances made by any of the said particular Receivers to any [person whatsoever] of any thing touching the premises appointed to him or their charge, shall be a good and effectual discharge for every of the said particular Receivers and other [persons whatsoever] aforesaid against the king's highness, his heirs, and successors for ever.

XVI   Also it is ordained that the said Treasurer shall yearly account before the said Chancellor and such two or more of the said Auditors as the said Chancellor shall appoint. And that every of the said particular Receivers shall yearly account before one of the said ten Auditors to be assigned to him by the said Chancellor,[5] and that every of the said particular Receivers for the year to be ended at the feast of St Michael the Archangel shall make and finish his account before the 20th day of March next after the same feast ensuing, and that the Treasurer shall yearly finish his account before the last day of April next after that following.

XVII   Also it is enacted by authority aforesaid that the said Chancellor, by consent of the said Treasurer, Attorney, and Solicitor, or two of them, shall divide to every particular Receiver such portion as every of them shall receive of the said religious houses, manors, lands, tenements, and all other hereditaments aforesaid, and shall also proportion the said religious houses and other the premises in ten parts and shall assign to every part thereof one of the said ten Auditors.[6] And that every of the said ten Auditors, as they shall be assigned, shall yearly ride to the part to him to be limited between the feast of St Michael the Archangel and Christmas, and take the accounts of all bailiffs, reeves, farmers, tenants, and occupiers of the manors, lands, tenements, and other hereditaments within the limits of his assignment.

XVIII   Also it is enacted by authority aforesaid that the said Auditors

[5] See section XVII and note.

[6] Both Auditors and Receivers were, in their patents of appointment, allotted certain areas: see Introduction, pp. 92–3.

and particular Receivers at all times upon warning given to them by the said Chancellor shall assemble together, as well for the ordering of the said religious houses, manors, lands, tenements, and other the premises as of the tenants of the same, from time to time as the case shall require, as [well as] for the viewing and determination of the said account to be made thereof.

XIX   Also it is ordained by authority aforesaid that all the accounts of every year to be ended at the feast of St Michael the Archangel, as well of the said particular Receivers, bailiffs, reeves, farmers, tenants, and occupiers of the said houses, manors, lands, tenements, and other hereditaments aforesaid as of the said Treasurer, shall be well and perfectly engrossed in parchment by the said Auditors and delivered to the said Chancellor safely to be kept to the king's use every year yearly [sic] before the first day of May next ensuing the said feast of St Michael the Archangel, upon pain to forfeit and lose their offices.

XX[7]   [The Auditors and other officers of the court to have such 'diets, rewards, profits, and commodities' and expenses as do the officers of the duchy of Lancaster.]

XXI   Also it is ordained by authority aforesaid that all reparations and building which shall be done from time to time in or upon any [of] the premises shall be done and made by order and commandment of the said Chancellor, by the consent of the said Treasurer, Attorney, and Solicitor, or two of them. And that the said Treasurer from time to time upon his account shall be allowed, as well of such fee as shall be limited unto him for exercise of his office, as of and for all such sums of money as he shall pay to any patentee or patentees of any office, fee, or annuity that shall be granted or given under the seal of the said court, and also of all such sums of money as he shall pay to any other person or persons by virtue of the king's warrant or bill assigned, and also of such sums of money as he shall be commanded to pay by any bill assigned and subscribed with the hands of the said Chancellor, Attorney, and Solicitor, or two of them, upon such considerations as shall be thought convenient by their discretions. And that the said Auditors taking the accounts of the said Treasurer or of any of the said particular Receivers shall have power and authority to allow to the Treasurer the premises, and every part thereof, and also to allow to every particular Receiver and other accountants as well their fees and wages, and all other such sums of money as they or any of them shall pay for, in, and about any building or reparations, as [well as] all other honest and reasonable petitions and allowances, in as large and ample manner and after such form, fashion, and condition as the king's auditors of his Duchy of

---

[7] Sections xx–xxiv in the original engrossment are on a separate sheet, headed by the King's sign manual. They all concern various 'loose ends' which clearly emerged after the main provisions had been completed.

Lancaster do, may do, or have been accustomed to do, without any bill or warrant to be sued for the same.

XXII   Also it is enacted by authority aforesaid that all manner of process that shall be made out of the king's Exchequer to or against any person or persons for any farms, rents, issues, or profits concerning the premises or any part thereof limited by this act to be in the survey, order, and governance of the said court and the ministers thereof shall be clearly void and of none effect.

XXIII   Also it is ordained and enacted by authority aforesaid that the said Chancellor and Treasurer shall yearly declare to the king's highness the state of the clear yearly value of the said houses, manors, lands, tenements, rents, pensions, reversions, and other hereditaments, and how, where, and to whom [the revenues] be employed, and what remaineth thereof in the hands of the said Treasurer.

XXIV   Provided always and be it enacted by the authority aforesaid that all such manors, messuages, lands, tenements, rents, reversions, and other hereditaments which in any manner of wise shall come to, or be in the hands or possession of, our said sovereign lord the king, his heirs, or successors by authority of the said former act of parliament, set, lying, and being as well within the county palatine of Lancaster, as [well as] all other manors, lands, tenements, rents, reversions, and hereditaments, with their commodities and appertenances, set, lying, and being within this realm of England, Wales, or either of them out of the said county palatine, which be or were appertaining or belonging unto the said monasteries or any of them, which were of the foundation of our said sovereign lord [the king], or of any of his right noble progenitors as Duke or Dukes of Lancaster, may, at the free will, liberty, and pleasure of our said sovereign lord, be assigned, limited, and appointed unto the order, surveying, receipt, letting, and setting of the chancellor and officers of his said Duchy of Lancaster, in as large and ample manner and form as the said chancellor and officers of the said Duchy have, use, and exercise at this present time of, upon, and in any manors, lands, tenements, or hereditaments appertaining or in any wise belonging unto the said Duchy, this act or any thing therein contained to the contrary notwithstanding.

26. Ministers' Accounts

(a) From the roll of accounts of the Bailiffs and Collectors of Rents of the lands of the late monastery of Cockersand, Lancashire, and others, Michaelmas 1538 to Michaelmas 1539: PRO, Special Collections, Ministers' Accounts, Henry VIII (SC 6), 7304, printed, in translation from the Latin, in W. Farrer, *Chartulary of Cockersand Abbey*, iii, pt. 3, Chetham Society, NS 64, 1909, pp. 1182–90. The Premonstratensian Abbey of Cockersand was dissolved on 29 January 1539 (*LP*, XIV i, 163). John Kechyn, lately the abbey's Receiver, acted as a special local Receiver for the Cockersand lands and accounted for them to William Blithman, Augmentations Receiver for the bishopric of Durham and the archdeaconry of Richmond.

[m. 1] . . . .

THE LATE ABBEY OF COCKERSAND: The account of John Kechyn . . . for the farm of the site of the late monastery, with the demesne lands, and of the grange called Pilling, with lands belonging, late in the occupation of the said monastery, £33 6s 8d, but he does not account because they have been let by the Crown to John Burnell and Robert Gardiner;[1] nor for £40 being the farm of the rectory of Garstang belonging to the late monastery, with the glebe, tithes and other commodities, also let by the Crown, to John Burnell and Robert Gardiner . . . as follows:

Indenture made between Henry VIII, King of England [etc.] on the one part, and John Burnell and Robert Gardiner on the other part, witnesseth that the King, by the advice and consent of the council of his court of Augmentations, has granted and to farm demised to John and Robert the site of the monastery of Cockersand now dissolved, with all houses, buildings, barns, gardens, orchards . . . and two crofts of arable land called Lez Crokes, one croft of land called Le Rye Croft containing 22 acres and three closes of moor, moss, and pasture called Le Mylne Pasture, Le Mosse Close and Bagger Close, containing 24½ acres, and the pasture called Lez Pilling, together with all common rights, commodities, and profits to the premises belonging, lying in the parish of Garstang, late in the abbot's own occupation and reserved to his use, also the rectory of Garstang appropriated to the late monastery and all manner of tithes, oblations, profits, and emoluments belonging to the rectory; reserving to the King all large trees and woods growing upon the premises and also the advowson of the vicarage of Garstang[2] and all

---

[1] The rent was paid direct to the Receiver, William Blithman. In 1544 Kechyn bought the site, etc.: *LP* XVIII ii, 241, g. 2.

[2] The next presentation had been granted by the abbey in 1538 to John Kechyn: *VCH Lancs.* VII, p. 297.

such buildings within the site of the late monastery which the King shall hereafter cause to be pulled down and carried away; to hold to John and Robert and their assigns from the feast of St Michael the Archangel last past for the term of 21 years, rendering yearly at the aforesaid court of Augmentations £73 6s 8d, namely for the site of the late monastery and the lands £33 6s 8d, and for the rectory £40,[3] at the feasts of the Annunciation of the Blessed Virgin Mary and St Michael the Archangel by equal portions. The said John and Robert are to be discharged of all rents, fees, annuities, pensions, portions, and sums of money payable out of the premises except the rent reserved; all the houses and buildings to be sufficiently repaired and maintained, in timber only, during the said term, by John and Robert, who shall lawfully take upon the premises sufficient hedgebote, firebote, ploughbote and cartbote every year necessary to be expended there. Dated at Westminster 28 March in the 30th year of King Henry VIII [1539]

Courts: No profits from pleas or perquisites of courts arose this year

Sum total of the farm: £73 6s 8d, charged in the account of William Blithman, the King's Receiver there

[m. 1d.] MITTON RECTORY, Yorkshire: The account of Thomas Burgoyne, farmer there . . . by letters patent as follows [*in English*]: Indenture made 20 September . . . [1538] between the abbot of the monastery of Our Blessed Lady St Mary the Virgin of Cockersand in the county of Lancaster and the convent of the same place on the one part, and Thomas Burgoyne gentleman, one of the King's auditors of his duchy of Lancaster, on the other part, witnesseth that the said abbot and convent . . . have granted and to farm let . . . to the said Thomas all that their rectory and parsonage of the parish church of Mitton . . . with all tithes of corn, hay, hemp, flax, wool, and lambs . . . all offerings, mortuaries, and other spiritual profits, emoluments, and commodities . . . and the advowson of the vicarage . . . to hold from the feast of St Michael the Archangel now next coming . . . unto the end and term . . . of four score and one years . . . paying therefor yearly . . . thirty and five pounds[4] of lawful English money at the feasts of St Lawrence the Martyr [10 August] and St Nicholas the Bishop [6 December] in winter . . . by even portions, the first day of payment thereof to begin at the feast of St Nicholas next coming . . . the same Thomas being discharged from the payment of all rents, farms, pensions . . . and the said abbot and convent shall well and sufficiently repair, sustain, maintain, and keep the chancel of the church of Mitton aforesaid and the quire, chapel, and all other houses and buildings as oft as need shall require

---

[3] In 1535 the site and demesnes were valued at £6 10s and the rectory at £19: *VE* v, p. 261.

[4] In 1535 Mitton rectory was valued at £26 16s 8d: *loc. cit.*

during the said term ... [clauses of protection in respect of any leases previously granted, of distress, re-entry for non-payment of rent, etc.][5]

Sum £35

Discharge of Rent: In discharge of rent due on the feast of St Nicholas the Bishop because the feast fell before the last day of January ... [1539] on which day the monastery came to the King's hands by reason of surrender, and so in discharge £17 10s.

Pensions:[6] In pension to Thomas Kellett, perpetual vicar there, at £13 6s 8d a year, namely in allowance of such pension for the terms of Easter, the Nativity of Saint John the Baptist, and St Michael the Archangel which fall within the time of this account, £10; and in pension to Giles Parker, chaplain and curate of the church or chapel of Waddington within the said parish at 26s 8d a year; and in pension to the archbishop of York at 40s a year according to the agreement made upon the appropriation of the rectory, payable at the feast of Saint Michael only, in allowance of such pension, 40s; ... to the Dean and Chapter of York ... 20s; ... to the deacons of York ... 20s; ... to the archdeacon of York, 7s 6d; and to the archbishop of York, 4s, for sinodals and procurations due on the feasts of Easter and Saint Michael the Archangel; ... to the said Dean and Chapter out of the rectory ... payable at Easter only, in allowance 7s 6d; and in money yearly paid in buying bread and wine used within the parish church there in celebration of divine service, at 20s yearly, in allowance for three-quarters of a year falling within the time of this account ... 15s

Sum £17 8d.

Delivery of Money: Delivered to John Kechyn, the King's Receiver there, by his recognisance, 9s 4d

Sum   9s 4d

Sum of allowance and delivery £35, which corresponds with the sum of receipts

[m. 2d.] MANOR OF WEST HOUGHTON: the account of Sir Thomas Langton, farmer there ...

Free farms ... 32s; Farm of the manor ... with all lands, and with burgages, etc. in the town of Preston in Amounderness, ... [let by the abbot for 99 years to Sir Thomas Langton, knight, of Walton in le Dale, for a fine of 100 marks and rent of £55 14s 11½d][7]

Sum total £57 6s 11½d

---

[5] Burgoyne's lease was challenged and in August 1540 he was granted a new one by the Crown for 21 years: LP xv, 1032, p. 557.

[6] There is a note in the margin that these will have to be confirmed by the court of Augmentations.

[7] The date of this lease must have been within a year of the dissolution of Cockersand for it was called in question and annulled by the court of Augmentations, Langton having admitted that the customary 100 hens had been omitted from the rent: Haigh, Lancashire Monasteries, pp. 110–11, 127–8.

Discharge of rents . . . because they fell due before the day of the surrender of the late monastery . . . Total £29 9s 5¾d
Reward: In allowance to the auditor's clerk for writing this account, 2s
Delivery of Money: In money charged upon Thomas Langton knight
as part of the farm of the manor of West Houghton, unpaid on this
account, 55s 5¾d

Delivered to John Kechyn, the King's Receiver there, £25

Total £27 15s 5¾d

Sum of allowances and delivery, £57 6s 11½d, which sum corresponds
with the receipts

[m. 3, *inter alia*, contains the text of a lease by the abbey on 16 November
1537 to Henry Audley of St Albans of the manor of Hutton, for 99 years,
at a rent of £23 18s 3d during his life and £30 11s 7d for the remainder
of the term from his heirs or assigns.[8]
m. 4 contains the text of a lease by the abbey on 3 September 1538 to
Sir Robert Hesketh of Rufforth, Lancashire, of property in Tarleton
and Sullam, for 99 years, for a fine of 20 marks and the customary
rent of £4 19s 8½d. Hesketh had also obtained a 61-year lease of
another messuage in Tarleton 'in consideration of divers large sums
of money paid to the abbot and convent . . . towards the repair of their
monastery'.]

(b) From the accounts of the Bailiffs, etc., of the lands of the late priory
of Bath, Somerset, Michaelmas 1538 to Michaelmas 1539: PRO, SC 6,
3144. The priory surrendered on 27 January 1539: *LP* XIV i, 148.
[Translated from Latin]

[m. 19d.] MANOR OF COMBE: The account of Edith Pole, bailiff . . .
Assized rents: .   .   .   .   .   Total:-   £7 19s 10d
Farm of the manor: And for £7 14s 4d for the farm of the barn of the
manor of Combe . . . [etc., as in lease of 1528, Doc. 2] as let to William
Pole, his wife Edith, and their son Thomas for their lives and that of the
longest liver, Viz:- the price of 16 quarters of corn @ 5s 4d, 65s 4d;
22 quarters of barley @ 2s 8d, 58s 8d; the price of the carriage of wood
@ 16d a load, 5s 4d; the price of feeding one ox . . . 5s; and £6 for the
farm of the flock of 360 sheep . . . Total, £13 14s 4d
Rents in kind: And for 3s 9d . . . the price of 32 hens @ 1½d collected
from the tenants by ancient custom . . . 3s 9d
Perquisites of court: .   .   .   .   .   .   nil

Total   £21 17s 11d

Allowed on the same account for cash delivered to the use of the priory

---

[8] It was sold to a Berkshire man in 1546: Haigh, p. 127.

o

from this manor for the Christmas term before the time of the dissolution of the same on the oath of the accountant [Edith Pole], £5 13s 5d
And she owes £16 4s 6d

The account for 1539–40 (*ibid.*, 3145) shows Edith Pole, who had
presumably outlived both her husband and her son, paying up in full,
including the arrears.

(c) From the roll of accounts of the Bailiffs, Farmers, Collectors of Rents,
etc., of lands administered by the court of Augmentations in the
county of Warwick, Michaelmas 1546 to Michaelmas 1547: Birming-
ham Reference Library, Roll 168255, printed in translation by
W. B. Bickley, Dugdale Society, II, 1923, pp. 84–90. The Particular
Receiver for Leicestershire, Northants., Rutland, and Warwickshire
was George Gifford. This roll contains the accounts not only of what
remained with the Crown of the lands of the former Warwickshire
religious houses but also, for the first time, the accounts of property
in the county belonging to houses elsewhere, and of attainted and
other Crown lands: see Introduction, p. 94.

[m. 22] MEREVALE, late monastery in the county of Warwick: Lands and
possessions of the same late monastery of Merevale . . . the account of
Nicholas Alcock, bailiff there, by Amyas Hill his deputy . . . Arrears:
none, because this is the first account since the [re-]establishment of the
court aforesaid.[1]

Rents and farms within the town and lordship of Mancetter, with the
rectory there:

But he answers for 49s 4d for rents of tenants at will of the lord there,
viz. of one messuage with garden adjacent in the tenure of John King,
8s; of one cottage with garden in the tenure of Robert Fossecote, 3s; of
one cottage with garden adjacent let to John Chekley, 4s; . . . and for
16s 8d for the farm of one pasture or close there . . . with appertenances,
as let by indenture under the conventual seal of the said late monastery,
dated 19 March 21 Henry VIII [1530] to one Robert Greene for term
of 43 years . . .; and for 4s for the farm of one cottage . . . let to Richard
Alein by conventual indenture dated 12 April 28 Henry VIII [1537] for
a term of 61 years . . .; and for 6s 8d for the farm of one close there let
to John Glover by conventual indenture . . . 14 March 14 Henry VIII
[1523] for a term of 40 years; . . . and for 30s for the farm of a tenement
lying on Watling Street on the west side near the end of the bridge of
Witherley with garden, orchard and two closes . . . as let to Alice Glover,

---

[1] The court of Augmentations was itself dissolved in 1547 and re-erected in
amalgamation with the court of General Surveyors. Outstanding arrears were
dealt with separately.

late wife of John Glover, and John Glover her son by conventual indenture 12 January 26 Henry VIII [1535] for a term of 62 years; . . . and for
12s for the farm of one croft . . . lying near the Cross, let to William
Ludford by conventual indenture 3 June 30 Henry VIII [1538] for a
term of four score years; . . . and for 40s for the farm of all tithes of
grain accruing within the lordship of Hartshill . . . as let to William
Findern by conventual indenture dated 12 March 25 Henry VIII [1524]
to hold during the life of the same William and for one year after his
decease (which William yet lives) and after his death to the aforesaid
William Ludford for a term of four score years; . . . and for £20 11s 4d
for the farm of . . . the rectory of Mancetter as let to farm to Amyas
Hill, gentleman, by indenture under the sale of the court of Augmentations dated 28 July 36 Henry VIII [1544] for a term of 21 years . . .

Total   £31 3s 4d

Kingsbury, Curdworth and Shernford   .   .   3s 6d
[The site and demesne of the late abbey, rents detailed, but he answers
only for the rent of £27 3s 10d reserved in the Crown grant of the
property on 2 December 1540 to Sir Walter Devereux, lord Ferrers]

Total   £27 3s 10d

[m. 23] Court profits: .   .   .   .   Total nothing

Sum total of the charge £58 10s 8d, from which [he claims allowance
for his own fee, £4; that of a clerk, 4s; payments for bread, wine, wax,
and oil for the church at Mancetter, 6s 8d; for deliveries of cash to
William Sheldon, Receiver, £52 19s 11d; and for repairs this year, 20s.
There follows a list of former Merevale property in other counties for
which he no longer answers.]

27. Receivers' Accounts

(a) The account of John Scudamore, one of the Particular Receivers of the court of Augmentations, for the county of Hereford, to Michaelmas 1536: PRO, Exchequer, Augmentations Office, Miscellaneous Books (E 315), 278, fos. 134–152. The entries relating to Clifford, a Cluniac priory, are given virtually in full, the rest in summary only. Monmouth lay outside the county but within the diocese of Hereford. [Translated from Latin]

[fo. 134] THE OFFICE OF RECEIVER OF SUPPRESSED LANDS IN THE COUNTY OF HEREFORD

The account of John Scudamore esquire, ... for one whole year, together with a declaration of all goods, grain, cattle, money and jewels, debts, lead, and bells appertaining to the same late religious houses at the time of their suppression, as appears below:

ARREARS: None, because this is the first account

MONMOUTH: Rents and farms ... £49 16s 2d; [fo. 135] Movable goods and silver plate ... £16 6s 11½d; Debts [due to the house] ... £30 15s 2d; Lead and bells ... £11 6s

MONASTERY OF DORE: Rents and farms ... £100 7s; [fo. 136] Movable goods and silver plate ... £71 9s 8¾d; Debts ... £5 15s 8d; Superfluous buildings sold by the commissioners to John Scudamore esquire ... £4; [fo. 137] Lead and bells ... £24 1s 8d

CLIFFORD: Rents and Farms: And he is charged with £7 5s 3d received per Nicholas Hugh, late prior of Clifford, from the issues and profits of Hardwick with 'le Heye', including £6 5s 3d received per the lord prior from the tenants and farmers there and 20s from multure [*payment for grinding*] from a certain mill occupied by and reserved in the hands of the said prior, as appears in his account thereof, exhibited and examined, and due since the aforesaid act [of suppression]. And he is likewise charged with 71s 6½d received per the aforesaid late prior from the issues and profits of the foreign bailliwick of Clifford in the county of Hereford per the hands of the tenants and farmers there, due since the act of suppression ... And he is charged with £11 10d received per the aforesaid prior from the issues and profits of demesne land, including 70s for a meadow called 'le Bache meadow' and £7 10s 10d [for land] in the hands of the said prior and unbuilt upon ... And he is charged with £15 9s 4d received per the abovenamed prior from the issues and profits of the rectories of Bronllys and Llandefalle [*Co. Brecon*] per the hands of William Vaughan esquire, farmer there, including 100s due before the act of suppression and £10 9s 4d rent due after the act ...

And he is likewise charged with £10 received per the abovenamed prior from the issues and profits of the rectory of Frampton [-on-Severn, Gloucs.] per the hands of the farmer there, including 100s due before the act of suppression and 100s due since the act . . . And he is charged with £13 7s received per the said prior from the issues and profits of the rectory of Clifford per the hands of the tenant and farmer there, including 16s 8d due before the act and £12 10s 4d rent due since the said act of suppression . . . And he is charged with 29s 4d received per the abovenamed prior from the issues and profits of the tenants and farmers in Siefton and Hylhall in the county of Shropshire due since the said act, [all of which] as appears in his [the prior's] accounts thereof made, exhibited, and examined: Total   £62 3s 3½d

Movable Goods and Silver Plate: And for £13 4s 10d received by the said Particular Receiver for goods, grain, cattle, ornaments, and other movable goods sold . . . to various persons, including 104s 8d paid to the same Particular Receiver by the hand of James Whiteney and £8 2d . . . by various other persons, as appears more particularly specified in the inventory. And he is charged with £7 15s 9d for part of the goods [etc.] sold to the aforesaid James Whiteney by the aforesaid commissioners, and in the hands of the said James still remaining and not yet paid for, as appears in the said inventory . . . And he is charged with £11 18d for goods, grain, and cattle used by the said late abbot towards the expenses of his household between the survey and the suppression, including 12s 4d for goods deficient and dead of murrain, 10d for the price of one hamper remaining with the evidences of the house aforesaid, and £10 8s 4d for goods, grain, and cattle there used in the period aforesaid, as appears in the said inventory. And for 43s 4¾d received by the abovesaid Receiver, the price of 11¾ ounces of money, jewels and plate, silver, gold, parcel gilt and white, as appears in the inventory aforesaid

.   .   .   .   Total   £34 5s 5¾d

Bells: And he is likewise charged on his account with 36s, for the price of one bell weighing two hundredweight, at 18s the hundredweight, remaining and not yet sold, as appears in the inventory: Total   36s

[fo. 138] ACONBURY: Rents and farms . . . £61 7s 3½d; [fo. 139] Movable goods and silver plate . . . £119 19s ½d; Bells . . . £6 5s; Superfluous buildings sold by the commissioners to John Scudamore, 33s 4d . . .

SUM TOTAL, £611 7s 9¼d, from which [he claims to be allowed]:

[fo. 141] PENSIONS FOR GOVERNORS: The same accounts for an annual pension or rent granted among other things to Thomas Clybery, former abbot of Dore in the county aforesaid, of £16 13s 4d a year granted under convent seal dated 11 February [1525]   .   .   £16 13s 4d

RENTS RECEIVED by the Governors of the suppressed religious houses and due before the act of suppression:

Monmouth £8 11s 8d

Clifford: And in payments to Nicholas Hugh ... by the hands of the farmers and tenants of the rectory of Bronllys and Llandefalle, 100s, and by the hands of the farmer of the rectory of Frampton, 100s, and by the hand of the farmer of the rectory of Clifford, 16s 8d   £10 16s 8d
Aconbury . . . 20s   Total   £20 8s 4d
[fo. 142] ALLOWANCES OF RENTS of divers lands and rectories in the hands of the Governors for the use of their households:
Dore: £17 16d
Clifford: ... 20s for the multure from the watermill in Hardwick together with 70s profit from a meadow called 'le Bache meadow' and £7 10s 10d profit from the site with demesne there, and issues arising, in the period aforesaid converted to the use of the household there, besides certain grain sold to the king's profit as appears in the inventory
.   .   .   .   £12 10d
Aconbury . . . £11 3s 4d   Total   £40 5s 6d
ALLOWANCE OF RENTS AND FARMS received by the Governors of the religious houses suppressed towards the maintenance and support of their households:
Monmouth: ... £37 2s;   Dore: ... £52 8s 10d
[fo. 143] Clifford: And in payments made to Nicholas Hugh, late prior of Clifford aforesaid by the hands of farmers, tenants, and collectors of rents and farms there this year, due since the said act, during the time of this account, in and towards the maintenance, relief, and hospitality of his house there, and charged above among other things as rents of Clifford . . . £39 5s 9½d
Aconbury: ... £38 7s 11d   Total   £167 12s 6½d
EXPENSES OF THE KING'S COMMISSIONERS: And in payments by the said Particular Receiver this year for the costs and expenses of Rowland Moreton, John Scudamore, and Richard Palmer, esquires, and Robert Burgoyne, Auditor, commissioners of the lord King's court of Augmentations [sic] in the county of Hereford aforesaid, riding and residing in various places there ... and also the costs and expenses of John Scudamore esquire, riding from his house in the county of Hereford, [fo. 144] including the carriage of gold plate from Monmouth, Dore, Clifford, and Aconbury to London and delivering it to the Treasurer there of the court of Augmentations, 60s, in all as it appears in the book of detailed expenses of the four commissioners   .   .   .   £37 19s 1d
ALLOWANCES FOR GOODS AND MOVABLE CHATTELS SOLD BY THE GOVERNORS of the aforesaid religious houses between the first survey and the dissolution: Dore: ... £4 10s
ALLOWANCES FOR CATTLE, GRAIN, AND OTHER MOVABLE GOODS USED BY THE GOVERNORS in their household before the dissolution:
Dore: ... £7 2s
Clifford: ... nine young pigs slaughtered, 9s; ... thirteen quarters of

rye, £4 11s 8d; 40½ quarters of oats, £4 12d; and sixteen cartloads of hay, 26s 8d, as appears in the inventory . . . £10 8s 4d

Aconbury: . . . £6 2s   Total   £23 12s 4d

ALLOWANCES FOR BEASTS AND CATTLE DEAD OF MURRAIN, with movable goods deficient and spoiled between the survey and the dissolution: Monmouth: . . . 3s 4d; Dore: . . . 20s 4d; Clifford: . . . one ox, and one horse dead of murrain, 12s 4d; . . . one chest sent to the Treasurer with the evidences, 10d . . . 13s 2d; Aconbury: . . . 59s 6d

Total   £4 16s 4d

ALLOWANCES FOR VARIOUS MOVABLE GOODS given to various people by the aforesaid commissioners: . . . certain ornaments of the church charged in the survey among the movable goods of Aconbury . . . given to the parish church . . . and a vestment worth 15s sent to the Lord President of the Council of the lord King in the Marches of Wales at the King's castle of Wigmore . . . 26s

PAYMENTS TO THE RELIGIOUS AND THEIR SERVANTS with their liveries due at the dissolution of houses of religious: Dore: . . . to four religious, 66s 8d and to 15 servants there, 108s 7d; [fo. 146] Clifford: . . . to two religious, 25s, and to 11 servants there, 103s 11d; Aconbury: . . . to six nuns, 45s 6d, and to 16 servants there, 103s 5d

REWARDS from the lord King to the religious and their servants: Dore: . . . five religious, £6 13s 4d, and 14 [sic] servants 17s 4d . . .

Clifford: And in rewards of the said lord King aforesaid given to the religious and the servants of the late priory of Clifford . . . by the Particular Receiver, by consent of the commissioners aforesaid, that is to say, to two monks, 60s, and to ten servants there, 16s 8d . . .

Aconbury: . . . six nuns, £7 6s 8d and sixteen servants, including a certain decrepit woman, 36s

Total   £20 10s

PAYMENTS TO THE GOVERNORS and other persons at the time of the dissolution for the expenses of their households between the survey and the dissolution: Dore: . . . 100s 4½d;

Clifford: in payments made by the said Particular Receiver with the assent of the commissioners . . . for the diet, costs, and expenses of the household, including 5s paid to Robert Game for things necessary for the church . . . 102s 5d; [fo. 147] Aconbury . . . £7 3s 11d

Total   £17 6s 8½d

DEBTS of the religious houses: Dore: . . . £4 14s 10d; Clifford: . . . £4 5s

Total   £8 19s 10d

NECESSARY EXPENSES: . . . carrying letters, 5s; purchase of parchment and paper, 4s 4d; salary of a clerk, 10s; purchase of bags for the ministers' accounts, 2s; purchase of money bags, 2s 4d; costs and expenses of the Particular Receiver riding from his house in the county of Hereford to London and returning, taking six days at 2s per day, 12s [crossed through]; salary of the Particular Receiver's clerk, 10s; and costs and expenses of the Auditor, Receiver, and other persons at the time of the audit this year at Ross, £11 15s ...

Total £14 8d [amended to £13 8s 8d]

DELIVERY OF GOLD PLATE, JEWELS, AND MONEY to the Treasurer of the foresaid court from the suppressed religious houses in the county of Hereford: ... Clifford: ... gold plate, 3½ oz, parcel gilt, 5¼ oz, white plate, 3 oz ... 43s 4¾d; ... [Total] £36 10s 7¼d

And in the price of a certain ornament of the church delivered to the aforesaid Treasurer from the priory of Monmouth, together with a velvet cope of crimson colour and a pallium of the colour of Baudekyn crimson, valued at 100s and charged in the survey among the movable goods of Monmouth, and from the priory of Aconbury a vestment of cloth of gold ... valued at 66s 8d

Total £44 17s 3d

[fo. 149] TOTAL OF ALLOWANCES AND DELIVERIES aforesaid
£445 3s ¼d [corrected to £444 11s ¼d]
and he owes £166 4s [corrected to 16s] 9d which is charged in his next account under the heading of arrears

RESPITES: . . . . . . Total £12 3s
and there remains besides £154 21d [corrected to £154 13s 9d]

[fo. 150] GOODS, CATTLE, MOVABLE GOODS NOT YET SOLD
. . . . £10 14s 1d
LEAD remaining [on the steeples of Monmouth and Dore priories] 30s
BELLS remaining £32 2s
Total £44 6s 1d
and he owes besides £109 15s 8d [corrected to £110 7s 8d]

[fos. 151–2] Arrears £39 3s 2d

(b) The account of John Aylworth, Particular Receiver of the court of Augmentations, for the county of Devon, Michaelmas 1558 to Michaelmas 1559: PRO, Exchequer, Land Revenue, Receivers' Accounts, Series I (LR 6), 4/6. The account is given in broad outline only except for those parts relating to the property late of Buckfast Abbey which are given in full. [Translated from Latin]

THE ACCOUNT OF JOHN AYLWORTH ESQUIRE, Receiver-General [sic] of all those lordships, manors [etc.] in the governance of the court of Augmentations ... in the county of Devon ... [Michaelmas 1558 to Michaelmas 1559] ARREARS: £374 13s 4d

CASH RECEIPTS IN THE SAID COUNTY OF DEVON: [From lands late of the priory of Totnes, £13 7½d; Cornworthy, £25 2s 2d; St Nicholas, Exeter, £6 11s 10½d; Frithelstock, £18 9s 1¼d; Pilton, £32 14s 2¾d; Barnstaple, £21; Plympton, £92 6s 1½d; St John's, Exeter, £37 5s 5½d]

Buckfast: And he renders account for 32s 4d from Sir Thomas Dennis for the annual tenth for the site of the said late monastery, as reserved in the letters patent of the late King Henry VIII to the same Thomas; and for £68 21½d from James Mawditt, bailiff of the manor of Buckfastleigh from the issues of his office as appears in his account;[1] and for 41s 2½d from John Southcote for the annual tenth for the manor of Kilbury, as reserved . . .; for the issues of the borough and escheated land of Kingsbridge he renders nothing . . .;[2] but he renders account for 37s 1d from John Wotton for the annual tenth of the manor of Englebourne . . .; and 4s 6½d from John Fry for the annual tenth from the manor of Mainbow . . .; and for 31s 4½d from Humphrey Colles for the annual tenth for the manor of Downe [St Mary] . . .; and for £34 2s 1½d from William Edwards, bailiff of the manor of Heathfield for the issues of his office for this year;[3] and for 10s 1½d from Sir Thomas Dennis for the annual tenth of the manor of Brownston . . .; and for 23s 6d from Sir Thomas Dennis for the annual tenth from the manor of Petrockstow as reserved in the letters patent of the late King Henry VIII to Henry Dennis; and for 24s 10d from John Southcote for the annual tenth of the manor of Trusham . . .; for the issues of lands in various places he renders nothing . . .;[4] but he renders account of 2s 10d from John Southcote for the annual tenth of divers tenements in Spitchwick . . . Total £112 10s 9d[5]

[Torre, £23 17s 11d; Polsloe, 119s 1¼d; Hartland, £30 5s 4d; Buckland (including 46s 4d from Richard Grenville [sic] for the site), £23 19s 4½d; Dunkeswell, £75 13s 9½d; Newenham, £94 8s 11½d; Canonsleigh, £14 17s 5d; Forde, £47 17s 2½d; Tavistock, £311 9s 10¼d; Grey Friars, Exeter, 4s; Plymouth, nil;[6] Cleeve (Som.), 104s 8d; Taunton (Som.), £13 6s 8d; Montacute (Som.), 57s 9d; Bridgwater (Som.), 23s; Cannington (Som.), 18s 3d; Barlinch (Som.), 12s; Shaftesbury (Dorset), 20s; Sherborne (Dorset), £4 17s 1d; Breamore (Hants.), 6s 1d; Tewkesbury (Gloucs.), 25s 10½d; St Dogmells (Pembroke), 40s; Lilleshall (Salop.),

[1] According to the corresponding Ministers Accounts (PRO, SC 6/Elizabeth, 490) Mawditt had begun the year with arrears of £12 odd but carried forward at the end only just over £7.

[2] These had been granted to John and Bernard Drake on 4 September 1557, by which time tenths were no longer reserved: Youings, *Devon Monastic Lands*, p. 122.

[3] Edwards carried no arrears and he paid up in full, except for allowances by way of fees and expenses: Ministers Account, *as above*.

[4] Including arrears the sum of 46s 2d was owing.

[5] The account no longer comprehends even the main abbey properties. Sir William Petre had compounded for the rents reserved on his grants of the manors of Brent and Churchstow: Youings, *op. cit.*, pp. 74, 85.

[6] Sums of 26s 8d and 20s were due for the two friaries there for this year and for eighteen previous years: Ministers Account, *as above*.

32s; Studley (Warwicks.), 18s 9d; Syon (Middx.), £47 17s 8d; Merton (Surrey), 28s; Christchurch (London), £25 10s 6d; Quarr (I. of W.), 43s 4d; St John of Jerusalem, 29s 1d; Chantries, £319 6s 9¼d; Richmond lands, £166 4s 6d; Warwick and Spencer Lands, £10 9s 11½d; Glaston-bury (Som.), 54s ½d;   .   .   .   .   .   .   .⁷

SPIRITUAL LANDS AND POSSESSIONS . . .

Buckfast: And he renders account for £11 11s 4d from Richard Avery, farmer of the rectory of Buckfast⁸ from the issues of his farm this year: and for £15 5s 10d from Thomas Southcote, farmer of the rectory of Churchstow with the chapel of Kingsbridge . . .;⁹ and for 75s 4d from Roger Talland, rector of Zeal [Monachorum] and Robert Withbroke, incumbent of the church of Downe [St Mary], for pensions due to the late abbey   Total   £30 12s 6d . . .

                            Sum Total, with arrears: £3,761 12s 10½d [from which he claims to be allowed on account of various payments, largely non-monastic: Fees (£56 2s 8d), Pensions to churches (£31 16s), Annuities (£49 14s 2d) and Charities (£10 8s) and

ANNUAL FEES AND PENSIONS due . . . from . . . lands late of priory of Plympton . . . £199 13s 4d; Tavistock . . . £91 13s 4d; Buckland . . . £87;]

Buckfast: And in a fee to Sir Thomas Dennis, chief steward . . . at £6 13s 4d per annum, John Southcote, steward . . . at 53s 4d per annum, granted for their lives¹⁰ by letters patent by the late abbot and convent there, that is to say, allowed for this year £9 6s 8d; and in annuities, John Whiddon, 26s 8d; Maurice Donath, at £4 per annum, that is for the first half of this year because he died after the feast of the Annunci-ation of the Blessed Virgin Mary, 40s, Thomas Bever, 26s 8d, Robert Fulford, 40s, Edward Jenney, £6 13s 4d, Thomas Wincote, 40s, Richard Dennis, 53s 4d, John Ridgeway, 20s, John Aylworth, 66s 8d, Henry Williams, £6 13s 4d, Humphrey Colles, 40s, John Ashley, 26s 8d, and Mathew Prest, 106s 8d, all granted to the above for their lives by letters patent under the seal and exemplified by the court [of Augmentations] aforesaid,¹¹ that is, allowed for this year, as above, £37 13s 4d; and in pensions paid to divers persons in the late monastery, that is, to John Watts, 106s 8d, Thomas Gill, 100s, granted to them for their lives by

---

⁷ Twelve further, non-monastic, items follow.

⁸ The lease dated from 1 March 1537 and would expire in 1597.

⁹ This lease dated from 30 September 1538 and would run until 1598. The lessee also paid a stipend of £16 13s 4d to the vicar, 13s 4d to the bishop, and 2s to a clerk.

¹⁰ When these appointments had been made, in 1538 and 1537 respectively, each had included the man and his son: Youings, op. cit., p. 137.

¹¹ None of these conventual grants was earlier than November 1537: Youings, op. cit., p. 138.

letters patent dated 26 April ... [1539], that is allowed for this year as
above, £10 6s 8d[12]   [Total]   £57 6s 8d

.   .   .   .   .   .   [Sum] Total £962 11s

DELIVERED to the Exchequer of Receipt ... £200

NECESSARY EXPENSES ... £29 6s 8d

Total of Allowances and Deliveries: £1,339 18s 6d
and he owes   £2,421 14s 4½d

[Further allowances, including arrears of £244 17s 8d, reduce the debit
to £2,027 6s 6½d, for which the Receiver is exonerated pending the
settlement of his liability for the property of the late religious houses in
Somerset]

Winchester[13]   By me, Nicholas Luke

[12] At the time of the dissolution of Buckfast Abbey the total Crown liability
for pensions for the former monks had been £177 13s 4d: *ibid.*

[13] William Paulet, marquess of Winchester, Lord Treasurer of England.

Doc. 28 [p. 220]

[1] Each of the above, all of which had incomes of less than £200 a year, with the
exception of Stixwould, Blanchland, and Alnwick, which the king refounded,
was granted formal exemption by letters patent: *LP* XI, 385, 519, 1217; XII i, 311,
1103; XII ii, 191, 411, 1008; and XIII i, 646. Exemption was also granted to
Chatteris and Denney, Cambridgeshire and Grace Dieu, Leicestershire (*LP* XI,
385); Marrick, Yorks. (*ibid.,* 519); Heynings, Lincs. (*ibid.,* 1217); Studley, Oxon.
(*LP* XII i, 311); Cook Hill, Worcs., and Newcastle, Northumberland (*ibid.,* 795);
Whitland, Carmarthen (*ibid.,* 1105); Neasham, Durham and Burnham, Bucks.
(*LP* XII ii, 411); Swine, Yorks (*ibid.,* 1008); Arthington and Hampole, Yorks
(*LP* XIII i, 646); Kirklees, Yorks., (*ibid.,* 1115); and Nun Appleton, Yorks., (*ibid.,*
1519).

28. Treasurers' Accounts

(a) From the account roll of Thomas Pope, Treasurer of the Court of Augmentations, April 1536 to Michaelmas 1538, a list of fines paid for the exemption of religious houses from the Act of Dissolution of 1536: PRO, Exchequer, Augmentations Office, Treasurers' Accounts (E 323), 1, pt. i (summarized in *LP* XIII ii, 457), m. 4d. [Translated from Latin]

And [he charges himself with] £5,948 6s 8d . . . received in part payment of various sums of money owed to the lord King for fines or compositions . . . for toleration or continuation of monasteries, as follows:

The monastery of Bindon in the county of Dorset,	£300
The monastery of St James in the county of North-ampton,	£333 6s 8d
The monastery of De la Pré in the same county	£266 13s 4d
The monastery of nuns [*St Mary's*] in the city of Winchester	£333 6s 8d
The monastery of Huntingdon,	£133 6s 8d
The monastery of Biddlesden in the county of Buck-ingham,	£133 6s 8d
The monastery of Shap in the county of Westmoreland,	£266 13s 4d
The monastery of Charterhouse [at] Hull in Yorkshire,	£233 6s 8d
The monastery of Kyme in the county of Lincoln,	£200
The monastery of Stixwould in the same county,	£21 13s 4d

[Ulverscroft, Leics., £166 13s 4d; Polsloe, Devon, £400; Canonsleigh, Devon, £200; Newstead, Notts., £233 6s 8d; Beauvale, Notts., £166 13s 4d; Wallingwells, Notts., £66 13s 4d; Neath, Glamorgan, £150; Blanchland, Northumberland, £400; Strata Florida, Cardigan, £66 13s 4d; St Mary's, Chester, £160; Dale, Derbyshire, £166 13s 4d; Repton, Derbys., £266 13s 4d; Wormsley, Herefordshire, £200; Limebrook, Herefordshire, £53 6s 8d; Alnwick, Northumberland, £200; Lacock, Wilts., £300; St Thomas [Baswich], Stafford, £133 6s 8d; Croxden, Staffs., £100; Rocester, Staffs., £100; Hulton, Staffs., £66 13s 4d; Bruisyard, Suffolk, £60; St. Ann's, Coventry, £20; Polesworth, Warwicks., £50][1]

[He does not charge himself with fines unpaid because before the making up of his account all the monasteries concerned have been surrendered by their governors, or have been dissolved by Parliament.]

(b) From the Receipt Books of the Treasurer of the court of Augmen-

[1] See p. 219.

tations, 1540–41, PRO, Exchequer, King's Remembrancer, Misc. Books (E 164), 68.

[fo. 57] Item, received the 22nd day of January [1541] of Sir Richard Williams, alias Cromwell, knight, £666 13s 4d sterling, in part of payment of £2,963 4s 2d residue of the sum of £4,963 4s 2d due unto the king's majesty for the site of the late monastery of Ramsey in the county of Huntingdon, and for the manors of Ramsey [etc., as granted in March 1540: *LP*, xv, 436, g. 20]

. . . .

[fo. 64] Item, received 14 August [1540] of Sir Richard Gresham, knight, £5,537 11s 8d in part of payment of £11,137 11s 8d sterling due to the king's majesty for the gift, grant, and clear purchase of the site and demesnes of the late monastery of Fountains, . . . [etc.] and also for the site of the late monastery or priory of Swine . . . and also for the site of the late monastery of Nunkeeling . . . [as granted in October 1540: *LP*, xvi, 220, g. 2]

. . . .

[fo. 64v.] Item, received 20 November [1540] of Sir Ralph Sadler, knight, by the hands of Henry Whitereson the sum of £300 sterling in part of payment of the sum of £736 sterling due unto the king's majesty for the purchase of the site of the late monastery of Selby . . . [as granted in August 1540, *LP*, xv, 1027, g.40].
Item, received 10 March [1541] . . . [as above] £368 sterling, parcel of the sum of £436 residue of the said sum of £736 . . .[2]

. . . .

[fo. 76] Item, received 9 June [1540] of Augustine Steward, merchant, of Norwich, the sum of £81 sterling, being due to the king's majesty for the purchase of the site and garden of the late Blackfriars within the city of Norwich which the mayor, sheriffs and commonalty of the said city have lately purchased . . . [as granted on 1 June 1540: *LP*, xv, 831, g.72]

. . . .

[fo. 77] Item, received 3 February [1541] of Sir Edmund Bedingfield, knight, one hundred pounds sterling in part of payment of the sum of £161 19s residue of the sum of £561 19s due unto the king's highness for the purchase of the site and demesnes of the late monastery of Redlingfield in the county of Sussex . . . [as granted in March 1537: *LP*, xii i, 795, g.39]

. . . .

(c) From the account roll of Edward North, Treasurer of the court of Augmentations, 1539 to 1543, payments made, and allowed him, in respect of royal warrants: PRO, Exchequer, Augmentations Office,

[2] The date of the final payment has not been traced.

Treasurers' Accounts (E 323), 2B, pt. i, calendared in *LP*, XVIII ii, 231, pp. 123–8. [Translated from Latin]

[m. 80d. 1540–1] . . . And in cash paid by the same to Morgan Wolff, goldsmith . . . by warrant dated 6 January 1541 . . . £200; . . . to the same Morgan Wolff for the price of a chain or collar of gold . . . weighing 32¾ ounces and given to John Coziesleye knight, ambassador of the king of Poland, £73 17s 8½d, together with the price of another gold chain . . . given to a certain gentleman of Scotland for announcing to the king's majesty the birth of the prince of Scotland, £65 2s 6d . . . warrants dated 25 August, 1540 . . .; And in payments made by the said Treasurer to Lord Russell, President of the Lord King's Council in the West Parts . . . for fees and diets . . . for three quarters of a year ending at the feast of the nativity of St John the Baptist [24 June] by virtue of a warrant of the same lord King to the Treasurer . . . dated the last day of March 1539 . . . £927 10s . . . [m. 81 Total for the year, £7,525 4s 9d]
[m. 81d. 1541–2] . . . And in cash paid by the same Treasurer to Robert Acton esquire for various saddles and other stuff delivered by him to the King's Great Wardrobe . . . by warrant dated 12 March 1542 . . . £661 14s 8d; . . . And to Anthony Anthony and Christopher Gould for wages of various captains, lieutenants, deputy keepers and other soldiers of the King at various castles, fortresses, . . . [etc.] amounting to £1,361 15s 6d . . . [for the year 1540–41] and £32 [for 1541–2] . . . by warrant dated 26 June [1541] . . . with receipt dated 24 August [1541] [m. 82 Total payments by royal warrant for the year, £7,067 11s 9d]
[m. 82d. 1542–3] . . . to Henry Coldwell, goldsmith, for working and making five separate seals, that is to say the great seal of Ireland and the seal of the Exchequer of the lord King there, the seals of the King's Bench, Common Pleas and of the Exchequer of the lord King at Westminster, £63 10s 2d, as well as for 144 ounces of silver for the making of the said seals at 3s 8d the ounce, £26 9s 10d . . . in all £100; . . . paid by the Treasurer to the countess of Bridgwater by the hand of Lewis Torfote of London, gentleman, as a reward at the king's special command, . . . by warrant dated 24 February 1542, £66 13s 4d . . .
[m. 83 Total for the year, £6,158 0s 10d]
[m. 84d. Total for 1543–4, £1,703 14s 2½d]
[m. 85 Total payments for the four years, by royal warrant, £37,754 11s 7¼d]

29. Provision for Lay Servants

(a) The grant of a Corrody by the Priory of Kirby Bellars, Leicester-shire, to Marion Tomlinson, widow, 17 December, 1531: PRO, Exch., Augmentations Office, Misc. Books (E 315), 278, fos. 47–8. The text of the priory's grant comes from the copy inserted in his accounts for 1536, i.e. immediately after the dissolution of the priory, by the Crown's Particular Receiver for the region, George Gifford.

To all Christian people to whom this present writing shall come, William, the prior of Kirby upon Wrike [Kirby Bellars] and the convent of the same place, sendeth everlasting health in Our Lord. You shall know that we, with one assent and consent of all our chapter, for the benefits done unto us and in time to come after to be done, by God's grace, have given, and with this writing have confirmed, to our well-beloved in Christ Marion Tomlinson, widow, a corrody within our priory during the life of the said Marion, of us and our successors, under the form that follows. That is to say, every week when the baker does bake in our own house [Marion is to have] three casts of the best bread, and three of the second, and one brown loaf. Also to have three gallons of the best ale and two of the second in like manner. Also to have of the kitchen as one of the convent, except [*unless*] she hath milk of the day [*dairy*] house, that is to say, if she hath milk at the day house then to have nothing of the kitchen for that meal, and so in like manner at supper. Also the said prior and convent granteth unto the said Marion two houses next to the kitchen with the chambers over the said houses. Item, to have one load of coals and two loads of wood every year during her life. Also to have candles as shall be [thought] sufficient by the sight of the prior and convent. Also to have two hens and a cock at her own cost. In witness whereof the said prior and convent to this present writing have put their convent seal in the chapter house in the feast of St Lazarus [17 December] in the year of Our Lord God 1531. Also we are content that she shall have her daughter to keep her.

Pending a decision by the Court of Augmentations the King's com-missioners awarded Marion, because she was old, the sum of 26s 8d for the half year from Easter to Michaelmas 1536.

(b) FROM the account of John Freeman, Particular Receiver of the court of Augmentations for the former monastic lands in Lincolnshire, Michaelmas 1538 to Michaelmas 1539: PRO, Special Collections, Ministers Accounts, (SC 6), Henry VIII/2030. Sempringham, the motherhouse of the Gilbertine order, surrendered in September 1538 (*LP*, XIII ii, 375). The site of the priory was granted in January 1539 to Edward Fiennes, lord Clinton and Saye and his wife Elizabeth, who were expressly discharged in their letters patent from all 'encumbrances' except certain specified rents and fees (*LP*, XIV i, 191, g. 10). Smythe was still alive and enjoying his 'corrody' – although payment was temporarily in arrears – in 1552 (G. A. J. Hodgett, *The State of the ex-Religious in the diocese of Lincoln*, p. 58).

[m. 20] ALLOWANCES AND DEDUCTIONS arising from various abbeys and priories this year: . . . Payment of CORRODIES: . . . In consideration of the payment made by the same [Receiver] to John Smythe, lately the servant of the prior of Sempringham, as granted . . . by letters patent, the tenor of which follows in these words:

THIS INDENTURE made the second day of March in the 25th year of the reign of our sovereign lord King Henry VIII [1534], between us, John, the prior of the monastery of Sempringham in the county of Lincoln of the order of St Gilbert, and the convent of the same place, of the one part and John Smythe, servant to the said prior, of the other part, witnesseth that the foresaid prior and convent as well by their whole assent and consent as by the special licence of Thomas, the chief and head prior of the said order of Gilbert, have given and granted to the said John Smythe our servant, for his true and diligent service that he hath done and with God's grace hereafter shall do, a certain corrody or annuity during his natural life in manner and form following:—That is to say, a mansion or a dwelling house in the East Court of the said monastery, with an orchard and all other grounds as they be enclosed within the walls of the said house, with the appertenances. Also 40s of money yearly to be paid at two terms in the year, that is to say at the feast of the Annunciation of Our Lady and St Michael the Archangel, by even portions, and meat and drink and a livery when the said prior and convent and their successors shall give liveries to other of their servants, and the gate pasture, and feeding of twenty sheep yearly, winter and summer, with grass and hay according to the time of year for one horse. For the which corrody or annuity the said John Smythe do bind him by virtue of these presents to the said prior and convent and their successors so long as he shall live and be able, infirmities and sickness, reasonable and lawful cause and impediments to the contrary not letting him, to serve and keep the Quire night and day, according to such cunning and knowledge as God hath given him, in manner and form following, that is to say, New Year's Eve, Twelvth Eve, St Gilbert's Eve, Easter Eve, Ascension Eve, Whitsun Eve, Trinity Sunday Eve, Corpus Christi Eve, the Eve of the Assumption of Our Lady, Allhallows Eve, and the Eve of the Nativity of Our Lord, these principal feasts yearly to serve the Quire with the organs at matins, high mass, evensong, and compline, except before excepted, and every double feast, evensong, and high mass, and every [feast of] Our Lady and St Gilbert when they be served in the week day, high mass only, except before excepted, and also to do all such service besides as shall be meet for him [and] that be convenient, at the commandment of the said prior and his successors. Also the said prior and convent granteth for them and their successors to the said John Smythe every year liberty and licence for one month to sport him among his friends, at such time as he may best be spared from the Quire, at the discretion of the said prior and convent and their successors. And the said John Smythe shall uphold, repair, and make the mud wall of the foresaid house, except [that] the said prior and convent and their successors shall find [timber] and nails and cause mortar to be made and brought and laid at the foresaid house for repairing and making of the same, and all other reparations belonging to the same house shall be made at the only cost and charges of the said prior and convent and their successors ... Given in our Chapter House at Sempringham the day and year abovesaid. ALLOWED ... by the discretion of the King's officers ... 40s.[1]

[1] Smythe was apparently not compensated for the loss of his material emoluments.

30. The Settlement of Monastic Debts

FROM the first register of Decrees and Orders of the court of Augmentations: PRO, Exchequer, Augmentation Office, Misc. Books (E 315), 91. All the religious houses concerned were small and were dissolved in 1536 or early 1537.

[fo. 82v.] Memorandum, forasmuch as it is duly proved before the Chancellor and Council of the King's court of the Augmentations . . . that William Hale, gentleman, ought to have thirty pounds sterling due to him of the late monastery of Leiston in the county of Suffolk, by authority of parliament suppressed and dissolved, by an obligation of forty pounds made to the said William and Alice his wife for the surety of payment of thirty pounds by the late abbot and convent of the same late monastery under their convent seal bearing date [13 June 1530], it is therefore ordered and decreed by the said Chancellor and Council in the term of Holy Trinity [20 June 1537] that the said William Hale shall have the said debt of thirty pounds to be paid to him by the hands of the Treasurer of the revenues of the said Augmentations in and for full recompense and satisfaction of the said obligation.   .   .

[fo. 83] Memorandum, that [20 June 1537] it is ordered and decreed by the Chancellor and Council . . . that John Mills of the town of Southampton, esquire, shall have fifty pounds sterling in full recompense and satisfaction of divers and sundry debts due to him of the late monasteries ensuing, that is to say, a debt of thirty pounds and eleven pence of the late monastery of Breamore, a debt of eleven pounds of the late monastery of Netley and a debt of twenty and seven pounds, six shillings, and eight pence of the late monastery of Quarr in the county of Southampton [Hampshire], the said fifty pounds to be paid by the hands of the Treasurer in manner and form following, that is to say, at the feast of All Saints next coming, twenty and five pounds, and at the feast of Pentecost then next following [the] other twenty and five pounds in full payment of the said fifty pounds.

31. The Augmentations Officers in the Field

(a) One of a pair of indentures recording the receipt by Nicholas Sprake of 220 sows of lead lately stripped from the roofs of Cirencester Abbey, 13 July 1541: PRO, Exch., K.R., Church Goods (E 117), 14/28. The abbey had been surrendered on 19 December 1539: *LP* XIV ii, 705.

This bill made the 13th day of July in the 33rd year of the reign of our sovereign lord King Henry the eighth [1541] between Richard Paulet esquire, Particular Receiver of the Revenues of the Augmentation of the King's Crown in the county of Gloucester of the one party, and Nicholas Sprake, servant of Roger Basing esquire of Cirencester, yeoman [*sic*], of [the] other party, witnesseth that the said Richard Paulet the day of [the] making hereof has delivered unto Nicholas Sprake all the lead being sometime covered of and upon the church, cloister, and chapter house, with the aisles of the church, Our Lady Chapel, and all the gutters and covering of windows appertaining to the late dissolved monastery of Cirencester in the said county of Gloucester, the which lead now is molten into sows or blocks of lead containing in number eleven score with their weights marked upon them, all which said lead and every parcel thereof the said Nicholas promises and grants for and in the name of Roger Basing esquire safely and surely to keep to the king's use without waste, spoil, or concealment thereof, and every part or parcel thereof until such time as the said Nicholas by the aforesaid Richard Paulet or other officers of the said court of Augmentations thereof be discharged. In witness whereof the parties abovesaid to these indentures interchangeably have set their seals and subscribed their names the day and year abovesaid.

[*signed*] Nicholas Sprake

(b) A petition to Thomas Cromwell from some of the former tenants of the abbey of Vale Royal, Cheshire, *c.* 1538–9: PRO, State Papers Domestic (SP 1), 141/pp. 65–6. Vale Royal had been suppressed in September 1538. The Augmentations officers were apparently attempting to commute labour services as part of a policy of streamlining manorial administration.

To the right honourable the Lord Cromwell, Lord Privy Seal: Piteously complaining and showing unto your good lordship your poor and faithful orators and tenants of the lordships of Over and Weverham, belonging unto the manor of Vale Royal within the county of Chester, lately dissolved and surrendered to the King's Highness, that whereas your said poor orators have been lately enforced and compelled to do certain boons, otherwise called services, to the said manor by the space of two abbots' days[1] last past and not before, that is to say with wains, ploughs, and harrows in times of the year, and in harvest with hooks, and making of hay, and at Christmas gift hens, with other charges, the which boons and services began at the first of the free will and gentleness of the said tenants, and not of any duty or preserved customs before these days used, for the which services the said tenants then had bountiful dinners, and in divers times of the year other great relief and comfort of meat and drink for them and their servants, besides haybote, housebote, and timber necessary for plough and wain in recompense of the same services. And now, gracious lord, there is none such relief nor comfort of hospitality nor of timber to be had. And yet notwithstanding the officers [of the court of Augmentations] there have assessed and will convert the said services so lately begun into certain sums of money, to the great impoverishing and undoing of the said tenants, by reason whereof they shall not be able to do the King's Grace such service as they have done in times past, nor your good lordship, unless that your good lordship may be moved with pity unto them mercifully showed in this behalf. In consideration whereof, the premises tenderly considered, it may please your good lordship of your abundant goodness, being there head steward under the King's Highness,[2] that the said tenants may have their tenures in such large and ample manner as they have had in times past, and of their old accustomed rents. And the said poor tenants be and shall be at all times ready with their bodies and goods to do the King's Grace and your good lordship all such services as can lie in their power to do[3] and shall daily pray for the preservation of the King's Highness and your good lordship long to endure.

[1] i.e. during the last two abbacies.

[2] Cromwell's appointment dated from 6 June 1536, to take effect from the death of the earl of Shrewsbury, with a fee of £20, payable at once: PRO, Exch., Aug. Office, Misc. Books (E 315), 96, fo. 119.

[3] This was a more than formal phrase since the abbot had apparently urged his tenants not to support the King during the risings of 1536–7: LP xiv i, 639.

32. Request to Purchase

Letter to Cromwell from Sir Richard Grenville, Marshall of Calais, from Cornwall, July 1539: PRO, State Papers Domestic, Henry VIII (SP 1), 152, p. 242, calendared in *LP* XIV i, 1338. For the sequel see Doc. 34a.

... notwithstanding at my being with your lordship I showed you at that time [that] I would put your lordship to no suit to the king's majesty for me, neither for land nor fee ... but since I have bethought me that if I have not some piece of this suppressed land by purchase or gift of the king's majesty I should stand out of the case of few men of worship of this realm. As God knows I was and am as glad as any man of this realm of the suppression of these orgulous persons and devourers of God's word and takers away of the glory of Christ, and I reckon before this they were takers away of the wealth of this realm and spies to the devilish ['dewffelys'] bishop of Rome. And because my heirs shall be in the same mind for their own profit, I will gladly, if it might stand with the king's majesty's pleasure, buy certain parcels of this suppressed land in these parts, and I will send the king's majesty good sufficient sureties for the payment of his money, and sell part of my inheritance to pay part of the money in hand. The land that I desire to have of the king's highness be this: the priory of Launceston with the meadows and gardens, with a parcel of the demesnes called Newhouse, valued latterly by the king's surveyors at £14, and another little parcel of land called the manor of Norton, worth by the year £19. All that I desire is £33, and if it [might] stand with the king's majesty's pleasure to give me the purchase of £8, I will give his grace after the rate of 20 years' purchase for the rest, which will grow to five hundred pounds. ... Nor I do not this for no covetousness but to stand in the case of others. And the lands stand not far from my lands. I have written to Master Wriothesley desiring him to put your lordship in remembrance of this matter ... Writing at my poor house at Stowe the last day of July, by your own assured to command while I live.

Richard Grenville

33. The Third Commission to Sell Crown lands, 1543

A Commission under the King's Privy Seal to certain specified Crown officers to sell Crown lands, including former monastic lands, up to the annual value of £10,000 a year: PRO, Chancery, Patent Roll (C 66) 739, m. 19, calendared in *LP* XVIII i, 623, g. 29. This is the third of a series of such commissions, the first of which was issued to Cromwell and Rich in December 1539: *LP* XIV ii, 780, g. 36.

Henry the eighth, [etc.], to our right trusty and wellbeloved councillor Sir Richard Rich knight, Chancellor of our court of Augmentations of the Revenues of our Crown, Sir Richard Southwell knight, one of our General Surveyors of our lands, Sir Edward North knight, Treasurer of our said court of Augmentations . . ., Sir John Williams knight, Master of our Jewels, Sir Thomas Moyle knight, one other of our said General Surveyors of our lands, William Whorwood esquire, our General Attorney, Walter Hendley esquire, our Attorney-General of our said court of Augmentations, Henry Bradshaw esquire, our General Solicitor, and William Stanford esquire, our Attorney-General of our court of General Surveyors, Greeting. Whereas divers manors, lands, [etc.] by sundry and divers ways and means, as by act of parliament, attainder, surrenders, and otherwise, are come to us and be in our hands and possession, part thereof, by the advice of our Council, we think meet and convenient, towards the supportation and relief of our great charges being presently at hand to be employed for the defence, maintenance, and safeguard of this our realm and the common wealth of our loving subjects inhabiting the same, to put to sale, divide, distribute, and impart amongst the said our loving subjects, to such as intend to purchase and buy the same of us, and for certain other causes and considerations us specially moving. For accomplishment whereof know ye that we, trusting in your service, fidelities, and approved wisdoms, have appointed and assigned you eight, seven, six, five, or four of you, whereof you the said Sir Richard Rich or you the said Sir Richard Southwell or you the said Sir Edward North to be one, and by these our present letters patent do give unto you . . . full power and authority to bargain and sell and fully to conclude and agree for us in our name to our said subjects such of our said manors, [etc.] being as well within the survey of our said court of Augmentations . . . as of our said court of General Surveyors of our lands, amounting in the whole to the whole and clear yearly value of ten thousand pounds or under as shall seem to you ... most meet and convenient by your discretions. The same bargains and sales not to be made of any one manor, farm, or other hereditaments being certified to you by the auditor thereof to exceed the clear yearly value of forty pounds ... The same bargains and sales of the premises not before excepted, except [also] of such houses, cottages, tenements, and gardens whereunto no lands do appertain or belong being aswell in London as in other cities, boroughs, towns or places and [also] except manors, lands, tenements, rents, reversions, or services being heretofore granted for term or life or lives without any rent to be paid therefore, to be made after the rate of twenty years' purchase at the least, or more by your discretions, according to the particular values and certificates thereof to be made by the said auditor of the same, which said values and certificates made by them or any of them as is aforesaid shall be a sufficient warrant and discharge to you our said commissioners and every of you at all times for the value thereof. Always foreseeing and having respect by your discretions to the woods, advowsons, and other commodities of the same manors, [etc.] so to be sold, the value and price of the same woods to be certified by my [sic] officers of the same woods, and that the said certificate shall be likewise a sufficient warrant [etc., as above]. And such houses, tenements, cottages, and gardens whereunto no lands do appertain or belong as is aforesaid, being either in possession or reversion, the bargains and sales thereof to be made by the discretions of you our said commissioners ... and for such price as you ... shall think, judge, or esteem upon the certificate of the said auditor or auditors the same houses, [etc.] to be worth, which said certificate so to be made shall be a sufficient warrant [etc., as above]. And of the said manors, lands, tenements, houses, rents, reversions, or services being granted for term of life or lives without any rent to be paid therefore as is aforesaid the said bargains and sales thereof to be made after the rate of ten years' purchase at the least, or more by your discretions, according to the particular values and certificate thereof to be made in manner and form aforesaid. The moiety or half of the money for the which the premises or any parcel thereof shall be sold as is aforesaid, houses, [etc.] to which no lands do appertain only excepted, to be paid forthwith upon the said bargain to the Treasurer of our said court of the Augmentations ... to our use, and the other half or residue thereof to be paid to the same Treasurer within three months next after the bargain and sale made thereof. And that you the said Sir Richard Rich by recognisance or obligation to the king, or you the said Sir Richard Southwell or you the said Sir Edward North by your discretions by obligation to the king in the absence of the said Sir Richard Rich, shall take sufficient surety for the payment of the said residue so to be paid within three months next after the said sale. And that the money coming of such houses [etc.] in cities [etc.] to the which no lands do appertain to be paid to the said Treasurer of the Augmentations at such days and times as you our said commissioners . . . shall by your discretions think most meet and convenient for utterance and sale of our said houses, [etc.] . . . [The commissioners to take sufficient sureties for the same]. And that the buyers thereof, their heirs, and assigns shall hold the same manors, lands, and tenements so by them to be bought, . . . houses, [etc.] to the clear yearly value of four pounds whereunto no lands do appertain only excepted, . . . of us our heirs and successors by the tenure of knight service in chief, and also by one yearly rent amounting to the tenth part of the clear yearly value thereof, after and according to the certificate of the auditors thereof to you made, to us and our heirs and successors in our said court of the Augmentations of the Revenues of our Crown yearly to be paid for ever. And of houses [etc.] whereunto no lands do belong or appertain as is aforesaid, not exceeding the clear yearly value of four pounds, and also of every piece or parcel of land not exceeding the yearly value of forty shillings, the buyers thereof, their heirs and assigns shall hold the same of us, our heirs, and successors, by a tenure in free burgage or in socage, or otherwise as it shall seem best by the discretion of you our said commissioners as is aforesaid, and by one yearly rent amounting to the tenth part of the yearly value thereof, to us, our heirs and successors yearly to be paid for ever in form aforesaid. Provided always that the same yearly rent of the tenth part of the premises shall not be paid nor reserved unless the manors, [etc.] so to be sold came to our hands by reason of suppression or forfeiture of any ecclesiastical person or persons. Provided also that the money to be due to us for the same purchases shall be severally contained within the letters patent to be made to the said parties thereof, and that the bills and warrants whereupon the letters patent of and for the same purchases shall be made shall be always subscribed with the hands of you eight, seven, six, five or four of you, whereof you the said Sir Richard Rich or you the said Sir Richard Southwell or you the said Sir Edward North to be one, and from time to time at our pleasure to be signed with our hand and sign manual. Provided also that this commission shall not extend to meddle with any mere gift or exchange, or with any purchase being mixed with any gift or exchange to be made or given by us to or with any of our subjects, or with any sale of any lands, tenements, or hereditaments whereof days be given contrary to the form and effect of this commission, but that the same during our pleasure shall be rated and ordered always by the Chancellor and Council of our said court of Augmentations for the time being in such form as heretofore hath been used and accustomed. Provided also that after the manors, [etc.] to the said yearly value of ten thousand pounds appointed by this commission in form aforesaid to be sold [have been] bargained, sold, and purchased, according to the effect of these our letters patent, that then and from henceforth and immediately thereupon this commission to cease and be void and no longer to continue. In witness whereof . . . Westminster . . . 6 May [1543]   By writ of privy seal.

34. Particulars for Grants

(a) Particulars for the grant to Sir Richard Grenville of Bideford of the site, church, and demesne of Buckland Abbey, Devon, and of the rectory of Morwenstow, Cornwall, late of St John's Hospital, Bridgwater, Somerset: PRO, Exch., Aug. Office, Particulars for Grants (E 318), 510, calendared in Youings, *Devon Monastic Lands*, pp. 18–19. The letters patent are dated 26 May 1541 and Grenville paid a first instalment of the purchase price, £130, in May 1542, and £102 7s 7d just over a month later. The sum of 15s 9d was still outstanding in 1551. The Buckland estate, the abbey church almost certainly already converted into a commodious residence, was sold by Grenville's grandson and heir, the famous Elizabethan sea-captain, to Sir Francis Drake in 1580 for the sum of £3,400 (Plymouth City Archives, Drake MSS., 1, 2, 6).

[m. 3][1] The former Monastery of Buckland in the county of Devon. The site of the said former monastery with demesne land appertaining to the same: Farm of the site there, with apple orchards, gardens, lands, meadows, feedings, and pastures called Calves parke[2] and Barne parke, 5 acres; Dedeham, 70 ac.; Quarry parke, 11 ac.; Conyger, 26 ac.; Wyndemyll parke, 8 ac.; Long parke, and a small meadow adjoining, 17 ac.; Longlands, 60 ac.; Vyntens, 18 ac.; Oxenham, 4 ac.; Sowthefelde, 40 ac.; Penmarshe parke, 5 ac.; Okewell, $2\frac{1}{2}$ ac.; Hyer Bickeham and Lower Bickeham, 110 ac.; together with certain arable land called Hayleball, 60 ac.; Long parke, 7 ac.; and Ruggemyll parke, $2\frac{1}{2}$ ac.; and certain meadows there called Cawsey Mede, 1 ac., and Shepewaishe, $1\frac{1}{2}$ ac.; and pasture, 120 ac., and a wood called Haileball Wood, with all and singular appertaining thereto, per annum £23 3s 5d[3]

Certified by Mathew Colthurst [Auditor]

[m. 4] The former Priory of Bridgwater in the county of Somerset The rectory of Morwenstow ... Cornwall: The farm of all sheaf tithes appertaining to the aforesaid rectory, let to Hugh Pruste for a term of 80 years by indenture dated 8 July ... [1538], payable at the feast of St James, [£10]; with 30s farm of the house of the rectory aforesaid with demesne land appertaining thereto, let to John Stanbury by indenture; 8s rent from one cottage in the tenure of the said Hugh Pruste; 16d free rent of certain land in Hawke Marche; $6\frac{1}{2}$d for certain

---

[1] Membranes 1, 2, 5, etc. relate to a later grant to Grenville.

[2] Field names are here given in their original spelling.

[3] This was the rent reserved on a Crown lease made in December 1539 for 21 years: PRO, Exch., Aug. Office., Misc. Books (E 315), fol. 33.

land called Campis Crosse in the tenure of John Littelston and 3d rent of a tenement in the tenure of John Broke appertaining to the said rectory, per annum £12 1½d

Certified by Mathew Colthurst 28 January ... [1541] for Richard Grenville knight: The sum of all premises in both schedules over and besides [the woods] are worth yearly £35 3s 6½d. Therefrom for the tenth, £3 10s 4½d and there remains clear £31 13s 2d. Therefrom for the king's gift £20 to him and his heirs for ever, and there remains clear £11 13s 2d, which after 20 years' purchase doth amount to the sum of £233 3s 4d, to be paid in [the] form following, that is to say, in hand £100 and at Christmas then next £133 3s 4d.

Rychard Ryche[4]

Memorandum a recognisance for the woods
Memorandum the king must discharge the said Grenville of all incumbrances except the rent reserved.

(b) Particulars for the Grant of former monastic lands in Staffordshire and Shropshire to John Leveson of Wolverhampton, merchant: PRO, E 318, 711. John traded in wool and was a member of the Calais Staple.

[m. 2] PART OF THE POSSESSION OF THE LATE PRIORY OF BREWOOD in the county of Staffordshire:

Brewood ... it is valued in a rent of assize or free rent from John Moseley for his lands there, per annum, 1d; ... from Thomas Johnson, 7d; the farm of a pasture there called Dawploke, let to Roger Fowke by indenture, so it is said, at a rent per annum of 1d   [Total]   9d
Horsebrook and Stretton ... it is valued in a rent of assize or free rent from Richard Whitmore ... 3d; for a parcel of land or a croft there, let to Richard Bromehall at the will of the lord, per annum 8d; ... a messuage with land, meadow, pasture ... let to John Tomkyns, so it is said, at a rent of 16s   [Total]   16s 11d

[Sum total]   17s 8d

Memorandum, the King's highness hath no more land nor tenements in Brewood and Horsebrook belonging to the late monastery other than above mentioned, to the Auditor's knowledge
Item, the premises lieth not nigh any of the King's majesty's houses, forests, chases, and parks which be kept for the access of his highness, to the Auditor's knowledge
Item, there be no spiritual promotions belonging to the premises
Item, there have been no other particulars delivered of the premises heretofore

[4] Rich was here acting in his capacity as Chancellor of the court of Augmentations as the grant was part gift: see Doc. 33, p. 232.

Memorandum, for the Woods and underwoods growing on the premises

Examined by Robert Burgoyne [Auditor] [?] day of March ... [1545] for John Leveson of Wolverhampton, Merchant:

The rents and farms in Brewood in the county of Stafford, 9d, and in Horsebrook and Stretton in the same county, 16s 11d, in all by the year, parcel of the possession of the late priory of Brewood in the said county, 17s 8d; which rated at 20 years' purchase doth amount to the sum of £17 13s 4d, to be paid all in hand

Woods: nil   The tenure in socage

Memorandum, the King's majesty must discharge the premises of all incumbrances except leases, and except such charges as the tenants and farmers are bound to discharge

[signed] William St John   Robert Southwell   Edward North [m. 3 Woods] ... will hardly suffice for timber to repair the houses standing upon the same ... nil

Examined by me David Clayton [*Surveyor of Woods*] [mm. 4–7] PARCEL OF THE POSSESSIONS OF THE LATE MONASTERY OF HAUGHMOND in the county of Shropshire:

Manor of Hardwicke in the county of Shropshire: it is valued in rents and farms in Grinshill ... £4 13s 10d; ... in Hadnall ... 65s 2d; ... in Haston ... 29s; ... in Smethcote ... 5s: in Astley ... 32s 8d; ... in Consawe in the parish of St Mary, Shrewsbury ... 4s; ... in Muckleton ... 24s; ... in Edgebolton ... 27s; ... in Besford ... 8s; ... in Acton Reynold ... 10s; ... in Balderton ... 24s; ... in Stiple ... 16d; ... in Hardwicke, the farm of a Grange called Hardwicke adjoining Hadnall, in the tenure of Richard Tyler, with a room on the west there reserved for the use of the late abbot of the late monastery of Haughmond ... and an assart adjoining Smethcote called 'the abbot's brutche', let to Richard Tyler by indenture under the conventual seal of the late monastery of Haughmond dated the last day of December ... [1538] ... for a term of 81 years ... £4 6s 8d, and for the assart ... 6s 8d: court profits ... with heriots, reliefs, and other casualties arising in an average year, 5s

[Total]   £21 11s 4d

The said manor of Hardwicke is no more in value than is before expressed

Rectory of Shawbury in the county of Shropshire: it is valued in the farm of the tithes of grain ... let to Edward Littleton esquire by indenture under the seal of the court of Augmentations ... dated the last day of May ... [1540] for 21 years ... and paying rent of £6 10s; and in the farm of the tithes of grain in the town of Shawbury, let to Richard Corbett gentleman by indenture under the convent seal of the monastery of Haughmond dated 17 December ... [1535] for 24 years ... and paying rent of 40s; and in the farm of the tithes of grain in the town of

Wytheford, let to Roger Lancashire and his wife Alice . . . by indenture under convent seal . . . dated 13 August . . . [1535] for 60 years . . . rent of 13s 4d   [Total]   £9 3s 4d
[mm. 7d–8 Further property late of Haughmond Priory, all crossed through]
[m. 8d–9] Memorandum . . . [as above]
Item, what fines have been paid for any parcel of the premises the said Auditor knoweth not

Examined by me Robert Burgoyne

[m. 10 WOODS] County of Shropshire:
The manor of Hardwicke with certain lands and tenements in Grinshill, Hadnall . . . [etc.] in the said county . . .:
In Hardwicke Park Close be five acres of wood growing by parcels; Hardwicke Coppice containeth three acres; in Hardwicke Common be six acres of wood growing by parcels; in Lady Mosse be six acres of wood growing by parcels. Total of acres: 20, whereof 3 acres of six years' growth, 5 acres of forty and sixty years' growth, most part usually cropped and shred, reserved to Richard Tyler, farmer of the site of the said manor for his firebote, hedgebote, ploughbote, cartbote, and housebote which he hath been accustomed to have in the same; 6 acres of sixty years' growth, most part usually cropped and shred, £4; and 6 acres residue of eighty years' growth, £6; the wood of every acre aforesaid valued as appeareth, which is in the whole:- £10
The Spring of the Wood or ground of eight acres aforesaid not valued because they be reserved, and of twelve acres residue not valued because the wood is old and groweth by parcels, and the said farmer and tenants there have and occupy the herbage of the same as parcel of their farms for their yearly rents charged in the particulars of the valuation of the lands:- nil
There be growing about the situation of the said manor, twenty seven messuages, and three tenements there, and in the lands pertaining to the same, and other the lands aforesaid, 800 oaks of sixty and eighty years' growth, most part usually cropped and shred, whereof 500 reserved to the tenants there for their firebote, housebote, and hedgebote which they have been accustomed to have in the same, and 300 residue valued at 3d the tree, which is in the whole:- 75s
The parsonage of Shawbury . . . [etc. 55s, all crossed out]
                                [Total]   £16 10s [amended to £13 15s]
Examined by me David Clayton
[m. 9d] 24th day of February . . . [1545] for John Leveson of Wolverhampton:
The manor of Hardwicke with the appertenances in the county of Shropshire, parcel of the possessions of the late monastery of Haughmond by the year, £21 11s 4d

The parsonage of Shawbury in the same county of Shropshire with the tithes and profits belonging to the same by the year, £9 3s 4d

Total: £30 14s 8d, whereof deduct for the tenth, 61s 6d, and so remaineth clear £27 13s 2d, which rated at 20 years' purchase is £553 3s 7d. Add thereto for the woods growing upon the premises £13 15s, and so the whole sum for the purchase of all the premises is £566 18s 4d,[1] whereof in hand £300 and at Midsummer next the rest, being £266 18s 4d

The tenure knight service

Memorandum the King must discharge . . . [as above]

[signed] William St John   John Baker   Edward North

Enrolled by John Hanby

[m. 1] Memorandum that I, John Leveson, gentleman, do desire and require to purchase of the King's majesty the manor, rectory, advowson,[2] [etc.] mentioned in the particulars hereunto annexed, being of such yearly value as in the same particulars is expressed and declared. In witness whereof I, the said John Leveson, to this present writing have put my seal the 24th day of February in the 36th year of the reign of our sovereign lord Henry the eight [etc.] . . . [1545].

[signed] by me John Leveson

(c) Particulars, dated 24 February 1544, for the Grant, dated 20 November 1544 (*LP* XIX ii, 690, g. 34) of property in Wiltshire, all late of Malmesbury Abbey, including the site, church and other abbey buildings, to William Stumpe, for the sum of £1,517 15s 2½d: PRO, E 318, 1074. The delay in the issue of the letters patent seems to have been due to some delay in the issue of the warrant for the Great Seal.

[m. 2] Malmesbury, late monastery in the county of Wiltshire

Parcel of the possessions of the said late monastery now in the hands of the lord king:

Hamlet of Rodbourne, member or parcel of the manor of Cowfold . . . [eighteen customary holdings, with works (23s 2d), etc., totalling £30 1d, less 5s for the fee of the collector of the rents, leaving clear per annum . . . £29 15s 1d]

William Berners, auditor

What commodities the tenants take of their holdings aforesaid the said William Berners knoweth not

---

[1] If to this be added the £17 13s 4d on m. 2 the total comes to £584 11s 8d, as in Leveson's letters patent of 20 May 1545: *LP* XX i. 846, g. 59.

[2] No payment seems to have been made in this case for the right of presentation.

[m. 3 Valuation of various meadows, etc., part of the abbey manors of Malmesbury, Burton, and Thornhill, in Malmesbury, worth £6 5s 10d and crossed through by the commissioners.]

Memorandum that the manor of Malmesbury besides the parsonage there is of the clear yearly value of £65. Memorandum the said manors of Burton and Thornhill be of the clear yearly value, with the herbage of the park there which now is reserved for the king's studs, of £42[1]

[m. 4] Manor of Brinkworth in the county of Wiltshire ... [in rents, etc., valued at £36 18s 3¾d, less 10s for the fee of the bailiff, leaving clear per annum] ... £36 8s 3¾d

The Certificate of the Auditor to the contents of Master Chancellor's letters:

> Memorandum the king's majesty hath the patronage and advowson of the parsonage of Brinkworth aforesaid. Item the manor lyeth adjoining to the king's forest of Bredon and in distance from the two parks which the king's majesty hath in Cowfold and Thornhill reserved for his grace's studs four miles, and from the queen's manor and park of Festurne, one mile.
>
> Item what fines hath been given for the farms above mentioned or any of them the said auditor knoweth not.
>
> Item there is none other particular delivered of the said manor to any person before this time.

William Berners

[m. 5. Valuation of Woods, including some items cancelled by the commissioners.]

The manor of Brinkworth with the appertenances, parcel of the possessions of the said late monastery:

> There be growing about the said tenements and hedges enclosing lands pertaining to the same 100 oaks and elms, cropped and shred, of 80 years' growth, whereof 80 [are] reserved for timber for housebote to repair the said tenements which they have had in the said manor by custom of old time used, and 20 trees residue valued at 4d the tree, which is in the whole 6s 8d.

The hamlet of Rodbourne ... 120 elms and ashes of 80 years' growth, whereof 100 reserved ... and 20 trees residue valued at 2d the tree, which is in the whole 3s 4d.　By me William Colles

[m. 6] County of Wiltshire

The late monastery of Malmesbury: the sum of the value of all the houses and buildings of the said late monastery:

> Assigned to remain, that is to say, the late abbot's lodging and the new lodging adjoining, with kitchen, larder, buttery, pantry, and houses of office, with lodgings thereupon builded pertaining to the

---

[1] Stumpe was evidently not to be allowed to purchase even a part of these valuable estates: see Doc. 33, p. 231.

same. The abbot's stable, with the wool houses, the gate and houses over the same enclosing the quadrant of the said buildings, the barn at the Spytell gate and the outer gatehouse of the Basse court, priced at £40.

Appointed to be razed and sold, that is to say, the church with the cloister and chapel adjoining, £50; the dormitory with the chapter house, £5; the frater and library, £5; the farmery with the lodging adjoining, £13 6s 8d; the sextery end, 40s; the cellarer's chamber with the Sqyer chamber, the Saint Mary house with the chantry and convent kitchen with all the houses there, the guests' stable with houses adjoining and the steward's lodging, £40; . . . in all £115 6s 8d

[Total] £155 6s 8d[2]   William Berners, Auditor
Memorandum that in all the premises the lead and bells be no parcel of the value.

The site of the said monastery with the mill within the same and certain pieces of land and pasture parcel of the possessions of the same late monastery . . . 18 acres, lately in the occupation of the abbot, 60s a year; 2 acres called the Castle Mead in the tenure of Robert Cove, 7s a year; 6 acres in closes . . . 5s.

Copyhold tenement . . . in Westport Street, Malmesbury, and lands . . . 14s 8d; [house and garden] called Saint White's Hermitage on Burton Hill in the parish of Birport . . . 1 rood . . . 4d.

[Total] £4 7s   William Berners, Auditor
[m. 7] 24 February 35 Henry VIII, for William Stumpe
Manor of Brinkworth valued clear per annum, £36 8s 3¾d
Manor of Rodbourne valued clear per annum, £29 15s 1d

[in all] £66 3s 4¾d, less for the tenth, £6 12s 4¼d
And remains besides clear per annum, £59 11s ½d, which rated at 21 years' purchase doth amount to the sum of £1,250 11s 10½d

Item, for the site of the house of Malmesbury with all the buildings of the same, the garden, and orchard £4 7s, less for the tenth 8s 8½d [leaving] clear 78s 3½d, which, together with the buildings of the same with the church, frater, cloister, chapter house, garden, and orchard, the lead and bells only reserved, is rated at £266 13s 4d.[3] And then the whole sum that the said William Stumpe must pay, with the woods, is £1,517 15s 2½d, to be paid in form following, that is to say, in hand £1,000 and at the first day of June £517 15s 2½d.

Memorandum the king must discharge the said William Stumpe of all incumbrances except leases and the rent before reserved, and except

----

[2] As it relates to buildings this is a capital valuation.

[3] How this figure was arrived at is a mystery. Deducting £155 6s 8d as the price of the buildings there is left the sum of £111 6s 8d, which is about 30 years' purchase of the site, etc.

20s, the fee of the bailliwick of Brinkworth, and 10s for the fee of the [bailiff of the] manor of Rodbourne.

Richard Rich	Richard Southwell
Edward North	John Williams

[m. 1 Request to purchase the above lands, dated 24 February 1544 and signed by Stumpe.][4]

[4] Through him the abbey church was handed over to the parish of Malmesbury.

35. A Licence to Alienate

Letters Patent, 26 September 1544, licensing William Riggs and Leonard Brown to alienate certain property in Dorset formerly belonging to the abbeys of Abbotsbury and Milton to Robert Martyn: PRO, Chancery, Patent Roll (C 66), 756, m. 33. The four messuages, etc., concerned were part of a very large grant, made by the Crown to Riggs and Brown in August of the same year, of property in Lincolnshire, Essex, Huntingdonshire, Bedfordshire, Devonshire etc. (*LP* XIX ii, 166, g. 21), most of which they subsequently disposed of in small parcels.

The King to all to whom, etc., greeting. Whereas by letters patent under our great seal of the Augmentations [*sic*] bearing date at Hampton Court 14 August [1544], for certain sums of money in our said letters patent recorded and specified, among other things we gave and granted to our beloved subjects William Riggs and Leonard Brown, and the heirs and assigns of the said William, all those our four messuages and tenements and one cottage with their appertenances situated, lying, and being in Westhorppe and Southover in the parish of Tolpuddle in our county of Dorset, formerly appertaining to the late monastery of Abbotsbury in our county of Dorset, and now or formerly in the tenure or occupation of Sir Thomas Trenchard, his wife Edith, and Henry and John Martyn or their assigns or the assigns of any one of them, and all and singular lands, [etc.] with their appertenances everywhere in the said parish of Tolpuddle ... together with all that our manor of Burdeleston ... in our county of Dorset, with its rightful members and appertenances everywhere, formerly appertaining to the late monastery of Milton ... in the said county of Dorset now dissolved ... as well as the advowson, gift, and free disposal and legal *persona* of the rectory and parish church of Burleston in our said county of Dorset, appertaining to the late monastery of Milton ... together with all those our meadows, feedings, and pastures with their appertenances lying and being in Burdelston [and] Littlepuddle alias Thorpe, and one meadow of ours called White Meade in the parish of Wodesford in the said county of Dorset, and all our wood lying in Thorpe aforesaid ... formerly appertaining to the said monastery of Milton ... which manor, [etc.] they held of us in chief for the service of one fortieth part of a knight's fee, rendering to us our heirs and successors of and for the aforesaid messuages [etc.] five shillings and eight pence, and of and for the said manor of Burdelston ... fifteen shillings ... Know that we of our special grace, and for three pounds eight shillings and eight pence paid to us in our Hanaper, have granted and given licence, and by these present grant and give licence, for us and our heirs as far as in us lies to the said William Riggs and Leonard Brown that all those said tenements ... in the county of Dorset which they hold of us in chief they may give and grant, sell, hand over, demise, alienate or [dispose] by fine in our court of King's Bench, or by any other method, at the will of the same William and Leonard, to our beloved subject Robert Martyn of Athelhampton[1] ... in the parish of Puddletown in the said county of Dorset, his heirs and assigns, to hold the premises ... of us and our heirs for the service due and of right accustomed for ever ... In witness thereof ... Katherine, queen of England and regent of the same, at Westminster, 26 September [1544]

[1] The price at which the property changed hands was of no concern to the Crown.

36. A Speculator Unmasked

FROM the testimony of Henry Whitereson of Hackney, before the court of Augmentations in May 1545, concerning the career of Leonard Beckwith, Particular Receiver for Yorkshire: PRO, Exchequer, Augmentations Office, Miscellaneous Books (E 315), 113, fo. 29, printed by G. W. O. Woodward in 'A Speculator in Monastic Lands', *EHR*, lxxix (1964), pp. 778–83. Selby Abbey, a Benedictine house in Yorkshire, was dissolved in December 1539 and within a year the site was granted by the Crown to Sir Ralph Sadler for £736. In December 1540 Sadler obtained a Crown licence to alienate the property to Beckwith: *LP* xv, 1027, g. 40; xvi, 379, g. 40; and *supra*, Doc. 28b. Meanwhile the real risk, as we see in this document, had been assumed by Whitereson.

... at such time as the said Sir Ralph Sadler did conclude with the king's highness and sued out the letters patent for the bargain and sale of ... [the site and demesnes of Selby Abbey], and of the granges of Thorpe and Stayner, the same Sir Ralph did promise and grant to this deponent that this deponent should have the premises for the sum of £110 more than the said Sir Ralph did and should pay to the king's highness for the same. And so this deponent did agree ... and gave to the said Sir Ralph Sadler the sum of £110 over and above ... and then this deponent, having a commission of the said Sir Ralph Sadler to bargain and sell the premises, or to do with the same what he would, did ride into Yorkshire, minding to make money of woods of the premises, and of leases to be made of the granges ... and within three days of the coming of this deponent to his house at Wilberfoss this deponent fell sick there of a great ague ... and for that cause devised with his friends to sell certain woods of the premises to make money towards the later payment of the money due to the King's Majesty for the said purchase and ... sent for one William Rydeard ... and Henry Smyth ... and desired them to sell as much woods at Selby as would amount to 200 marks or £200, and also to practise for him who would give best fines for leases to be made for the term of 21 years of the granges ... And the said William and Henry went to Hull and Beverley and declared that they had commission to sell the woods at Selby, and thereupon certain persons ... came thither and saw the woods, but the said William and Henry ... made relation to this deponent that they could not make above £60 of wood ...

[Whitereson went on to relate how his 'friends' also endeavoured to sell the site and demesnes for him but could only get an offer of £800.] ...

And afterwards this deponent being sick rode to York to Dr Stevens house, and so there being Sir Leonard Beckwith ... the said Sir Leonard Beckwith said to this deponent that he heard say that this deponent had bought Selby of Sir Ralph Sadler ... and after divers communications thereof this deponent agreed for the bargain and sale of the premises to the same Sir Leonard for the sum of £1040, whereof £520 to be paid at Wilberfoss at All Soul's Day then next and £520 to be paid ... at Candlemas ...

37. The Conversion of Titchfield Abbey

FROM a letter to Thomas Wriothesley, 2 January 1538, from John Crayford, clerk, and Roland Latham, the king's commissioners for the dissolution of Titchfield Abbey: PRO, State Papers Domestic (SP 1), 128, fos. 25v–27v., calendared in *LP* XIII i, 19. The enrolled copies of the deed of surrender are dated 28 and 18 December 1537 (see *supra*, p. 66) and the letters patent of Wriothesley's grant of the site, etc., 30 December (*LP* XII ii, 1274, 1311, g. 40). Before Christmas Crayford and Latham informed Wriothesley that the conversion of the buildings into a house suitable for his residence would cost at least 300 marks (*ibid.*, 1245). This correspondence is particularly interesting because a considerable part of Wriothesley's conversion can still be seen and the layout of most of the conventual and secular complex of buildings on the site has been recovered by archaeological field-work: see plan on opposite page.

... As for pantry, buttery, cellar and larder no man in Hampshire hath better and more handsome couched [*lying*] together.[1] The kitchen is large and old and may with little charge be made new in the same place. The hall is devised to stand in plan covenable [*conveniently*] for the premises and the door to appear in the great court which will be square, every way a hundred foot. A gallery of 13 foot broad and the same length with the court if you list, and as much for servants' lodging abated. All houses of offices sufficiently had without charge now towards you was in vain if the church should be altered as you devise. You shall understand that the church is furthest south from all other lodging, joining to the garden and orchard, so the kitchen there and the sink must be aligned with your rosemary and lavendar, etc.[2] ... All the church must [come] down with the steeple, only that portion which is north from the steeple and knit with the dorter to stand,[3] for your dining parlour and chapel beneath, and for lodging above of two storeys if you list,[4] leaded and [em]battled above with fair crests and prospects east, west, and south upon your garden, orchard and court. It was too long to write all. To be brief, you may have with reasonable charges an house for the King's grace to 'bate' [visit?] and for any baron[5] to keep his

---

[1] The sub-vault of the Frater on the north side of the cloister.
[2] Wriothesley apparently wished to make a kitchen in the western part of the abbey church, but this would have been adjacent to his pleasure garden.
[3] i.e. the North transept.
[4] The eastern range.
[5] Wriothesley was not made a baron until 1544.

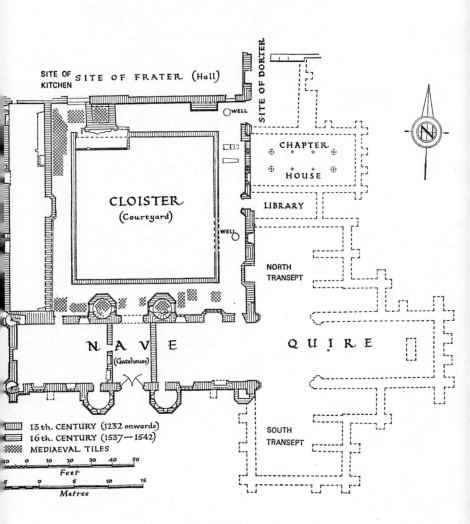

PLAN OF TITCHFIELD ABBEY, HAMPSHIRE
(after W. H. St. J. Hope and HMSO Guidebook, 1969)

hospitality in . . . The frater may be lodging as you write and the side of the court all above.[6] Under that almost the whole length is there a buttery, vaulted right well, for 60 ton of beer or wine. Next unto that eastward the pantry, within that the cellar for wine, both vaulted, answering to both. Southward [southeastward] and next under this the hall,[7] fifty foot or more in length as you will, the high desk [*dais*] to join with that portion of the church that shall stand, in the which, as is said, beneath, next to the high desk of the hall your dining parlour, etc. . . . Mr Sherlond was here on Sunday and from East Mean 14 miles off some half a dozen of neighbours to visit your manor and view our hospitality. Whereas thay had meat, drink and lodging and have promised to return and buy marble stones, altars, images, tables, etc., upon the [proceeds of] which we propose to levy our Christmas charges. Mistress Wriothesley, nor you neither, be not meticulous nor scrupulous to make sale of such holy things, having example of a good, devout bishop of Rome called Alexander, whose epitaph is writ after this sort: Vendit Alexander cruces altaria Christi vendere jure potest, emerat ille prius. Mistress, your husband will open the sense of these two verses. As for plucking down of the church [it] is but a small matter, minding (as we doubt not but you will) to build a chapel. . . . For lack of time and opportunity to make a new plat [*plan*] I have sent your own again, corrected as we think meet . . .

The work, under Crayford's supervision, occupied many months. Stone was brought, via Southampton, from Caen in Normandy. The steeple, quire, presbytery and north and south transepts of the abbey church were removed and over the middle bay of the nave a great tower gatehouse was erected. The chapter house in fact became Wriothesley's chapel and the abbey frater his great hall. (For more extensive extracts from Crayford's letters and details of the conversion see W. H. St John Hope, 'The Making of Place House at Titchfield near Southampton in 1538', *Archaeological Journal*, LXIII, (1906), pp. 231–44)

[6] i.e. an upper storey to the north alley of the cloister.
[7] This was to be newly built.

38. The Former Religious in a Secular World

FROM a letter to Cromwell from Richard Ingworth, bishop of Dover, 10 March 1539: State Papers Domestic (SP 1), 144, fo. 85, printed in J. W. Clay, *Yorkshire Monasteries, Suppression Papers*, Yorks. Archaeol. Soc., Record Series, xlviii (1912), pp. 68–9.

Further, my good lord, in these parts within the diocese of York the poor men that make surrender of their houses be hardly ordered by the bishop's officers, at the bishop's commandment, so that they cannot be suffered to sing nor say in any parish church without they show their letters of their orders, my letters or their capacities notwithstanding, and the charges of these letters of their orders be so great that the poor men be not able to bear it. Some must go a hundred miles to seek them, and when they come there the charges of for giving the register is so great that they be not able to pay it. So they come home again confounded. I have been with my lord of York and showed to him your lordship's letter that your commandment is that they which so have surrendered their houses should be suffered without interruption to sing and say in any church. The bishop made many objections and said that it must be known whether they were priests or not, and I certified him that we that received the houses make due search which were priests and which were none and so made certificate to your lordship and your lordship to the king's grace, so that by that means their capacities were granted, wherefore I desired him to accept their capacities from the king's grace with so much favour as the bishop of Rome's capacities before had been received, for the which there was never search made but straight obeyed. He at the last granted that so many as showed my hand should be allowed until that their capacities might come, but there be many that be put out by other commissions that have not my hand. Wherefore your lordship should do a charitable deed to write your letters to the bishop . . .

39. Another Statutory Half-measure

'An Act that such as were religious persons may purchase', 31 Henry VIII, c. 6: *Statutes* III, 724–5.

Be it enacted by authority of this present parliament that all and singular such religious persons, as well men as women, professed of what order, rule or habit so ever they were, which be or hereafter shall be put at their liberties from the danger, servitude, and condition of their religion and profession whereunto they were professed, by reason of suppression, dissolving, forfeiture by attainder, rendering or otherwise giving up to the hands of the king's majesty or any other the same monasteries, abbeys, priories, or other religious houses or places wherein the same religious persons were professed, shall by authority of this present parliament, from and after the first day of the same parliament, and from and after the time that they were or shall be put at such liberty, have free liberty to purchase to them and their heirs, in fee simple, fee tail [*sic*], for term of life, for years, or at will, manors, lands, [etc.] in like manner and form as though they or any of them had never been professed nor entered into any such religion. And furthermore that they, the same religious persons and every of them, shall be made able by authority of this present act to sue and be sued in all manner of actions, plaints and suits whatsoever they be, of or for any matter or cause growing since and after the time of their several deraignments or departing out of their religion, in all courts and places within this realm as other the king's subjects be . . .

[II. No such former religious person to enjoy any such right accruing before his or her departure from religion] . . . nor that any of the said religious persons being priests, or such as have vowed at twenty-one years or above, and thereto then consented, continuing in the same any while after, not duly proving by witness or other lawful means some unlawful coercion or compulsion done to them or any of them for making of any such vow or constraining them to remain in their religion, be enabled by virtue of any words, clause, or sentence before in this act expressed, to marry or take any wife or wives, but that they and every of them be clearly excluded and put from the same to all intents and purposes, any thing before in this act contained to the contrary hereof notwithstanding.

40. Proceedings in Court

Bill of complaint, with answer and replication, in a case concerning tithes due from certain woods late of Westwood Priory, Worcester-shire: PRO, Exchequer, Augmentation Office, Proceedings (E 321), 13/63. Westwood had been a small Benedictine nunnery, dissolved in 1536–7. John Packington had been granted a lease of the site and the rectory of Westwood in March 1537, valued at £22 a year and regarded by him as part of his meagre fee as the King's Justice in North Wales (*LP* xii ii, 775 and xiii i, p. 580). Two years later he purchased not only the site and rectory but most of the rest of the priory lands, including Westwood Wood with eighteen coppices (*LP* xiv i, 651, g. 44). Assuming that he claimed the right to collect tithes from 1537, the case dates from 1541–2.

To the right worshipful Sir Richard Rich knight, Chancellor of the court of Augmentations: Sheweth unto your mastership John Packington that where the king our sovereign lord by his letters patent under his great seal gave and granted unto your beseecher and to his heirs the late suppressed priory of Westwood in the county of Worcester with all the demesne lands thereunto belonging, and the parsonage of Westwood aforesaid appropriated to the same late priory, with all manner of tithes, oblations, and other profits to the same late priory and parsonage belonging, as by the said letters patent amongst other things more plainly appear, all which tithes, oblations, and profits be to be taken in and upon the demesne lands belonging to the said late priory and no other place, except certain tithes in Caverich and Wichbold which be not above the yearly value of 6s 8d, and the same tithes and oblations were rated and valued to your said beseecher upon the said grant for 50s yearly. So it is that one Gilbert Wheeler which hath in farm and lease 18 coppices of wood, parcel of the said demesne, for term of certain years yet enduring of the demise and grant of Dame Joyce, late prioress of the late suppressed priory, the tithe of which coppices your beseecher is entitled to have by force of the grant. And so it is that the said Gilbert fellith every year one of the said coppices and hath not tithed nor paid the tithes of the same to your beseecher, but hath detained and kept the same tithe to his own use by the space of these four years, which amounteth to the sum of £4 and above, and albeit your said beseecher hath often and many times required the said Gilbert to tithe the tenth part of the said wood or else to agree with your said beseecher for the same, which to do he at all times hath refused, and yet doth, contrary to right and conscience. In consideration whereof that it may please your good mastership to grant unto your beseecher the king's most gracious letters to be directed to the said Gilbert, commanding him by the same personally to appear before your mastership in the king's court of Augmentations at Westminster, at a certain day by your mastership to be appointed, to make answer to the premises, and your beseecher shall pray for the preservation of your estate long to continue.

The Answer of Gilbert Wheeler to the bill of complaint of John Packington: The said Gilbert saith ... that one Joyce, late prioress of the said suppressed house of Westwood, was seised of the said valetts and coppices of wood comprised in the said bill of complaint in her demesne as of fee, in the right of her said monastery, and also saith that the parsonage of Westwood was appropriated to the said priory, and by reason thereof the said prioress [was] late seised of the said parsonage as *parson in persona*, and so being thereof seised the said prioress, as prioress of the said house and also *parson in persona* of the said parsonage, by the assent and consent of the convent, and for the sum of 43 marks truly contented and paid for a fine for the same by one John Wheeler now deceased, and also for £4 of increase of yearly rent over and above that as it hath been let to farm in time past, by their deed indented, and sealed with their convent seal, dated in the said monastery the 10th day of December the 24th year of the reign of our sovereign lord king Henry the eighth [1532] demised and granted and to farm leased all the said coppices and valetts in the said bill of complaint expressed to the said John Wheeler, to have to him and to his assigns during the term of 60 years then next following, yielding and paying for the same [the] rent contained in the said indenture, as by the same indenture made between the said late prioress and the said John Wheeler ready to be shown more plainly doth appear, by reason whereof the said John Wheeler was possessed of the premises according[ly]. And he so being possessed made the said Gilbert Wheeler his executor and died, after whose death the said valetts and coppices of wood came to the hands and possession of the said Gilbert as executor of the said John Wheeler, and the said Gilbert also saith that the said valetts and coppices of wood have been at all times discharged for payment of any tithes thereof, by force whereof the said Gilbert entered into the premises and occupied the same as lawful is for him to do, without that that any tithe have to be paid for the said woods, or ought of right to be paid, or that any tithe ought or have been used to be taken in and upon the demesne lands belonging unto the said prioress, or that the said complainant of right ought to have any tithe of the said land, ...

The Replication of John Packington to the Answer of Gilbert Wheeler: The said John saith that truth it is that as long as the said 18 valetts and coppices were in the hands and possession of the said late prioress that she could not have the tithes of them, and further the said John saith and averreth every thing in his said bill of complaint to be true, and that one of the said coppices is fallen yearly by the said defendant at the age of 18 years, and not above, and that the defendant hath fallen four of the said coppices within these 5 years and not tithed to your beseecher for the same. And forasmuch as the said valetts be out of the hand of the said late prioress and be now in the hands and possession of the defendant, being a temporal person, by the lease of the said late prioress, yielding yearly therefore £10, and also for that there is no discharge expressed in the said lease that the defendant should be discharged of tithes for the said valetts, and also forasmuch as the same tithes were rated and valued to the king's highness to the yearly value of 50s and so granted by his highness to your beseecher, which is confessed by the defendant in his answer to be true, for all which causes your beseecher prayeth that the defendant may by the order of this honourable court be compelled to make payment for the said tithes which is behind unpaid by the space of four years which amounteth to the sum of £4, all which matters the plaintiff is ready to prove as this honourable court will award and prayeth as he in his said bill of complaint hath prayed.

BIBLIOGRAPHY

A select list of books and articles published since 1959 and not included in Dom. D. Knowles's, *The Religious Orders in England* III, 1959, pp. 498–506

Chambers, D. S., *Faculty Office Registers, 1534–49*, Oxford, 1966

Dickens, A. G., *The English Reformation*, 1964

Dickinson, J. C., 'The Buildings of the English Austin Canons after the Dissolution of the Monasteries', *British Archaeological Association Journal*, Series 3, XXXI (1968)

Haigh, C., *The Last Days of the Lancashire Monasteries and the Pilgrimage of Grace*, Manchester, 1964

Hockey, S. F., *Quarr Abbey and its Lands, 1132–1631*, Leicester, 1970

Hodgett, G. A. J., *The State of the ex-Religious in the diocese of Lincoln*, Lincoln Record Society LII (1959)

Hodgett, G. A. J., 'The unpensioned Ex-Religious in Tudor England', *Journal of Ecclesiastical History* XIII (1962)

Jack, S., 'The last days of the Smaller Monasteries in England', *Journal of Ecclesiastical History*, XXI (1970)

Kew, J., 'The Disposal of Crown Lands and the Devon land market, 1536–58', *Agricultural History Review* XVIII ii (1970)

Oxley, J. E., *The Reformation in Essex to the death of Mary*, Manchester, 1965

Richardson, W. C., *A History of the Court of Augmentations*, Baton Rouge, 1961

Swales, T. H., 'Opposition to the suppression of the Norfolk Monasteries', and 'The redistribution of the Monastic Lands in Norfolk at the Dissolution', *Norfolk Archaeology* XXXIII (1962–6)

Thorpe, S. (Mrs S. Jack), 'Monastic Lands and their Administration on the eve of the Dissolution', *Trans. Leicestershire Arch. and History Society* XLI (1965–6)

Williams, Glanmor, 'Landlords in Wales: The Church', in *The Agrarian History of England and Wales* IV, 1500–1640, ed. J. Thirsk, Cambridge, 1967

Williams, Glanmor, 'The Dissolution of the Monasteries in Glamorgan', *The Welsh History Review* III i (1966), reprinted in the same author's *Welsh Reformation Essays*, Cardiff, 1967

Woodward, G. W. O., 'The Exemption from Suppression of certain Yorkshire priories', *EHR* LXXVI (1961)

Woodward, G. W. O., 'A Speculation in Monastic Lands', *EHR* LXXIX (1964)

Woodward, G. W. O., *The Dissolution of the Monasteries*, 1966

Youings, J. A., 'Landlords in England: The Church', in *The Agrarian History of England and Wales* IV, 1500–1640, ed. J. Thirsk, Cambridge, 1967

Youings, J. A., 'A rare survival: Letters Patent granting a pension to a Lincolnshire nun in 1539', *Archives* VII, no. 36 (1966)